D1419525

The Dilemmas of Lenin

The Dilemmas of Lenin

Terrorism, War, Empire, Love, Revolution

Tariq Ali

VERSO

London • New York

First published by Verso 2017
© Tariq Ali 2017

All rights reserved

1 3 5 7 9 10 8 6 4 2

Verso
UK: 6 Meard Street, London W1F 0EG
US: 20 Jay Street, Suite 1010, Brooklyn, NY 11201
versobooks.com

Verso is the imprint of New Left Books

ISBN-13: 978-1-78663-110-7
ISBN-13: 978-1-78663-113-8 (US EBK)
ISBN-13: 978-1-78663-112-1 (UK EBK)

British Library Cataloguing in Publication Data
A catalogue record for this book is available from the British Library

Library of Congress Cataloging-in-Publication Data
A catalog record for this book is available from the Library of Congress

Typeset in Sabon LT by Hewer Text UK Ltd, Edinburgh
Printed in the UK by CPI Mackays

For those who will come after: the gateway to the future can only be unlocked by the past

CONTENTS

CONTENTS

ACKNOWLEDGMENTS

This book was written to put Lenin in proper historical context. It has been immensely pleasurable to reread his key texts and related material. One reads them differently now than in the last century, but they retain their power. Usually I write a book after a great deal of discussion with audiences at public lectures and meetings. This time, my only companions were books. Of these (listed in the Further Reading section), I must single out the remarkable work of the late John Erickson, a military historian par excellence, whose studies of the Red Army and its command structures from 1917 to 1991 have no peer in any language.

For brief discussions on particular subjects I must thank Perry Anderson; Robin Blackburn and Susan Watkins, my colleagues at the *New Left Review*; and Sebastien Budgen, editor at Verso, Paris, who, as usual, sent me extremely useful texts to digest. For reading the manuscript and suggesting useful alterations and elucidations I am grateful to David Fernbach, a comrade of almost fifty years, and Leo Hollis, my editor at Verso, London – whose grandfather, Christopher Hollis, was an early biographer of Lenin who certainly would not have agreed with most of my assessments. Mark Martin at Verso, Brooklyn, and Rowan Wilson and Bob Bhamra at Verso, London, ensured a smooth transition on the production front. Many thanks as well to Ben Mabie at Verso, Brooklyn, for preparing a first draft of the Glossary of Personal Names.

T. A.
28 October 2016

INTRODUCTION

On Lenin

Here I stand, I can do no other.
Martin Luther

Why Lenin? First, because this is the centenary year of Europe's last great revolution. Unlike its predecessors, the 1917 October Revolution transformed *world* politics and, in the process, remade the twentieth century with a frontal assault on capitalism and its empires, accelerating decolonialization. Secondly, today's dominant ideology and the power structures it defends are so hostile to the social and liberation struggles of the last century that a recovery of as much historical and political memory as is feasible becomes an act of resistance. In these bad times, even the anti-capitalism on offer is limited. It is apolitical and ahistorical. The aim of contemporary struggle should be not to repeat or mimic the past but to absorb the lessons, both negative and positive, that it offers. It is impossible to achieve this while ignoring the subject of this study. For a long time during the last century, those who honoured Lenin largely ignored him. They sanctified him, but rarely read his work. More often than not, and on every continent, Lenin was misinterpreted and misused for instrumentalist purposes by his own side: parties and sects large and tiny who claimed his mantle.

The Lenin cult, which he loathed even in its most incipient form, was a disaster for his thought. His texts, never intended or written as a catechism, were mummified, making it difficult to understand his political formation. This phenomenon must be situated at the confluence of two historical processes. Lenin was a product of

Russian history and the European labour movement. Both posed questions of class and party, of agency and instrument. The synthesis developed by Lenin was thus determined by the intermingling of two very different currents that can be characterised, broadly speaking, as anarchism and Marxism. He played a crucial role in the triumph of the latter.

That is why, before moving on to discuss some specific problems confronted by Lenin and the Bolsheviks, I will explain at length the history and prehistory of both currents. Without this excavation, it's not easy to understand the dilemmas that confronted Lenin.

It takes imagination to misread Lenin and Trotsky or present them as liberals underneath the mask. Whatever one might think of them, the lucidity of their prose leaves little room for political misinterpretation. As Perry Anderson has recently reminded us, the fate of Gramsci, the third major thinker produced by the Communist tradition of the Third International, has been somewhat different and for specific reasons relating to his imprisonment by the Italian fascists.[1]

First things first. Without Lenin there would have been no socialist revolution in 1917. Of this much we can be certain. Fresh studies of the events have only hardened this opinion. The faction and later the party that he painstakingly created from 1903 onward was simply not up to the task of fomenting revolution during the crucial months between February and October 1917, the freest period ever in Russian history. A large majority of its leadership, before Lenin's return, was prepared to compromise on many key issues. The lesson here is that even a political party – specifically trained and educated for the single purpose of producing a revolution – can stumble, falter and fall at the critical moment.

This is where the Bolsheviks as a party were headed strategically and tactically before April 1917. No party can ever be right all the

---

1 In a new introduction to the book version of his essay 'The Antinomies of Antonio Gramsci', Anderson details the disgraceful attempts by anti-Communists and post-Communists alike to mummify Gramsci and even present him as a liberal-democrat, among many other things.

time. Nor can a political leader, not even one with the most exceptional qualities and strength of will. In this particular case, however, Lenin understood that if the moment were not seized, reaction would triumph once again. Events favoured him. He dragged a reluctant party leadership behind him by winning the support of grassroots Bolsheviks and, more importantly, soldiers completely alienated from the war. For the latter it was the slogans from frontline Bolshevik agitators that articulated what they themselves were thinking and whispering to each other in the trenches or as they participated in mass desertions. History handed Lenin a gift in the shape of the First World War. He grasped it with both hands and used it to craft an insurrection. It is revolutions that make history happen. Liberals of every sort, with rare exceptions, are found on the other side.[2]

The First World War was Lenin's initial dilemma. The person he admired the most and regarded as his mentor was the German socialist Karl Kautsky. It was the latter's capitulation to the war fever in Germany that shook Lenin. He had thought that an understanding of Marx was sufficient inoculation against most intellectual plagues, especially that of enthusiasm for imperialist wars. He solved the problem by an angry public break with the German Socialist Party, agreeing with Rosa Luxemburg's definition of it as 'a stinking corpse'. This, alas, turned out not to be the case. This 'corpse' weighs heavily on German workers to this day.

The next dilemma he was to confront concerned the path to revolution. After February 1917 this was not an abstract question. Lenin opted for a socialist revolution, creating mayhem inside his own party. At one point he denounced the old Bolsheviks as 'conservatives' mired in a centrist marsh. He won them back only

---

2 Domenico Losurdo's *Liberalism: A Counter-History*, London and New York, 2011, is replete with examples of liberal philosophy in practice. One of these is especially instructive. He points out that US recognition of Haiti after the American Civil War was purely instrumentalist. The United States, including Lincoln, had not yet abandoned the idea 'of depositing on the island of black power the ex-slaves, who were to be deported from the Republic that continued to be inspired by the principle of white supremacy and purity' (p. 153).

after they had realised that the Petrograd workers were politically ahead of them.

There have been long debates on the role of individuals in history. The eighteenth-century view that history was made by conscious individuals faced a strong challenge in the century that followed, and from many eminent pre-Marxist historians for whom no serious discussion of history was possible without analysing social and economic conditions. The view that social and material forces create the conditions in which individuals are transformed and act in a way that would be impossible in different circumstances was systematised by Marx and Engels and generally accepted for most of the twentieth century. This applies to individuals of all kinds: Napoleon and Bismarck as well as Lenin, Mao Zedong, Ho Chi Minh and Fidel Castro.

Had the English Revolution been delayed, Oliver Cromwell and his family would have crossed the Atlantic and settled in the dissenter stronghold of New England. Had the French Revolution not occurred, Bonaparte would have left France as he was planning to do and sought employment in the Russian Imperial Army. As Kropotkin wrote in his classic history of the French Revolution, a book that became part of the common heritage of the Russian revolutionary movement, context determined all:

> That is why the French Revolution, like the English Revolution of the preceding century, happened at the moment when the middle classes, having drunk deep at the sources of current philosophy, became conscious of their rights, and conceived a new scheme of political organisation. Strong in their knowledge and eager for the task, they felt themselves quite capable of seizing the government by snatching it from a palace aristocracy which, by its incapacity, frivolity and debauchery, was bringing the kingdom to utter ruin. But the middle and educated classes could not have done anything alone, if, consequent on a complete chain of circumstances, the mass of the peasants had not also been stirred, and, by a series of constant insurrections lasting for four years, given to the dissatisfied among the middle classes the possibility of combating both King and Court, of upsetting old institutions and changing the political constitution of the kingdom.

Without the First World War and February 1917, Lenin would have died in exile, one of the many Russian revolutionaries destined to miss the fall of the autocracy. Trotsky could easily have become a Russian novelist in the classic tradition. Even when conditions favour revolutionary upheavals, however, there are rarely organisations capable of taking advantage of them. Failed insurrections, uprisings and revolutions litter the history of our world. Why did Spartacus lose? Why did Toussaint Louverture win? Each answer is embedded in the history of the epochs in which they lived. Likewise, Lenin.

It was the Iron Chancellor in newly created Germany who insisted on underplaying his own role, arguing the intelligent conservative position in an address to the North German Reichstag in 1869:

> Gentlemen, we can neither ignore the history of the past nor create the future. I would like to warn you against the mistake that causes people to advance the hands of their clocks, thinking that thereby they are hastening the passage of time. My influence on the events I took advantage of is usually exaggerated; but it would never occur to anyone to demand that I *should make history*. I could not do that even in conjunction with you, although together, we could resist the whole world. We cannot make history: we must wait while it is being made. We will not make fruit ripen more quickly by subjecting it to the heat of a lamp; and if we pluck the fruit before it is ripe we will only prevent its growth and spoil it.

Bismarck's heirs or, to be more precise, German artillery fire prematurely ripened the fruit in Russia. Lenin was confident that once the fruit trees of Germany and Russia had been grafted together, the rest of the continent, with the exception of Britain, would be rotten-ripe for revolution. Whatever else, he was not shy of making history, of compressing the experience of a decade into a single day. Events did not unfold quite as he had expected in the rest of Europe, but for contingent reasons rather than objective conditions.

This book is a contextualisation without which the history of the Russian Revolution is incomprehensible.

For instance, the terrorist phase of the nineteenth century, to which a sizeable section of the liberal intelligentsia were committed, came to an end when the leadership of the People's Will voted unanimously for the only item on the agenda: to execute Alexander II without further delay. The execution was successfully carried out under the command of Sofiya Perovskaya; during the ensuing repression, the small groups that had survived were crushed. The impact of these events on *all* the Russian political parties that emerged during the first decade of the twentieth century should not be underestimated.

Wishful thinking on the part of liberal historians and ideologues has helped sustain the view that had it not been for the Bolshevik 'aberration', the course of Russian democracy would have flowed smoothly and fed into the Western European marsh. What democracy has ever flowed smoothly? This did not happen in 1991 any more than it would have in 1917. In reality, given the relationship of forces and the continuing war, the most likely eventuality would have been the rise to power of a hard-core military dictatorship through mass pogroms and large-scale repression, with Entente support designed to keep Russia in the war.

The February Revolution produced a weak government that was incapable of dealing with the crisis and committed to the war. There were only two forces that could have filled the vacuum: the Bolsheviks, after they received a vigorous reeducation course from Lenin, and Generals Kornilov, Denikin, Kolchak and Wrangel and Wrangel's cohort, who led the Whites during the civil war that followed the revolution.

When there is no revolutionary party or one that has been defeated and decapitated, it is reaction rather than reform that triumphs. This pattern has remained constant from Cavaignac and Louis Napoleon to Groener, Noske, Mussolini and Hitler, from Suharto to Pinochet and in the work of virtually every American president.

Why would Russia have taken a different course had there not been a revolution or if the Red Army had lost the civil war?[3] Liberal

---

3   For my views on the Stalinist aftermath of the revolution, see Tariq Ali, ed., *The Stalinist Legacy: Its Impact on Twentieth-Century Politics*, London and Boulder, 1984, and Tariq Ali, *Fear of Mirrors*, London and New York, 2016 (a recently republished novel).

and conservative historians often belittle the events of October 1917 as a 'coup'. This was not the case. True, the urban proletariat on which the revolution based itself was a minority of the population, dominated by a peasantry that dotted the large rural hinterlands of the country and that supported the Bolshevik decrees on land ownership immediately after October. Without this growing support among the poor peasants, the Bolsheviks could not have won the civil war. Lenin's dictum that the strategic majority needed for success must have a decisive preponderance of force in the decisive place at the decisive time had a relatively restricted meaning in Russia.

It was only after the Bolsheviks won majorities in the soviets that they set the date for the insurrection. Lenin can be denounced for basing himself exclusively on the workers, but here he was following the instructions of the founding elders of the movement, Marx and Engels. This was also the reason he dissolved the Constituent Assembly in November 1917. Here the Bolsheviks argued that the soviets were a higher form of democracy and that they were not going to waste time debating the Social Revolutionaries (SRs) in a chamber that had been overtaken by revolution. The Bolshevik vote in these elections, however, did signify huge support in the towns. Out of a total of 37.5 million votes cast, 16 million (mainly in the rural areas) voted for the SRs, 10 million (mainly in the urban areas) for the Bolsheviks and 1.3 million (of which 570,000 were in the Caucasus) for the Mensheviks.

Revolutionary periods invariably encompass a huge fluctuation of political consciousness that can never be registered accurately by any referendum. The fact that the garrisons in Petrograd and Moscow came over so rapidly to the Bolsheviks' side related to the acceleration of disasters on the front. The peasants in uniform, politically radicalised by the war, simply did not wish to fight any longer for a regime that was not interested in them, their families, their welfare or the conditions in which they fought. Lenin's pithy slogan embodying the Bolshevik transitional programme – 'Land, Peace and Bread' – was brilliant (as even his many enemies were forced to acknowledge). Behind each word lay a set of ideas encompassing Bolshevik strategy.

No revolutionary vanguard party can ever triumph on its own. This is why those addicted to the word 'coup' have little understanding of revolution. Whether we ever see one again (a different matter and a different discussion), proletarian revolution as conceived by Marx and Lenin is a gigantic *awakening* of the millions of exploited, who believe in their own capacity to emancipate themselves.

Fractures in the state, divisions in the ruling class and indecision on the part of the intermediate classes pave the way for dual power, which, in Russia, led to the creation of new institutions and later, in China, Vietnam and Cuba, rested on revolutionary armies with varying class compositions that were locked in battle against their respective state machines.

In the Russian case, Lenin spelt this out with customary clarity a few weeks before the October Revolution:

> To be successful, insurrection must rely, not upon conspiracy and not upon a party, but upon an advanced class. That is the first point. Insurrection must rely upon a *revolutionary upsurge of the people.* That is the second point. Insurrection must rely upon that *turning-point* in the history of the growing revolution when the activity of the advanced ranks of the people is at its height, and when the *vacillations* in the ranks of the enemy and in the ranks of the weak, half-hearted and irresolute friends of the revolution are strongest. That is the third point. These three conditions for raising the question of insurrection distinguish Marxism from Blanquism. Once these conditions exist, however, to refuse to treat insurrection as an *art* is a betrayal of Marxism and the revolution.

After the debacle of the July Days, when the masses had attempted to lead the party during an unripe situation, the Bolshevik press was banned, some of its leaders imprisoned and Lenin exiled to Finland. It was from there that he sent the most urgent political letters in revolutionary history, pleading, explaining, arguing that July was a temporary setback, that the masses would rise again and the party must be prepared. He pointed out, accurately, that it was Marx who 'had summed up the lessons of all revolutions in respect to armed uprisings in the words of Danton, the greatest master of revolutionary policy yet known: *de l'audace, de l'audace, toujours de l'audace.'* In a more truculent mood he would provoke Menshevik and Bolshevik critics by quoting Napoleon: 'First engage, then see.'

Two key members of the Bolshevik Central Committee – Kamenev and Zinoviev – were not convinced and strongly opposed the insurrection, publishing its date in Gorky's newspaper. In fact it was hardly a secret that the Bolsheviks were planning a revolution. Lenin had said as much when he arrived at the Finland Station. His rage when the Bolshevik versions of Rosencrantz and Guildenstern on the Central Committee revealed the date of the planned insurrection is understandable – the element of surprise being crucial in all wars, including social and political conflicts – but in the end, it didn't matter at all. The insurrection still took place, proving that a ruling class in total disarray is helpless against masses that are raring to move forward, even when its members know the date of the revolution.

Why is insurrection an art? Because an armed uprising against the capitalist state or occupying imperialist armies has to be choreographed with precision, especially during its final stages.[4] The armed workers' militias and soldiers have to be coherently led in order to achieve victory. The final decision was left to the Military Revolutionary Committee of the Soviet, which was chaired by New Bolshevik Leon Trotsky and had a Bolshevik majority. And the victory, too, was reported to the Soviet, then in session at Smolny, Petrograd.

Every upheaval has its own peculiarities, but there are broad similarities between revolutions as well. The three great revolutions in European history all went through two distinct phases, each taking a more radical turn in the second and final act. Colonel Thomas Pride's purge of the House of Commons on 6 December 1648 was the precursor to the trial and execution of Charles Stuart, the key dividing line in the English Revolution that made further

---

4   This was as true of Petrograd in 1917 as it was of Beijing in 1949, Havana in 1960, Hanoi in August 1945 and Saigon in 1975.

compromise impossible. The Jacobin ascent to power in the French Assembly (or descent, given where they sat) in 1793 played a similar role in accelerating the revolutionary process, with the public execution of Louis Capet and Marie Antoinette in October of that year. Lenin's *April Theses* paved the way for the revolution in October 1917.

The difference between these revolutions lay in the following: whereas events pushed Cromwell and Robespierre forward, in Russia it was Lenin who consciously used events – in his case, the disintegration of the Russian autocracy as a result of the First World War – to push the workers and soldiers in Petrograd and Moscow toward a successful insurrection. When Lenin invoked Cromwell and Robespierre, it was not for ideological reasons – the Puritans were guided by the 'word of God', the Jacobins by metaphysical virtue – but because both were master strategists. Both were leaders of bourgeois revolutions, and both had their own differences with their respective moneyed classes. And, more importantly, both had to arouse the yeomanry, artisan classes, plebeians and sans-culottes in order to move forward. Like them, Lenin understood that to secure what was attainable, one had to aim at the unattainable, to storm paradise, to climb to the summit of an unconquered mountain.[5]

Each of the three revolutions was confronted with the need to create brand-new armies to fight civil wars and defend the revolutionary state. Promotion in these armies was on the basis of merit

---

5 Bertrand Russell wrote, 'Only once I saw Lenin: I had an hour's conversation with him in his room at the Kremlin in 1920. I thought he resembled Cromwell more than any other historical character. Like Cromwell, he was forced into a dictatorship by being the only competent man of affairs in a popular movement. Like Cromwell, he combined a narrow orthodoxy in thought with great dexterity and adaptability in action, though he never allowed himself to be led into concessions which had any purpose other than the ultimate establishment of Communism. He appeared, as he was, completely sincere and devoid of self-seeking. I am persuaded that he cared only for public ends, not for his own power; I believe he would have stood aside at any moment if, by so doing, he could have advanced the cause of Communism.'

rather than class. The New Model Army of the English Revolution was moulded by the patrician General Fairfax; it came into its own, however, when the aristocracy was shunted to one side and Essex, Manchester and Waller were replaced by second sons, yeomen and so forth. Colonel Pride, who emptied the den that was the House of Commons of corruption and class privilege, was the son of a brewer. To these examples one could add the return of a group of exiles from New England, who came back to strengthen both the Ironsides and the revolution. Cromwell was clear on what was needed: 'I had rather a plain russet-coated captain that knows what he fights for and loves what he knows, than that which you call a gentleman, and is nothing else.' Fleetwood, Okey, Lambert, Widmerpool, Harrison, Disborough, Ireton, Rainsborough, Goff, Whaley and Joyce all fit the bill.[6]

A century or so later the French revolutionary army was built on a similar pattern. Its most capable generals were plucked from the ranks or from the streets and rapidly promoted to replace the military nobility. In 1789, some of the most famous and highly regarded officers of the revolutionary and later the Napoleonic armies were in lowly positions. Davout, Desaix, Marmont and MacDonald were subalterns; Bernadotte (who later refounded the Swedish monarchy) was a sergeant-major; Hoche, Marceau, Lefebre, Pichegru, Ney, Masséna, Murat and Soult were non-commissioned officers; Augereau was a fencing master; Lannes was a dyer; Gouvion Saint-Cyr was an actor; Jourdan was a peddler; Bessières was a barber; Brune was a compositor; Joubert and Junot were law students; Kléber was an architect; Marrier did not see any military service until the revolution.[7]

It was the same with the Red Army created after the revolution and welded into a fighting force by Leon Trotsky, one of the few examples in history of a militarised intellectual. His famous appeal for the creation of a Red cavalry ('Proletarians to Horse') indicated the composition of the new army. In fact, the problem was a lack of officers experienced in basic military technique; a

---

6   John Rees, *The Leveller Revolution*, London, 2016.
7   V. Duruy, *Histoire de France*, Paris, 1893, t. II, pp. 524–5.

number of tsarist officers were press-ganged into service under the watchful eyes of political commissars (the equivalent of Agitators in the New Model Army). One of them, serving in the imperial army, was an autodidact and a military leader of genius whose story, long forgotten, requires a brief retelling, not least because Lenin and Trotsky regarded him as a vital third arm, necessary to continue politics by other means. This was Mikhail Tukhachevsky. His role in the civil war showcased his astonishing military capacities.[8]

The difference between Lenin and his revolutionary predecessors lay in this: both Cromwell and Robespierre embraced the revolution once they were confronted by its actuality. It would have taken place even without them. Lenin had begun working for a revolution twenty-five years before 1917. For twenty-four of those years he had worked underground, in prison, in exile. He had done so without imagining that he would see one in his lifetime. In January 1917, still in exile, he confessed to a Swiss audience that he and the generation to which he belonged might never witness success. They were fighting for the future. Milton had declared that Englishmen loyal to the king were not free men, that royalism was a form of moral slavery. For Lenin it was the same, with regard to believers in capitalism, empires and the autocracy. A much bigger enemy than the English monarchy had to be confronted and defeated globally. He, if not his party, was fully prepared for what needed to be done, in keeping with his view that at all times one must '*aussprechen, was ist*': speak of what is and avoid transforming wishful thinking into the truth. A hard-headed revolutionary realism, Lenin argued throughout his political life, was crucial in times of victory, defeat and transition. It is this clear-sightedness that explains many of the decisions he made during his lifetime. He never grasped the enormity of his own contribution as a theoretician, but the Hungarian philosopher György Lukács did so. In an emotionally charged essay written just weeks after Lenin's death in 1924, he described him 'in a world historical sense [as] *the only theoretician equal*

8 For further details, see Chapter 11.

to Marx yet produced by the struggle for the liberation of the proletariat.'[9]

Lenin was decisive not only in ensuring the success of the revolution against a majority of the Central Committee, but also in safeguarding the infant republic by making all necessary concessions to the Germans at Brest-Litovsk that would have seriously truncated revolutionary Russia. Once again he was in a minority on the Central Committee. Once again he fought back. His opponents within and outside the party accused him of betrayal. He admitted it was a 'shameful' peace, but was convinced that it was necessary to secure a respite for the revolution. The left faction, that included Bukharin and Kollontai, demanded a revolutionary war against Germany; Trotsky argued for masterly inactivity that he described as 'neither war nor peace'; Lenin supported accepting the territorial demands of the kaiser. It would only be a temporary retreat, as the German Reich would soon be overthrown by the German workers. In any event, it would be impossible to fight the German armies and Russian reaction at the same time. The Treaty of Brest-Litovsk was a necessary expedient. The German high command was already extremely annoyed by the fact that the Bolshevik delegation was led by uppity Jews who, on arrival, had authorised the distribution of subversive leaflets urging German soldiers to mutiny. Once again history refused to completely contradict Lenin.[10] Germany lost the war and came close to a revolution, but never went beyond getting rid of its monarchy.

---

9   György Lukács, *Lenin: A Study on the Unity of His Thought*, tr. Nicholas Jacobs, London, 1970, emphasis added. In a 1967 postscript, Lukács was critical of some assertions he had made in the earlier text, but none related to his general view of Lenin as a thinker who had laid the foundations for an autonomous Marxist political theory. As for Lenin's character, Lukács quoted Hamlet's praise of Horatio: *And blest are those, / Whose blood and judgement are so well commingled, / That they are not a pipe of Fortune's finger / To sound what stops she please.*

10   The best account of Brest-Litovsk can be found in Isaac Deutscher, 'The Drama of Brest-Litovsk', in *The Prophet Armed*, Oxford, 1959.

For five critical years from 1917 to 1922, Lenin had remained at the helm of the state. War Communism had been necessary to win the civil war. No mean achievement. The White armies had dissolved but the decline in revolutionary fervor was only too visible. The setbacks in Hungary, Poland and Germany were accompanied by the temporary restabilisation of capitalism in 1921. The March Uprising in central Germany that year was a disastrous, desperate and irresponsible last-ditch effort by Zinoviev and Béla Kun to arouse the German masses. Carried out with the imprimatur of the Communist International, it completely misjudged the situation and undermined the already weak German Communist Party. The frontiers of the Soviet state were now settled. The revolution in Europe had receded. The cream of the Russian working class was either dead or exhausted. Revolutionary politics was at its lowest ebb.

This necessitated a new plan. The result was the New Economic Policy (NEP), a state-invigilated reentry of small-scale capitalism. NEP was conceived as a transitional measure to revive the economy, at which it succeeded, improving food supplies and distribution networks. But while NEP was taking effect, the country was hit by a series of natural disasters, including droughts, sand blizzards and an invasion of locusts in the southern provinces. Famine struck, affecting the lives of millions. With it grew the black market, squalid as ever, but, for the moment, untouchable. Many workers fled to their villages. The proletariat had dispersed. The revolutionary dictatorship was now truly functioning in a vacuum. This fact made the character and capacities of individual leaders much more important than institutions like the party and the soviet. The Bolsheviks, at this point, resembled the Jacobins. Slowly the social and economic situation improved, but by that time the party that had created a revolution resembled a bureaucracy more with each passing day. Some felt that there was no alternative. Not Lenin.

The last dilemma he was to confront was also the most difficult. Felled by a stroke, he was ordered to rest both physically and politically and forced to step back from overseeing and guiding the daily life of the new state. Lenin was a bad patient. He refused to stop reading the newspapers or thinking about politics. While attending what would be his last party congress in April 1922, he felt alienated from the direction the state was taking. He accepted his share of responsibility and, while recognising the role of material causes in setting the party on this path, he was shaken by how far along it the party had gone and concerned with the subjective factor, namely the party and its leadership. 'Powerful forces', he wrote, 'had diverted the Soviet state from its "proper road"'. Lenin's last writings were a courageous attempt to make the party change course. He thought of historical examples of a nation's defeat when the vanquished had managed to impose their culture on the victors, defeating them in spirit. He felt that the old tsarist bureaucracy had managed to conquer his colleagues, who had easily adopted the old methods of governance, if not the cultural practices, of their past oppressors. Yes, he did write about all of this, as I detail in the concluding chapters of this book. And he apologised: 'I am, it seems, strongly guilty before the workers of Russia.' It was almost as if he had been rereading Engels's essay 'The Peasant War in Germany':

> The worst thing that can befall a leader of an extreme party is to be compelled to take over a government in an epoch when the movement is not yet ripe for the domination of the class which he represents and for the realisation of the measures which that domination would imply. What he *can* do depends not upon his will but upon the sharpness of the clash of interests between the various classes, and upon the degree of development of the material means of existence, the relations of production and means of communication upon which the clash of interests of the classes is based every time. What he *ought* to do, what his party demands of him, again depends not upon him, or upon the degree of development of the class struggle and its conditions. He is bound to his doctrines and the demands hitherto propounded which do not emanate from the interrelations of the social classes at a given moment, or from the more or less accidental level of relations of production and means of communication, but from his more or less penetrating insight into the general result of the social and political movement. Thus he necessarily finds himself in a dilemma. What he *can* do is in contrast to all his actions as

hitherto practised, to all his principles and to the present interests of his party; what he *ought* to do cannot be achieved. In a word, he is compelled to represent not his party or his class, but the class for whom conditions are ripe for domination. In the interests of the movement itself, he is compelled to defend the interests of an alien class, and to feed his own class with phrases and promises, with the assertion that the interests of that alien class are their own interests. Whoever puts himself in this awkward position is irrevocably lost.

Lenin, of course, never represented the 'alien class'. But some of his colleagues did and, as Lenin was only too aware, other observations made by Engels were apposite. Some of Lenin's last writings were hidden from the Russian people for thirty-three years. And those who revealed them were incapable of implementing the prescriptions. Lenin had seen what had happened to the Party when it was confronted with the task of running a country. He was mortified by the degree of bureaucratisation that had taken place. Before the revolution he had been strongly criticised by Rosa Luxemburg and intemperately so by Leon Trotsky over his conception of the Party as a heavily centralised, clandestine organisation. He had defended himself ably and without resorting to Marx, though he obviously was familiar with this passage from *Capital*:

> In all kinds of work where there is cooperation of many individuals, the connection and the unity of the process are necessarily represented in a will which commands and in functions, which, as for the leader of an orchestra are not concerned with partial efforts, but the collective activity.

In his famous addendum to *What Is to Be Done?* Lenin had utilised the image of an orchestra to illustrate how to organise the party from a central apparatus:

> In order that the centre can not only advise, convince and debate with the orchestra – as has been the case till now – but really to direct it, we need detailed information: who is playing which violin and where? What instrument is being mastered and has been

mastered and where? Who is playing a false note (when the music starts to grate on the ear) – and where and why? Whom to relocate to where and how in order to correct the dissonance?

What this concept assumes is a strong will but also an interplay of equality, democracy and authority inside the party and, by extension, in society as a whole. This is why Lenin believed that a revolution in Germany was so vital and that, had it been successful, it would have helped the Soviet Republic move forward much more easily both economically and politically. As for the ability of a party to work in clandestinity, this was important not just for Russia, but for the Communist-led resistance movements in France, Italy, China, Vietnam and Yugoslavia throughout the Second World War as well. The leaders and parties in these last three countries went on to make revolutions.

In one of his last injunctions, Lenin insisted that if one was defeated politically through a combination of one's own mistakes and circumstances, one must learn from the defeat in order to understand why it had occurred and then start one's work again. Socialism was an approximation and was not born fully formed; therefore socialists must openly admit their mistakes. Without this, they would never progress. Neither Khrushchev nor Gorbachev had the vision or the capacity to start again. Had Lenin lived another five years, the country and the party would have moved forward differently. The New Economic Policy would have been dismantled with greater care, and the brutal leap to industrialisation might not have transpired. Nor would Lenin have killed off the bulk of Old Bolsheviks on the Central Committee and the country as a whole. To what extent and with what degree of success he would have implemented change will always remain a subject for debate.

Putin's Russia will not be marking the centenary in either February or October. 'These dates are not in our calendar,' Putin said to a leading Indian newspaper publisher and editor. Other Russians, including some of Putin's opponents, do not even accept that there was a 'Russian' Revolution. It was, according to them, all the work of the Jews.[11] One of the few who are above criticism these days is Stalin, largely because of the 'Great Patriotic' War and partially because his methods of rule are envied by many Russian nationalists today. Mummifying Lenin and his ideas was a lasting 'achievement' of the Stalin period. Time, then, to bury Lenin's body and revive some of his ideas. Future generations in Russia might realise that Lenin still has a bit more to offer than Prince Stolypin.

---

11   I cannot help but recall a trip to a film conference in Moscow in the late '80s in the company of Fredric Jameson. After we had watched a Soviet documentary on Afghanistan that was littered with references to the Orthodox Church, we were approached by an eager postgraduate student who introduced himself as a great admirer of Fred and a regular reader of New Left Review. What did we think of the film? 'Too much church, too many baptisms and funerals', I said. The student was shocked. He protested that we had no idea of Russia. The Church was a vital component, the heart of the country. And the Bolsheviks, I asked? 'They were Jews.' The Mensheviks? 'They were Jews.' Is there no such thing as a Russian of Jewish origin? He didn't quite understand the question. Realising belatedly that neither Jameson nor I were too impressed, he wandered away.

The poet Vladimir Mayakovsky committed suicide in 1930. In one of his last poems, written in 1929 and titled 'Conversation with Comrade Lenin', Mayakovsky aired his concerns about the activities of the Party in the wake of Lenin's death:

Conversation with Comrade Lenin

Awhirl with events,
    packed with jobs one too many,
the day slowly sinks
    as the night shadows fall.
There are two in the room:
      I
      and Lenin –
a photograph
    on the whiteness of wall.

The stubble slides upward
    above his lip
as his mouth
    jerks open in speech.
      The tense
creases of brow
    hold thought
      in their grip,
immense brow
    matched by thought immense.
A forest of flags,
    raised-up hands thick as grass . . .
Thousands are marching
      beneath him . . .
        Transported,
alight with joy,
    I rise from my place,
eager to see him,
    hail him,
      report to him!
'Comrade Lenin,
    I report to you –

(not a dictate of office,
>> the heart's prompting alone)
This hellish work
> that we're out to do

will be done
> and is already being done.
We feed and we clothe
> and give light to the needy,

the quotas
> for coal
>> and for iron
>>> fulfill,
but there is
> any amount
>> of bleeding
muck
> and rubbish
>> around us still.

Without you,
> there's many
>> have got out of hand,

all the sparring
> and squabbling
>> does one in.
There's scum
> in plenty
>> hounding our land,

outside the borders
> and also
>> within.

Try to
    count 'em
        and
            tab 'em –
                it's no go,

there's all kinds,
    and they're
        thick as nettles:
kulaks,
    red tapists,
        and,
            down the row,
drunkards,
    sectarians,
        lickspittles.
They strut around
        proudly
            as peacocks,
badges and fountain pens
            studding their chests.
We'll lick the lot of 'em –
            but
                to lick 'em
is no easy job
    at the very best.
On snow-covered lands
        and on stubbly fields,
in smoky plants
    and on factory sites,
with you in our hearts,
        Comrade Lenin,
            we build,
we think,
    we breathe,
        we live,
            and we fight!'

Awhirl with events,
        packed with jobs one too many,
the day slowly sinks
        as the night shadows fall.
There are two in the room:
                I
                and Lenin –
a photograph
        on the whiteness of wall.[12]

---

12   Translated by Dorian Rottenberg, 1929.

SECTION ONE

Terrorism and Utopia

1

Terrorism versus Absolutism

The land of the knout and the pogrom. Tsarist Russia – patriarchal, sumptuous, barbaric – buttressed ideologically by the Orthodox Church (with its genetic anti-Semitism) and its own self-belief, defended militarily by stiff-necked braggadocio and geometric garrison towns, dominated economically by huge estates and a nobility dependent on the goodwill of a savagely oppressed peasantry, had long avoided both the revolutionary upheavals that had transformed England, Holland and France as well as the radical structural reforms from above that later united Germany. Because of this, Russia was rarely free from a dissent that sometimes emerged in the highest places. And the lowest. Russian absolutism created its opposites.

Later, over the course of the long nineteenth century, an oppositional *intelligentsia* (the word itself of Russian origin) emerged and continuously provided the country with liberal, Populist, anarcho-terrorist, pacifist, nationalist, socialist and Marxist thinkers who became a vital force in the history of Europe. It was a century that had given birth in Western Europe, Japan and North America to an accelerated industrial capitalism and its offshoot, imperialism. In normal conditions, there would be a reconciliation with the rising bourgeoisie whereby the latter would help to individualise the intelligentsia and in return would be provided with the bare necessities of civilised discourse. In Russia, however, the process was explosively uneven.

The outcome for the tsarist empire was dramatic: three revolutions – January 1905, February 1917 and October 1917 – within

An idealized depiction of serfs after the
Emancipation. In fact conditions remained grim.

the first two decades of the twentieth century. Just as defeat in the
Crimean War had pushed the tsar towards reforms, so the debacle
of the Russo-Japanese war of 1904–5 helped pave the way for
what Lenin described as the dress rehearsal of 1905. The 'Great'
War of 1914–18 made February 1917 inevitable. Lenin ensured
the success of October.

The apex of the system was the court. The tsar, whether in
Moscow or St Petersburg, exercised control of virtually every
aspect of life. He was assisted by a despised bureaucracy,
membership in which often altered class locations by opening the
gates to the lowest levels of the nobility. This upward mobility,
designed to ensure stability, occasionally had the opposite
effect. Everything was relative. The peasants and, later, the intelligentsia wondered whether the next ruler would be a good or a
bad tsar.

In 1796, understandably panicked by the tumbrils in Paris, Catherine's grandson and tsarevitch Grand Duke Alexander confessed to his French tutor 'that he hated despotism everywhere ... that he loved liberty ... that he had taken the greatest interest in the French revolution; that while condemning its terrible mistakes, he hoped the Republic would succeed and would be glad if it did.' The French Revolution was never too far from the thoughts of rulers and ruled in Russia.

A few years later Alexander conspired in a palace coup that did away with his father Paul I and dismantled some of the more odious structures of his reign. Alexander ordered the removal of gallows from public squares, authorised the import of foreign books and ended the state monopoly on the establishment of printing presses. He lived to regret the latter. Nothing fundamental changed. Despotism was inbred. The autocracy needed it to survive. For a while, however, Alexander was the best example of the 'good tsar' as far as many of his subjects were concerned.

Ever since the legal code of 1649 – a time when England was already engulfed in a bourgeois revolution – forbade peasants from leaving the land without authorisation, serfdom had gradually become entrenched in the absolutist system. Overnight, millions of people became tied to the land. This Russian form of servitude adversely affected the country on many levels, cutting it off from developments in Western Europe and delaying capitalism and modernisation till the twentieth century. When an 1861 imperial proclamation ended legal bondage, it was almost time to mark the centenary of the French Revolution.

Unlike the African slaves in North and South America or the West Indies, the Russian serfs lived in their own villages and were responsible for reproduction and the sharing of communal lands. In many other ways, however, their suffering was not dissimilar to that of slaves elsewhere. Contemporary historians argue that the serfs, unlike slaves, had 153 holidays a year, but leaving aside Easter, Christmas and numerous saint days, this probably had much more to do with the inclement Russian winters than a more benign dispensation on the part of their landlords. In 1800, for instance, the price of a serf fluctuated depending on the market and natural calamities but never rose higher than that of a pedigree dog, especially one imported from France or Germany. Young women were sold in the marketplace alongside horses, cows and used carriages. Advertisements such as the following in Moscow were common elsewhere in the country: 'For sale at Pantaleimon's, opposite the meat market: a girl of thirty and a young horse.' Liveried serfs worked in the households of rich families in huge numbers: the Sheremetievs had 300 house-serfs; the Stroganoffs, 600; the Razumovskys, 900. A similar pattern was repeated on different scales throughout the country. While some of the domestic serfs (the 'house niggers', in Malcolm X's memorable description of their Afro-American counterparts) shared the prejudices of their masters, many others imbibed a deep sense of bitterness and hatred. Serf memoirs published in the literary press after the abolition of legal bondage contain numerous details concerning the treatments to which they were regularly subjected. Sexual oppression against women and children was common. When the time came to rebel, serfs' congealed anger did not remain hidden. Class fought against class. And the serfs' numbers were huge. The 1825 census revealed that out of a total population of 49 million, a large majority – 36 million – were serfs. Anti-Semitism and pogroms were rife, reaching fever pitch when the autocracy felt threatened by serf unrest.

The roll-call of significant events in Russian history includes two giant jacqueries in the seventeenth and eighteenth centuries, followed by a semi-insurrection launched by radical army officers in St Petersburg in December 1825. These three events became deeply embedded in the historical memory of the entire country, their imprint reaching far beyond the more radical segments of the population. Each side of the social divide learnt its own lesson: the revolts were warnings of the destructive nature of the working class, or examples of their liberatory potential. Russian backwardness, as symbolised by the serf economy, had produced its own variant of upheavals. These did not, as in England and France, lead to full-blown revolution, but they established a pattern and strongly influenced Populist and anarcho-terrorist groups, especially the secret societies, that organised and carried out acts of terror against tsars, dukes, generals and senior bureaucrats in the second half of the nineteenth century and the early years of the twentieth. These were the early expressions of Russian Marxism that slowly developed into the Emancipation of Labour group and later the Russian Social-Democratic Labour Party, with its Bolshevik (majority) and Menshevik (minority) factions.

The peasant revolts grew out of a long tradition of rural discontent starting after the final victory over the Tatars in the 1380 Battle of Kulikovo and the birth of a Russia-wide tsarist autocracy. As the new absolutism grew in size and scale, it was accompanied by small peasant outbreaks, usually confined to clusters of small villages and bands of déclassé Tatars and their dependents that included ethnic Russians. All people of Mongol origin – Tatars, Kirghiz, Kalmuks – were treated as an inferior race and deprived of rights, and could be legally forced into serfdom by members of the Russian nobility, some of whom exercised this privilege. More popular with merchants was the legalised slave trade, formally prohibited only in 1828, that sanctioned the sale of children of Mongol origin throughout the empire and, no doubt, abroad. These conditions were instrumental in inciting the two large-scale rebellions that would make such a strong impression on peasants' political consciousness.

1918: Lenin dedicates a statue honouring
Stenka Razin.

The insurrections were led by the Don Cossacks: Stepan (Stenka) Razin (1667–71) and, a century later, Emilian Pugachev (1773–75), who took on Catherine II. The Cossack core of both insurrectionary groups rapidly expanded and embraced discontents of every sort. Both were ultimately defeated. Interestingly, both Razin and Pugachev had been born in the same South Russian village of Zimoyevskaya. Of the two, Razin was showier and more adventurous, a Cossack Robin Hood much given to tormenting and mocking his captives and extending his adventures to neighbouring Persia. Pugachev was more politically astute, pretending to be a popular deposed prince to whom he bore a resemblance. Mass movements in those days, not only in Russia, flourished on such myths. Pugachev took Tsaritsyn (later Stalingrad, today Volgograd), laid unsuccessful siege to Simbirsk (where Lenin was born), claimed to be defending a good tsar against the bad boyars and won the support of the Cossack *krug*, a representative though unelected assembly, for a march to the North. This triggered a wave of peasant uprisings en route, greatly enlarging the size of the army. After four years on the road and a betrayal by Cossack elders loyal to the tsar, Pugachev was captured and publicly decapitated in Moscow's Red Square. Some months later, his brother and elderly parents were eliminated in similar fashion. Punishing families to prevent revenge killings in the future is an old tradition.

The Volga rebellions typified the revolutionary traditions of the Russian peasantry, and radical poets and minstrels would glorify them for centuries to come. For all that the most popular jacqueries (as in China and India) linked themselves to a national history of resistance, they rarely transformed the living conditions of the people, offering temporary respite at best. Razin, for instance, pledged to 'wipe out the boyars and the nobles', but his efforts failed at a time when Russian cities were strongholds of reactionary sentiment, dominated by nobles and their retainers, state bureaucrats of every kind and the army. 'That is why', wrote Trotsky, 'after each of these grandiose movements ... the Volga washed the bloodstains into the Caspian Sea, and the tsar's and landlord's oppression weighed heavier than ever.'[1] Few decades that followed were unaccompanied by localised peasant risings.

The 1825 Decembrist uprising was the first major sign of urban discontent, a military revolt whose most radical leader, Pavel Pestel, was hugely influenced by the Jacobins and the French Revolution: Rousseau and Robespierre, Babeuf and Buonarotti. The ideological links between revolutionary Paris and the most radical sections of the Russian intelligentsia lasted for over a century following the Decembrist defeat; references to 1789, 1793 and 1815 are ubiquitous in the texts of Bakunin, Lenin, Trotsky and others. The impact of the December rebellion was electric. It enlarged the size of a small but active radical intelligentsia based in universities and literary circles. Pushkin, who had close friends among the Decembrist plotters, originally sent the eponymous hero of *Eugene Onegin*, badly disappointed in love, to join the Decembrists. Circumstances, however, compelled Pushkin to burn some of his verses and suppress others. This description of the vengeful tsar survived and was included in later editions:

> A ruler, timorous and wily,
> A balding fop, of toil a foe,
> Minion of Fame by chance entirely,
> Reigned over us those years ago.
> We knew him not at all so regal,
> When cooks, who were not ours, were sent
> To pluck our double-headed eagle,
> Where Bonaparte had pitched his tent.

The Decembrist mutiny was savagely crushed. Executions and imprisonment followed. Pushkin was distraught, but helpless. He was deeply touched when Maria Volkonskaya, a young woman he had known (possibly in the biblical sense) some years before in Tashkent, ignored the entreaties of her noble family and insisted on joining her imprisoned Decembrist husband, Prince Sergei

---

1 Leon Trotsky, *The Young Lenin*, tr. Max Eastman, New York, 1972.

Volkonsky, in Siberia. Pushkin knew she did not love Volkonsky, who was twice her age, but that only made her melancholic and courageous decision even more impressive in his eyes. It was, he reflected, the purest form of solidarity. He composed 'Message to Siberia' for Maria and, a week after her departure, pressed it into the hands of the wife of another Decembrist who was leaving Moscow to join her husband in internal exile:

> Deep in the Siberian mine
> Keep your patience proud
> The bitter toil shall not be lost,
> The rebel thought unbowed ...
>
> The heavy-hanging chains will fall,
> And walls will crumble at a word,
> And freedom greet you in the light,
> And brothers give you back the sword.[2]

Rural unrest and urban dissidence made reform inevitable. In 1861, Tsar Alexander II, while retaining the other structures of absolutism, abolished serfdom. A wave of joy engulfed the country-side, till the dark side of the ruling began to sink in: the former serfs were burdened with redemption payments to their former masters, for the land they had obtained after abolition as well as the lands they had worked for centuries. The redemption payments could not be enforced, however, and the peasants' spirits rose once again. The landlords were compelled to liquidate properties, marry into merchant families and invest in railways and factories in order to stay financially solvent, aiding the development of capitalism in Russia. The cities grew bolder and richer. Many began to ask why

---

2   This was the first poem I learnt by heart when I was about seven. I recited it at an early meeting of the Communist-led Progressive Writers Association in Lahore in the presence of many poets (including our great ones), literary critics and those who aspired to be both. These included Faiz Ahmed Faiz, Sibte Hassan, Sajjad Zaheer, Hameed Akhtar, Zaheer Kashmiri and Khadija Masroor.

the creators of serfdom had not been abolished as well and, as is often the case, the reform led to more radical demands. In the countryside itself, half the peasants had never owned land as individuals, only as a village collective. Consequently, many peasants had little incentive to improve the land and became poorer as time went by. Simultaneously, social differentiation in the countryside began to sharpen, producing a group of wealthier peasants (the kulaks).

The end of serfdom was not accompanied by similar political reforms. Apart from a slight improvement on the judicial level, there was, uniquely for a European power approaching the twentieth century, no form of popular representation whatsoever. The tsar was the supreme ruler, appointing and dismissing ministers at will and wielding the power of life and death. Most courtiers appeared genetically sycophantic. A cumbersome and inert state bureaucracy carried out the instructions of the tsar. Police officers saw themselves as servants of power, not justice. Where was the opposition? What was the people's will?

In 1860 the intelligentsia – an educated elite unconnected with the royal court – was infinitesimal, numbering between 20,000 and 25,000 in a largely peasant population of 60 million people. This social stratum began to regard itself as the only possible opposition to the autocracy. Its education, its ideals, its desire to do good, its passion for the Enlightenment and the French Revolution all created the basis for its politics in the decades that lay ahead. Many believed that the only way out was via 'the propaganda of the deed'. Terrorism was carried out by individuals or tiny groups of conspirators, but support for it was much broader. In 1866, the first attempt on Alexander II's life failed. The would-be-assassin, Karakazov, was in police custody when the tsar appeared. The conversation was brief but to the point.

'Why did you shoot at me?'

'Because', responded an unabashed Karakazov, 'you promised the peasants freedom and you deceived them.'

Lenin was born four years later in 1870. His generation grew up at a time when tsarist Russia was saturated with anarchist and radical ideas; women's emancipation and an end to patriarchy (detested parental control of young women) were frequently discussed within intellectual circles, and terrorist acts against the powerful were viewed with awe and sympathy. Much of this was a consequence of the absolutist political structures, which provided the Russian segment of the newly developing Social Democratic movement with its unique characteristics. But there were other and larger fish in the pond.

The late nineteenth century witnessed a flowering of radical anarchism on virtually every continent. For almost half a century prior to the Russian Revolution of 1917, the dominant tendency on the radical left in Europe and elsewhere was anarchism rather than Marxism or socialism. Prince Kropotkin and Enrico Malatesta were more popular than Marx and Engels. Activists were far more drawn to the direct-action philosophy preached by Bakunin and Nechaev; the principles of *The Revolutionary Catechism* were viewed by many radicals as much more attractive than the message of *The Communist Manifesto*. Targeted assassinations of tsars and princes, presidents and prime ministers cheerfully carried out by individuals or small groups were considered by young activists of the period to be far more glamorous and effective than building a radical political party.

Primitive 'anarchism' in rural Russia had long predated any theorist in the country or elsewhere. Individual responses to institutionalised brutality were not uncommon. It was not the big landlords who were usually the targets, but their intermediaries. Bakunin, Kropotkin and Nechaev arrived much later. The first two of this remarkable triumvirate imbibed anarchism during long years of exile. Both came from the nobility. Prince Kropotkin was born two decades before the abolition of serfdom and, in his wonderful *Memoirs of a Revolutionist*, describes vividly how his close and warm relations with the serfs belonging to his family opened his eyes to Russian realities and, much later, his mind to radical anarcho-Populist ideas. Kropotkin was descended from the princes of Smolensk and the house of Rurik that ruled Muscovy before the Romanovs. His father was one of the favourite generals of Nicholas I; Kropotkin's precociousness as a child attracted the tsar's attention at a royal gathering. Nicholas I ordered that Prince Kropotkin be enlisted in the Corps of Pages, the most exclusive military academy in the empire.

Kropotkin did well and was soon appointed the personal page of the new tsar Alexander II. When the latter issued the historic declaration that emancipated the serfs, Kropotkin's fondness for his new master turned to hero-worship. But not for long. His doubts began to emerge as soon as it became clear that members of the landed nobility were utilising the serfs' freedom to bleed them dry. As the mist clouding Kropotkin's political eyesight cleared, he began to notice the seamier aspects of court life: the endless intrigues, the jostling for power, the nauseating sycophancy, the embedded anti-Semitism. Gradually, his ambivalence turned to outright hostility. Collaboration with the autocracy became impossible. The Russian army lost a gifted future commander, and the radical intelligentsia was about to gain an illustrious new recruit.

Peter Kropotkin, the anarchist theoretician, whose history of the French Revolution formed an entire generation.

Kropotkin became close to the Populists, was imprisoned and went into exile, where he was greatly influenced by Bakunin's ferocious debates with Marx, even though one such debate revolved around Bakunin's agreement to translate *Capital* into Russian and subsequent failure to do so. It was 'too boring', he insisted, while refusing to return the advance he had received for the translation.

Kropotkin was much less attracted to the violent side of anarchism. Bloody revolutions, he argued, were sometimes necessary (and here he was thinking of the English, American and French revolutions), but were 'always an evil'; the means always infected the ends. His own description of anarchist utopia, as published in the much celebrated, cerebral 1911 version of the *Encyclopædia Britannica,* was elegant, couched in polite language and far removed from the terrorist conspiracies and violent prose of Bakunin and Nechaev as well as the actions of the anarchists on horseback, Durutti and Makhno:

> ANARCHISM (from the Gr. ἄυ, and ἀρχη, contrary to authority), the name given to a principle or theory of life and conduct under which society is conceived without government – harmony in such a society being obtained, not by submission to law, or by obedience to any authority, but by free agreements concluded between the various groups, territorial and professional, freely constituted for the sake of production and consumption, as also for the satisfaction of the infinite variety of needs and aspirations of a civilised being. In a society developed on these lines, the voluntary associations which already now begin to cover all the fields of human activity would take a still greater extension so as to substitute themselves for the state in all its functions. They would represent an interwoven network, composed of an infinite variety of groups and federations of all sizes and degrees, local, regional, national and international, temporary or more or less permanent – for all possible purposes: production, consumption and exchange, communications, sanitary arrangements, education, mutual protection, defence of the territory, and so on; and, on the other side, for the satisfaction of an ever-increasing number of scientific, artistic, literary and sociable needs. Moreover, such a society would represent nothing immutable. On the contrary – as is seen in organic life at large – harmony would (it is contended) result from an ever-changing adjustment and readjustment of equilibrium between the multitudes of forces and influences, and this adjustment would be the easier to obtain as none of the forces would enjoy a special protection from the state.[3]

The main carriers of anarchism were the newly rising intelligentsia, emerging in the 1860s, no longer confined to the nobility or the church, but increasingly dominated by less privileged sections of the urban population, the result of an education system

---

3 This entry was actually written for the 1910 edition, but included verbatim in the iconic 1911 *Britannica*.

that produced literates who could be of use to the regime.[4] Disregarding the tiny working class, some intellectuals began to refer to themselves as the 'intellectual proletariat' and saw their task as liberating the peasantry from the ideological and economic chains of absolutism. Razin and Pugachev had lacked knowledge and understanding. They had not experienced the Enlightenment or the French Revolution. The new intelligentsia could make up for these shortcomings, and lead the peasants to make a revolution that would get rid of the tsar and the nobility while bypassing the cities, dominated by merchants.

The 'To the People' movement was not a success. It had concentrated on the traditional zones of peasant unrest; neither the Don, the Dnieper nor the Volga regions were receptive. It was too soon after the 1860 reform. Most peasants trusted in God and the tsar and, despite the insatiable monkish greed for money, food and sex, the Orthodox Church remained a central point of reference. Consequently, the peasants were hostile to the city folk, the gentry, students and radicals of any sort. The city was not to be trusted. Not yet.

The first attempt was a disaster for the new radical-Populist vanguard: two large show trials, the 'Case of the 50' and the 'Case of the 193', meted out harsh punishments as a deterrent to others who might travel down the same path. But the rulings pushed the radicals in a different direction. One group decided that the previous experiment had failed because of attempts to lead the peasants and too-brief visits to the countryside. They would return and this time serve the people: educate them, teach basic hygiene, help in their daily labours and become part of their lives. Bakunin's ideas would have to wait.[5]

---

4 Lenin's father was one such educationalist, conservative but independent-minded and incorruptible. He lived in Simbirsk, the only city where merchants and nobility had managed to withstand the siege by the peasant armies in the sixteenth and seventeenth centuries.

5 The contrast with the Maoists of the twentieth century is noteworthy. During the 'Great Proletarian Cultural Revolution', the Red Guards were sent to the countryside to learn how the peasants lived. The event itself had more in common with aspects of Bakuninist ideology than with the model of the Paris Commune.

But the rapid growth of revolutionary circles in the cities brought the propaganda of the deed to the fore. Its principal ideologue was a provincial teacher, Sergei Nechaev, whose daytime job was teaching theology in a parish school. At night he devoured the texts of the French Revolution and won himself over to the anarchist cause. In 1866, he left his job and moved to St Petersburg to meet likeminded people. The city was still buzzing with a series of clandestine pamphlets titled *Young Russia* and distributed in the name of Peter Zaichnevsky, yet another admirer of the Jacobins, Mazzini and the Italian Carbonari, the leading exponents of 'revolutionary conspiracy' and terrorism. To this group must be added the name of Pierre-Joseph Proudhon, the French author of *What Is Property?* – the answer to which became more famous than the essay. It was Proudhon who first proposed the idea of a decentred socialism against a centralised state. Zaichnevsky had been translating Proudhon into Russian when he was arrested. His own particular contributions would have shocked poor Proudhon, not to mention Tolstoy and Kropotkin. Herzen, the intellectual father of Russian Populism, declared such views utterly repellent.

In *Young Russia*, Zaichnevsky recalled the heroism of Razin and Pugachev and called for a 'bloody and pitiless' revolution that went beyond the limited aims of their peasant forebears. Now, he argued, in his own version of the friend/enemy dichotomy, it was time to calmly and mercilessly exterminate the tsarist royal family, their courtiers and the nobility that sustained them:

We will cry 'To your axes' and then we will strike the imperial party without sparing our blows just as they do not spare theirs against us. We will destroy them in the squares, if the cowardly swine dare to go there. We will destroy them in their houses, in the narrow streets of the towns, in the broad avenues of the capital, and in the villages. Remember that, when this happens, anyone who is not with us is against us, and an enemy, and that every method is used to destroy an enemy.

This was the political atmosphere of the 1860s in the bohemian and political cellars of the Russian underground. The former theology teacher approved strongly of what was being proposed. Nechaev was one of the most charismatic, if somewhat unhinged, characters produced by Russian anarchism and the competition on this front was always fierce. He became a close collaborator of Bakunin and, according to George Woodcock (one of the more distinguished historians of anarchism), possibly his lover.[6] The combined political-sexual-emotional hold that Nechaev (in his early twenties) had on his ageing comrade is held responsible for Bakunin's ultraleftism and joint authorship of the *Catechism*. The authorship is disputed because of the violence of the language, the ultra-nihilism and political amorality, but the work was far from unpopular at the time. Nechaev, a fantasist in many ways, was not a loner, but a product of the dominant political culture of the period. The *Catechism* contained fanatical passages that offended some, but its tone and rhetoric were not so far removed from those of other clandestine pamphlets that circulated at the time. Numerous activists were lodged in the notorious Peter and Paul Fortress in St Petersburg and others were suffering in Siberia after the anarchist Karakazov had, in an audacious dress rehearsal, fired a few shots at the tsar. The legend of Nechaev was based partly on falsehood: he claimed he had escaped from the Peter and Paul Fortress and it was this that necessitated exile. No such escape had or could have taken place, as Nechaev was not being held there. Bakunin believed him and helped to carefully construct his reputation. He persuaded Ogarev to write a poem in praise of the young man (a work that circulated widely in Russia) while Bakunin produced his own profile of Nechaev, portrayed unambiguously as the prototype of the 1860s revolutionary:

---

6 George Woodcock, *Anarchism*, London, 1963, p. 159. Woodcock writes coyly and with mild homophobia: 'The fascination that Nechaev wielded over Bakunin reminds one of other disastrous relationships between men of widely differing ages: Rimbaud and Verlaine, or Lord Alfred Douglas and Oscar Wilde. There certainly seems to have been a touch of submerged homosexuality; indeed, it is hard to find any other explanation for the temporary submissiveness of the usually autocratic Bakunin to this sinister youth.'

[He is] one of those young fanatics who know no doubts, who fear nothing and who have decided quite definitely that many, many of them will have to perish at the hands of the government but who will not let this stop them until the Russian people arises. They are magnificent, these young fanatics, believers without God, heroes without rhetoric.

The *Catechism* itself was probably written by Bakunin, based on the actions of Nechaev and others. It expresses emotions, ideas and rules which are then given enormous power by the author's literary and political abilities, not all that different from those of his rival Marx but with one important difference. *The Communist Manifesto* is a distillation of the ideas of Marx and Engels, assembled partially from what they had learnt and rejected from Fichte and Hegel and from the theory and practice of the French Revolution, but largely from a synthesis that was working its way through Marx's brain based on analysing the development of capitalism. It was conceived as an internationalist text. The *Manifesto* was a call to delayed action when conditions were rotten-ripe; the transfer of power and authority from one social class to another, while it would require a revolution, would then lead rapidly to a new mode of production and distribution. The transition itself would be painless.

The *Catechism* is effectively a Russian text, written with the express purpose of recruiting new activists. Its most powerful feature, as in much of Bakunin's work, is a sense of urgency, of immediatism which itself is the consequence of a burning hatred for the tsarist autocracy and its dark realities. The text resounds with a call to destroy this system by a series of well-organised acts of terror, like those of the peasant leaders of past rebellions, that would arouse the masses. Bakunin often referred to this past in his many calls to action: 'The times of Stenka Razin are drawing near.' 'It is unlikely that there will be another popular hero like Stenka Razin; his place will be taken by the legions of youth without caste or name . . . collective and therefore invincible.' Who would carry out these actions? The revolutionary, the main subject of this incendiary pamphlet. To be such a person required a break with every aspect of bourgeois society, all its norms and taboos. There are no means towards such a pure end that were not permissible. *Omnia munda mundis.*

Mikhail Bakunin – revolutionary anarchist and
Marx's great political and theoretical rival.

The Revolutionary Catechism, as its name suggests, was a secular instruction manual for radical activists. Its first seven paragraphs (out of a total of twenty-six) concern psychology rather than political economy, a psychology that has reappeared in the twenty-first century and can be observed in full play, although Bakunin and Nechaev's caste of anarchist warriors differs in several important ways from current jihadi terrorist groups. These groups, who invoke Islam to carry out their deadly acts in the Middle East, Africa, Europe and elsewhere, have no clearly stated political aims and veer from one local potentate to another. The prevailing socioeconomic system poses no problems for them unless it prevents them from taking power. They often target the common people, including those of their own faith. As the paragraphs below indicate, though, there are more than a few analogies between these twenty-first-century jihadis and nineteenth-century anarchists:

Paragraph 1. The revolutionary is a lost man; he has no interests of his own, no cause of his own, no feelings, no habits, no belongings; he does not even have a name. Everything in him is absorbed by a single, exclusive interest, a single thought, a single passion – the revolution.

Paragraph 2. In the very depths of his being, not just in words but in deed, he has broken every tie with the civil order, with the educated world and all laws, conventions and generally accepted conditions, and with the ethics of this world. He will be an implacable enemy of this world, and if he continues to live in it, that will only be so as to destroy it the more effectively.

Paragraph 3. The revolutionary despises all doctrinarism. He has rejected the science of the world, leaving it to the next generation; he knows only one science, that of destruction.

Paragraph 4. He despises public opinion; he despises and hates the existing social ethic in all its demands and expressions; for him, everything that allows the triumph of the revolution is moral, and everything that stands in its way is immoral.

Paragraph 5. The revolutionary is a lost man; with no pity for the State and for the privileged and educated world in general, he must himself accept no pity. Every day he must be prepared for death. He must be prepared to bear torture.

Paragraph 6. Hard with himself, he must be hard towards others. All the tender feelings of family life, of friendship, of love, gratitude and even honour must be stifled in him by a single cold passion for the revolutionary cause. For him there is only one pleasure, one consolation, one reward, and one satisfaction – the success of the revolution. Day and night he must have one single thought, one single purpose: merciless destruction. With this aim in view, tirelessly and in cold blood, he must be always prepared to die and kill with his own hands anyone who stands in the way of achieving it.

Paragraph 7. The character of the true revolutionary has no place for any romanticism, sentimentality, enthusiasm or seduction. Nor has it any place for private hatred or revenge. This revolutionary passion which in him becomes a daily, hourly passion, must be combined with cold calculation. Always and everywhere he must become not what his own personal inclination would have him become, but what the general interest of the revolution demands.

The other paragraphs in the *Catechism*, more hair-raising in their details, deal with a variety of subjects, including how to treat each stratum of Russian society and the degree of hatred that must be expended on the upper echelons. The most intelligent personnel in high places pose the biggest threat to the revolution. For these worthies there is a single solution: extermination. Those who are of lesser intelligence should be left alone for the time being, since their stupidity only leads them to make decisions that enrage the people and push them in the direction of revolution. The majority of dignitaries are mere 'animals', in constant fear of losing their power and privileges; their punishment (outlined in Paragraph 19) is simple blackmail: 'We must get hold of their dirty secrets and so make them our slaves.'

The pamphlet concludes with a call to destroy the old state and for a revolution that 'annihilates all State traditions, order and classes in Russia'. The final paragraphs set out the parameters of what is required and how it should be achieved:

Paragraph 25. To do this we must draw close to the people: we must ally ourselves mainly with those elements of the people's life which ever since the foundation of the State of Moscow have never given up protesting, not just in words but in deeds, against anything directly or indirectly tied to the state; against the nobility, the bureaucracy, the priests, against the world of guilds and against the kulaks. We must ally ourselves with the doughty world of brigands, who in Russia are the only true revolutionaries.

Paragraph 26. All our organization, all our conspiracy, all our purpose consists in this: to regroup this world of brigands into an invincible and omni-destructive force.

In the fall of 1869, Nechaev returned to Russia and formed a clandestine group that could simultaneously spread the word and accomplish the deed. Notepaper of the still non-existent Central Committee of the People's Justice, adorned with an interlocking axe, dagger and pistol, was used to intimidate opponents. Up to this point, Nechaev had been regarded as a courageous and charismatic character, with numerous stories about his adventures (many of them untrue) circulating in the Russian underground. Soon after his return to Russia, however, he fell out with Ivanov, another member of his group, for reasons that remain obscure. Nechaev accused Ivanov of being a police agent (for which there was no evidence), charged him with, among other things, a 'breach of discipline' (which probably meant a disagreement with Nechaev) and then ambushed and killed him. The discovery of Ivanov's stabbed body a few days later created a huge sensation. Nechaev was accused of murder and, once again, fled into exile. Three hundred revolutionaries were arrested and seventy-four Nechaevites were tried in 1871, though many of them had not supported their leader's more outlandish tactics. Bakunin had broken with him in the summer of the previous year for a variety of reasons. He was shocked by the murder, and his vanity was wounded: he had been abandoned by his 'boy', who had turned to seducing liberal women to help destroy the bourgeois family. The institution survived the onslaught, though various individual families found themselves the poorer. Nechaev ruthlessly employed blackmail to raise funds for the anarchist cause and, on this particular issue, had Bakunin's support.

Sympathizers with the movement in Russia were horrified. One of them, Fyodor Dostoevsky, broke publicly and dramatically by devoting an entire novel, *The Possessed*, to the grisly episode. In the novel, the character Verkhovensky represents Nechaev, while Shatov is based on Ivanov. It's a savage portrayal and largely justified, but it did not succeed in destroying the appeal of Nechaev, whom many continued to regard as a heroic figure and a courageous revolutionary, not completely without reason. In 1872, Nechaev's whereabouts were betrayed to the Swiss police by a Polish revolutionary turned Russian spy. Due to the murder of Ivanov, the Swiss did not accept his status as a political exile this time and extradited him, as a criminal, to Russia.

Nechaev remained unbowed at his trial, refusing to accept the authority of the tsarist court. When he was taken for a mock execution, a quaint custom unique to tsarist Russia, he contemptuously rejected the services of a priest. As he was dragged away he shouted his defiance by invoking the peasant leaders Razin and Pugachev, who had strung up the Russian nobles as the French did much later. 'Before three years are over', he screamed, 'their heads will be hacked off on this very spot by the first Russian guillotine. Down with the tsar. Long live Freedom. Long live the Russian people.'

Alexander II read the report of the mock execution and scribbled a marginal note:

As a result of this we have every right to have him tried again as a political criminal. But I don't think that this would be of much use. And so the more prudent course is to keep him for ever [underlined by the tsar] in prison.

This was the sentence that Nechaev served.

The rest of his life was spent in isolation in cell number 5 of the Alexeyevsky dungeon in the Peter and Paul Fortress in St Petersburg, where he won over quite a few policemen, soldiers and warders. They were impressed by his intelligence and dignity. He used them to send supportive messages to various groups, including one to the central committee of the People's Will, on the eve of their fateful, unanimous decision to assassinate Alexander II. As Vera Figner later recalled in her memoirs, they were amazed and excited to hear that Nechaev was still alive. They wanted to postpone the planned assault on the tsar and free Nechaev instead, but he vetoed the plan, insisting that they stick to their original intention. After they had carried out the act, he suggested, there were other imprisoned revolutionaries – including Leon Mirsky, who had tried to assassinate the chief of police – who deserved the honour much more than him.

On 1 March 1881, the decision made by the leadership of the People's Will was carried out to the letter by a suicide bomber. The tsar, who had survived a number of attempts on his life, was duly assassinated. This emotionless account of the incident by Kropotkin sums up the story:

> In February, 1881, Melikoff reported that a new plot had been laid by the Revolutionary Executive Committee, but its plan could not be discovered by any amount of searching. Thereupon Alexander II decided that a sort of deliberative assembly of delegates from the provinces should be called. Always under the idea that he would share the fate of Louis XVI, he described this gathering as an assembly of notables, like the one convoked by Louis XVI before the National Assembly in 1789. The scheme had to be laid before the Council of State, but then again he hesitated. It was only on the morning of March 1 (13), 1881, after a final warning by Loris Melikoff, that he ordered it to be brought before the council on the following Thursday. This was on Sunday, and he was asked by Melikoff not to go out to the parade that day, there being danger of an attempt on his life. Nevertheless he went. He wanted to see the Grand Duchess Catherine, and to carry her the welcome news. He is reported to have told her, 'I have determined to summon an assembly of notables.' However, this belated and half-hearted concession had not been made public, and on his way back to the Winter Palace he was killed.
>
> It is known how it happened. A bomb was thrown under his iron-clad carriage to stop it. Several Circassians of the escort were wounded. Rysakoff, who flung the bomb, was arrested on the spot. Then, although the coachman of the Tsar earnestly advised the monarch not to get out, saying that he could still drive him in the slightly damaged carriage, Alexander insisted

upon alighting. He felt that his military dignity required him to see the wounded Circassians, to condole with them as he had done with the wounded during the Turkish war, when a mad storming of Plevna, doomed to end in a terrible disaster, was made on the day of his fête. He approached Rysakoff and asked him something; and as he passed close by another young man, Grinevetsky, threw a bomb between himself and Alexander II, knowing full well that both of them would be killed. They both survived but only for a few hours.

Alexander II lay upon the snow, bleeding profusely, abandoned by every one of his followers. All had fled. It was cadets, returning from the parade, who lifted the suffering Tsar from the snow and put him in a sledge, covering his shivering body with a cadet mantle and his bare head with a cadet cap. And it was one of the terrorists, Emelianoff, with a bomb wrapped in a paper under his arm and risking arrest and hanging, forgetting for these moments who he was, who rushed with the cadets to the help of the wounded man. The entire operation had been masterminded by Sofia Perovskaya, who had given the signal for the attack.

Thus ended the tragedy of Alexander II's life. People could not understand how it was possible that a Tsar who had done so much for Russia should have met such a death at the hands of revolution-ists. 'To me', wrote an intimate, 'who had the chance of witnessing the first reactionary steps of Alexander II, and his gradual deteriora-tion, who had caught a glimpse of his complex personality, – that of a born autocrat whose violence was but partially mitigated by education, of a man possessed of military gallantry, but devoid of the courage of the statesman, of a man of strong passions and weak will, – it seemed that the tragedy developed with the unavoidable fatality of one of Shakespeare's dramas. Its last act was already written for me on the day when I heard him address us, the promoted officers, on June 13, 1862, immediately after he had ordered the first executions in Poland.'[7]

---

7 James Harvey Robinson and Charles Beard, eds, *Readings in Modern European History*, vol. 2, Boston, 1908, pp. 362–3.

Nechaev lived on till December 1882. His behaviour in prison was exemplary, as attested to by many contemporaries who saw him at close quarters in the fortress. The short stories, memoirs and political pamphlets that he wrote disappeared. General Potapov, the head of the tsarist secret police, realising how useful this prisoner might be in dismantling the terror networks, visited him in his cell after the tsar's assassination and offered financial rewards and other inducements if Nechaev agreed to become an informer. The enchained prisoner rose to his feet, steadied himself, and used the entire weight of one arm to strike Potapov across the face, drawing much blood. Both his hands and feet were chained and he began to rot. Literally. Within two years Nechaev was dead. He was thirty-five years old.

Nineteenth-century Russian literature is rich in depictions of nihilists, terrorists, revolutionaries. As in life, so in fiction: a single character usually encompassed all three. In Dostoevsky, they were treated severely. Russian novelists did not shy away from politics. They regarded themselves and were seen by their readers as public intellectuals. The 1861 reform heightened the tempo. In the following year, Turgenev wrote *Fathers and Sons*. The distillation of politics into art transpired without any fuss and with tremendous effect. The novel depicts a generational conflict between liberalism and nihilism. The central character, Bazarov, marked a break for Turgenev. Till now his women had been strong and the men slightly pathetic, weak and self-centred (as in some of Pushkin's work). Turgenev identified himself and a majority of his peers as Hamlets, incapable of action, which was reflected in his work. Bazarov is a partial exception. He displays a sense of character and is a strong man, but even he, endlessly subjected to the patronizing and smug conceit of his father, is not allowed to triumph. No victory for the brave. Resigned to his fate, he dies passively, much to the anger of Turgenev's younger readers. By contrast, Ivan Goncharov's masterpiece, *Oblomov*, is the self-portrait of an entire social stratum and pitiless in its depiction. Lenin loved this novel. The average Russian nobleman is lazy, indolent, empty-headed and beyond redemption. The novel's success was celebrated by the entry of a new word into the Russian lexicon: *oblomovism*, used by liberals, anarcho-Populists and Marxists alike. In *The Precipice* (1869), Goncharov pillories a nihilist (a word invented by Turgenev as a virtual synonym for a radical student) without restraint. There is not the least trace of sympathy.

The emergence of a social-realist school of writers and critics was partially a response to these liberal writers and largely an attempt to connect with the growing movement of the *razochyny*. The two most prominent representatives of this increasingly radical wing of the intelligentsia were the essayist, historian and novelist N. G. Chernyshevsky and the fierce literary critic Nikolay Dobrolyubov. Both were sons of respected priests, both recorded happy childhoods; even as they rejected religion and the Orthodox Church in favour of science and materialism, they retained an affection for the moral atmosphere that had prevailed in their respective homes. It was the fierce honesty of their fathers that appealed to them. They loathed hypocrisy on every level: social, political, sexual. And their stinging prose left its mark. On one occasion, Turgenev accosted Chernyshevsky simply to inform him: 'You are a snake, but Dobrolyubov is a rattlesnake.'

Chernyshevsky's utopian novel *What Is to Be Done?* was written in the Peter and Paul Fortress, where he had been incarcerated because of his political beliefs. The hero is a dedicated and ascetic revolutionary (who could not be more different to Bazarov in *Fathers and Sons,* or the real-life Nechaev) who sacrifices all for the cause. Even his name, Rakhmetov, was chosen with care. He descends from a thirteenth-century Tatar family of the high nobility; the novelist paints a four-page pen portrait of the origins and history of the family. He took for granted that his readers were only too aware that many Tatars (who had by then turned Muslim) had fought under Pugachev against the tsar. A forebear had married a Russian woman, a common occurrence, and the resulting dynasty had retained many positions within the state apparatus. The fictional Rakhmetov's fictional grandfather had accompanied Alexander I to Tilsit. Given Chernyshevsky's deep knowledge of Russian history, it's likely that the character was based on a real person. What we are not told is that the name Rakhmet is of Arab origin, and means 'mercy'.

While the novel lacked the literary power of Dostoevsky, Turgenev or Tolstoy, it became the bible of the new generation in Russia, the 'young people' entering the struggle against the autocracy. It's difficult to recall a work of fiction that had an analogous impact on political consciousness elsewhere though, half a century ago, an American critic proposed a fascinating comparison.[8]

The fact that Lenin titled his first major political essay 'What Is to Be Done?' is not coincidental. He would have been amazed if a friend had predicted that one day, people would try to read the original in order to better understand its successor. The novel, too, was a call to action and written precisely for that purpose. Judged by its own criteria, it was a huge success. Its sympathetic treatment of women, in particular, was widely noted in a country where patriarchy, little different from contemporary Saudi Arabia, ruled supreme. In contrast to that unfortunate country, however, many women joined secret societies and participated in the acts decided upon by terrorist organisations.[9] As we shall see in a later chapter,

8 'Yet no work in modern literature, with the possible exception of *Uncle Tom's Cabin*, can compete with *What Is to Be Done?* in its effect on human lives and its power to make history. For Chernyshevsky's novel, far more than Marx's *Capital*, supplied the emotional dynamic that eventually went to make the Russian Revolution.' J. Frank, 'N. G. Chernyshevsky: A Russian Utopia', *Southern Review* 3, 1967

9 Article 107 of the Imperial Code of Civil Laws left little room for ambiguities. The hand of the Orthodox Church was far from invisible when it came to institutionalising the subservience of women to men. A woman needed her husband's (or father's) permission to get a passport or to work, to travel or live in a separate apartment. As in Saudi Arabia, she could own property, but inheritance rights were restricted. A divorce was both humiliating and virtually impossible (a husband's adultery and physical abuses were so common that the Church refused to accept these as grounds for permanent separation). Education was limited to home tutors or elite finishing schools for wealthy women. Most professions were closed to women. The Code insisted that a 'wife must obey her husband as head of the family, live with him in love and treat him with esteem, utmost respect, unlimited obedience and humility due to him as master of the house.' We can only speculate whether the Code would have allowed women the right to drive a car had such a contraption existed at the time.

revolutionary feminists openly acknowledged their debt to the ideas contained in Chernyshevsky's masterwork, including the role and function of the family and monogamy.

Lenin's text, first published in 1902, was an attempt to both critique and move beyond the tactical and strategic limitations of prior revolutionary organisations. A break was necessary. The Executive Committee of the People's Will (Narodnaya Volya) had scored its biggest success on 1 March 1881 by assassinating Alexander II, but also its biggest failure. It had successfully targeted the heart of the regime, but had burnt itself out in the process. The repression was heavy, the hanging chains of Siberia heavier still and though many young suicide terrorists were queuing up to join, the organisation was beginning to disintegrate. Its own leader, Zhelyabov, confessed that 'we are using up our capital' and while small groups spontaneously emerged in different parts of the country, they were, in the main, ignored by the radical intelligentsia. The reason was not simply fear (though that played its part) but a feeling that the basic outline of the original programme was, to put it at its mildest, faulty. The aim of the terror was to rouse the people from their torpor and trigger a mass uprising based on previous models (Razin/Pugachev), but this time under new conditions and in order to completely destroy the autocracy and its institutions. It never worked out and, in a grumpy mood, Lenin once characterised terrorists as liberals with bombs, suggesting that both held the opinion that propaganda alone, of deed or word, would be sufficient for the task that lay ahead. For the most part terrorist acts scared people and legitimated government repression.

Till now the Executive Committee had won the admiration and financial support of many intellectuals who felt that they were on the right track. Key members of the committee were at the house of Gleb Uspensky, a major pro-Populist writer, on 1 March, waiting for news of the operation. They drank to success and then withdrew to compose a powerful open letter to the dead man's son. The opening paragraph was suitably defiant, even while misjudging the writers' own strength. They informed Alexander III that 'the bloody tragedy which took place along the

Catherine Canal was not just the result of chance and was not unexpected. After everything that has been happening for the last ten years, it was inevitable.' They warned him that their struggle against the autocracy would continue, unless political prisoners were released and a national assembly convened via elections based on proportionality and without any restrictions whatsoever, including freedom of speech, press, assembly and electoral programmes. This would enable Russia to develop peacefully: 'We solemnly declare before our beloved Fatherland and the entire world that our party will of its own accord unconditionally submit to the decisions of a National Assembly.'

The initial reaction of the court to the death of the tsar was fear. When the open letter reached him, the new monarch burst into tears and had to be comforted by his tutor. But the autocracy was soon back on course. Tsarist ministers and advisers had noted the absence of uprisings or popular assemblies anywhere in the country. And the hard-line councillors of Alexander III turned their back on concessions of any sort and accelerated the counterreformation. A chain of legal proclamations sought to seal off free thought of any kind. Violations of these ordinances led to swift and brutal punishments. The mood in the country became despairing.

Having isolated themselves, the People's Will was dismantled by the repression and by the rapid dwindling of popular support. The end for leading members of the Executive Committee came in the month that followed the assassination of the tsar. Only one of them recanted. The others walked to the gallows with their heads held high:

Sofia Perovskaya, Kibalchich, Gesia Gelfman and Mikhailov, all confirmed the ideas for which they had sacrificed their lives. Sofia Perovskaya was outstandingly brave, Kibalchich revealed his true worth, and showed himself a man of genius, always concerned with the technical problem of the relations between ends and means. In his prison cell he went on designing a plan for a flying machine, which he regretted not being able to finish before he was hanged. Only Rysakov said that he was a peaceful socialist and he felt

remorse for his terrorist activities . . . At 9.50 in the morning of 3rd
April 1881, Rysakov, Zhelyabov, Mikhailov, Kibalchich and Sofia
Perovskaya climbed the scaffold. With the exception of Rysakov
they all embraced for the last time. Then they were hanged.[10]

There is a postscript to this story. Peter Kropotkin, the anarchist
philosopher, was living in comfortable exile in England when
the Russian Revolution erupted. Seventy-five years of age now,
the old man was incredibly excited and decided to go back. He
went first to visit his old haunts in Petrograd, but decided not
to stay there and moved instead to Moscow. He arrived quietly
without any fuss or fanfare. His daughter tried to persuade him
to move back to the old family house in the country, but Kropotkin
wanted to live in the capital. His daughter went to the offices
of Sovnarkom (the Council of People's Commissars) and met
with V. D. Bonch-Bruevich, secretary for the organisation and
Lenin's personal secretary. She described all the problems she had
encountered trying to find modest accommodation for her aged
father. Despite the chaos, it was an unwritten law that revolutionaries returning from exile would be provided with permanent
accommodation.

Bonch-Bruevich informed Lenin of the problem, who instructed
him to find accommodation for the old man immediately. Bonch-
Bruevich then visited Kropotkin to welcome him back. Kropotkin's
views came as a pleasant surprise. He supported the revolution
and declared that it had 'proved to everybody that a social revolution was possible'. He was totally hostile to the White Guards and

---

10   This is how Franco Venturi concludes his masterpiece, *Roots of
Revolution: A History of the Populist and Socialist Movements in 19th
Century Russia*, London, 1960. The original Italian edition was
published in 1952. It is undoubtedly the finest book to be written on the
Russian revolutionaries of the nineteenth century and their lineages.
Venturi, an anti-fascist who had fled to France with his parents from
Mussolini's Italy, was in Moscow in 1930 where he was allowed access
to all the nineteenth-century historical archives, then housed in the
Lenin Library. His Soviet colleagues, to his great regret, were denied
this access until de-Stalinisation in 1956.

anti-Soviet forces and commended the Bolsheviks for having moved on from February to October. As an anarchist, naturally, he did not agree with the organisation of the Soviet state or the role of the party, but was interested in reading Lenin's *State and Revolution*:

> I was told that Vladimir Ilyich wrote an excellent book about the State which I have not yet read, in which he puts forward a prognosis that the State would in the end wither away ... By this single shaft of light thrown boldly on the teaching of Marx, Vladimir Ilyich has earned the deepest respect ... I regard the October revolution as an endeavour to achieve the transition to communism and federalism.

Lenin asked to see Kropotkin and the two men met at the Sovnarkom offices in early May 1919. Bonch-Bruevich was present and his record of the meeting is instructive. Lenin admired Kropotkin not for his anarchism, but for his history of the French Revolution that had educated two generations of Russian radicals. Lenin regarded this book by Kropotkin as an indispensable classic and wanted it reprinted and placed in every library. The discussion opened with an exchange of views on the cooperative, with both men explaining their positions on this subject. Kropotkin complained of bureaucratic harassment of genuine cooperatives by local authorities, 'perhaps even people who yesterday were revolutionaries, changed as all authorities do, into bureaucrats, into officials, who want to twist their subordinates and who think that the whole population is subordinated to them.'

Lenin's response was immediate:

> We are against officialdom always and everywhere. We are against bureaucratisation, and we must pull up bureaucracy by its roots if it still nestles in our new system. But you know perfectly well that it is extremely difficult to remake people and that, as Marx used to say, the most inaccessible fortress is the human skull.

Kropotkin countered by pointing out that this explanation did not make things easier for citizens, since 'authority poisons everybody who takes authority on himself.'

Lenin replied by stressing that

you cannot make a revolution in white gloves . . . We are still making many, many mistakes; we correct all that can be corrected; we admit our mistakes – which sometimes result from plain stupidity . . . You should help us, let us know when you see that something is wrong; you can be assured that we shall welcome your remarks with the greatest attention.

After further debate on cooperatives, Lenin explained that 'we need enlightened masses and it would be good if, for example, your book on the great French revolution were published in a very large edition. This book is so useful for all.'

Kropotkin was flattered, but suspicious.

'But who would publish it? I cannot let the State Publishing House do it.'

'No, no,' interrupted Lenin. 'Why, of course not the State Publishing House, but a cooperative publisher.'

'Oh well,' said Kropotkin, 'if you find the book interesting and valuable, I agree . . . Perhaps one could find such a cooperative enterprise.'

'One can find it, one certainly can,' nodded Lenin. 'I am sure of this.'

The deal was done.

During the course of this conversation Lenin explained his views on anarchism and the decisive factor that helped him to solve the dilemma between anarchism and socialism.

It was the necessity of 'a mass struggle', he informed Kropotkin:

We do not need individual terroristic attempts and the anarchists should have understood long ago. Only with the masses, through the masses . . . All other methods, including those of the anarchists, have been relegated to the limbo of history – nobody needs them, they are no good, and they do not attract anybody – they only demoralise people who in one way or another have been drawn on to that old worn-out path.

When Kropotkin died a few years later he was given a state funeral. His remains were laid in the Hall of Columns in the House of Trades Unions. Tens of thousands paid their respects and attended his funeral.

It was the last state funeral of a non-Bolshevik.

Kropotkin had not agreed with the terrorist wing of anarchism but, like Lenin and others, he was part of its shared history. It is to the history of what came after that we must now turn.

2

The Elder Brother

When the People's Will decapitated the head of state in March 1881, the three oldest children of the Ulyanovs (Lenin's family name) in Simbirsk – Anna, Alexander and Vladimir – were aged fifteen, thirteen and eleven respectively. It was a formative period for all of them. Their reaction to the event in St Petersburg was not recorded, but it's safe to assume that they would have been, if not particularly surprised, shocked – though not to the extent of their liberal-conservative father, who denounced the terrorists as criminals, donned his official uniform and rushed off to attend Mass for the dead tsar at the local cathedral.

The oppositional political milieu had been dominated for so many decades by various forms of anarcho-Populism that its ideas were well-known and much discussed. Activist groups existed in nearby Kazan. Attempts to kill the tsar and other powerful figures of the autocracy were regular occurrences. Alexander II was not the first ruler to have been dispatched in this fashion. The fact that the Ulyanov family had never belonged to radical circles did not mean that the children were deaf to what was being discussed on the streets or at school. Even the parents had read magazines in which the ideas of the Populist intellectuals were prominently featured. Denunciations of the regicides became a ritual in schools and at church assemblies every Sunday.

Lenin's father was a conservative and a strong believer in both church and state. His energies as a schools inspector in the region were directed exclusively towards improving and enlarging educational facilities in the region. He was highly respected for his incorruptibility and his devotion to educating the children of poor peasants. At home he was a patriarch, a believer in strict routines and described as fair-minded. There is little doubt that he was mortified by the killing of the tsar, though the counterreformation that sought to reverse the gains made in education angered him greatly.

Alexander Ulyanov was described by his sister Anna as being very much like their mother in both looks and temperament: 'The same rare combination of extraordinary firmness and serenity, with wonderful sensitivity, tenderness and fairness: but he was far more austere and single-minded, and even more courageous.' This judgement was confirmed and strengthened by their private tutor, Kalashnikov, who would speak of Sasha's calm voice and gentle demeanour but added to this combination a powerful 'inner force' that was noticeable even at a young age.[1]

What of the middle brother? In *Lenin's Childhood*, his first and only published chapter of what was intended to be a full-scale biography, Isaac Deutscher drew on Anna Ulyanova's reminiscences to describe the very early years:

> At first the child appeared to develop slowly: he was big-headed and top-heavy, bulky and red-faced, started walking late, constantly tumbling down and knocking his head. But soon he made up for this initial slowness and as a toddler was exceptionally vigorous and nimble, a great rascal, full of mischief and a lover of noisy games. He did not play with his toys, says his elder sister, he broke them. At five he could read and write; then for four years or so a parish teacher tutored him at home until he was ready at the age of nine, to enter the local gymnasium.[2]

---

1   Leon Trotsky, *The Young Lenin*, New York, 1972, p. 38.

2   Isaac Deutscher, *Lenin's Childhood*, London, 1970, p. 12. In her brief introduction, the writer's widow, Tamara Deutscher, wrote: 'Paraphrasing Carlyle, Isaac said that his job as a biographer of Trotsky was to drag out his chief character "from under a mountain of dead dogs, a huge load of calumny and oblivion". In Lenin's biography, Isaac, detesting all orthodoxies, conceived his task as that of dragging his chief character from under a huge load of iconography and stifling orthodoxy.' Tragically, soon after he had begun to write the Lenin biography, Deutscher was felled by a heart attack in August 1967. He had just turned sixty.

The Ulyanov family: Sasha and Anna, resting on their father's shoulders; Lenin sitting on the right; Dmitri to the far left; Maria on her mother's lap.

The headmaster Fyodor Kerensky was, like the father of the brothers Ulyanov, both a conservative liberal and an exacting though stimulating teacher. The two men were good friends. Kerensky's son Alexander, a decade younger than Lenin, would be catapulted into the leadership of the Provisional Government after February 1917, only to be replaced by the Bolsheviks in October.

The bulk of the school's students hailed from the nobility and the upper echelons of the state bureaucracy. Middle-class kids formed just a third of the student body. The Ulyanov boys were spared the school fees (thirty rubles a year) as their father worked for the education department.

The headmaster was generous in his praise of the young Lenin, describing him as his best pupil and someone with the potential to become a classical scholar 'of genius'. Scholarly in the classroom but boisterous and quick-tempered during breaks, Lenin's progress, according to his older sister, greatly satisfied and pleased his father. There was just one worry: 'In those years father would sometimes say to mother that everything was coming to Volodya so easily that he might never acquire the ability to work.' When it was time for compositions in Latin and Russian, the headmaster's motto was '*non multa sed multum*': 'Not many but much' or, less literally, keep your words tight and your thoughts ample. Lenin stuck to this injunction all his life. He disliked flowery prose and the use of grandiose words designed to obfuscate rather than clarify. Latin became a passion bordering on obsession, and Cicero a favourite author. Lenin's oratory, too, in years to come, revealed the mark of the ancient Roman senate. In her own memoirs written after his death, his widow, Nadya Krupskaya, wrote that Lenin had confessed to three dangerous addictions during his youth: Latin, chess and classical music. All three had to be overpowered in order to do full-time revolutionary work, but the passion for chess and music never left him.

Sasha was much more interested in biology and chemistry. Young Volodya would often join him in his study where Sasha was experimenting with chemicals and bury himself in a book. Volodya recognised Sasha's worth and the temperamental qualities which he could never emulate. His short temper and intolerance of stupidity remained a constant throughout his life, and he found it difficult to control this side of himself. Deutscher writes:

His cousin, Veretennikov, recalls that when on one occasion Volodya, yielding to his satirical turn of mind, brought a simple and timid boy to tears with his mockery, he became contrite and did his best to soothe and console his victim.

Relations with his brother had become close. On occasions when they were both immersed in work and visiting cousins burst into the study demanding attention, the brothers would stand up and declaim in unison: 'Please oblige us with your absence.' It didn't always work. Sasha was strikingly handsome and female cousins enjoyed his company. He was also witty and polite, unlike his younger brother who, even as a teenager, could be scathing and extremely rude.

Both were self-contained. Neither had close friends at school. Nor did Lenin display any hint of rebelliousness while at the gymnasium. Till he turned sixteen, he was a conformist as far as politics and religion were concerned. Sasha was much more political and disdained religion, calmly refusing to attend Mass and upsetting his fervently Orthodox father. He had encountered the works of Chernyshevsky, Dobrolyubov and the radical essayist Pisarev. His sister Anna would later write of the forbidden fruits they tasted when she and Sasha were in their last two years at school:

I read together with Sasha all of Pisarev's works from cover to cover; they had a strong impact on us. These books were banned from libraries, but we borrowed them from an acquaintance, a doctor, who had the complete edition of them. These were the first forbidden books we read. We were so absorbed in them that when we finished the last volume we were deeply saddened to have to part from our beloved author. We walked in the garden and Sasha talked to me about the fate of Pisarev who was drowned – it was said that the gendarme who followed and watched him, saw him disappear in the waves, but deliberately did not call for help and let him die. I was deeply agitated . . . Sasha, walking by my side, lapsed into his usual silence, only his concentrated and darkened face showed how strong was his emotion also.

In 1883, a year after he finished at the gymnasium in Simbirsk, Sasha was admitted to the University at St Petersburg to study the natural sciences. Anna was already in the city. It was in the capital that Sasha and she could speak openly and engage in conversations on religion, which had been almost impossible in the backwater they had recently left. They had become atheists together. Later, after tragedy befell the family, it became clear that the two had discussed many things together in secret, but nothing that had made her suspicious. They discussed their parents, their siblings, life in the capital, the room he had rented which was equipped with 'silence, cosiness and the smell of an oil lamp'. He loved his academic work but kept aloof from student groups, telling his sister that 'they jabber a lot, but study little.' And for the first three years, Sasha did nothing but study. There was, in fact, very little else to do and since he was not addicted to either tavern life or brothels, he worked hard.

In 1884, the year Sasha reached the capital, the last radical Populist publication, *Notes of the Fatherland*, was banned. The following year the last issue of the old party's journal, *People's Will*, ceased to exist, following the example of the party that itself had been isolated and liquidated. The journal's farewell commentary was bleak in the extreme, but the regime was leaving nothing to chance. The overall atmosphere was oppressive, intellectual life was stagnant, a blanket of tsarist repression swathed the city. Police spies scoured the taverns and cafés in search of non-existent terrorists.

A senior state bureaucrat sent a scathing description of the court and life in the highest circles to an out-of-favour colleague: 'Everything there is dull-wittedness and idiocy, stupid routine and demoralisation. Nothing useful can be made from this rot and dirt.' The intelligentsia, too, was demoralised and, as is common in times of defeat, turned inwards to a 'life for ourselves'. They abandoned the peasantry, explaining that 'our times are not times for big tasks.' They abandoned the radical writers and artists, arguing that this was the time for 'pure art', drained of even the tiniest presence of reality.

The city was covered in snow in January 1887 when several hundred students gathered outside the Volkovo Cemetery to commemorate the twenty-fifth anniversary of Dobrylubov's death, carrying his portrait with the inscription 'Our Diderot'. They found the cemetery gates sealed and guarded by a platoon of Cossacks on horseback, their hands tight on sabres and whips. For a moment the students remained motionless; then they started singing 'La Marseillaise' and began to move forward slowly. The mounted Cossacks attacked them with whips. There were scuffles. Forty-two students were arrested and exiled from St Petersburg; the others scampered in all directions.

Sasha Ulyanov participated in this demonstration and was radicalised by the Cossack assault on peaceful and unarmed students. News from home was bad. His father had died, his family was dependent on a state pension, funds were low. He was only too aware of his responsibilities. But this event, trivial in itself, had a huge impact on him and other participants. Personal experience, much more than books, is often the most effective agent for transforming political consciousness. Student circles began to discuss a response. They agreed on a proclamation that was to be addressed to 'society' (which meant the liberal intellectuals), but even this did not get through. It was the police, perfectly aware of what was going on, who emptied the letter boxes on this occasion. Many students returned to 'normality'. Not Sasha and a few others. He agonised. Petitions were useless, they agreed. Others suggested that there was only one serious alternative: terrorism. Sasha insisted that careful thought must precede revolutionary action. His friends replied that reading and writing were not enough, that state violence was crushing them. The only response to state violence was revolutionary violence. The arguments were hardly original. They had dominated the 1860s and '70s.

But in those decades, terrorism was understood by many as a necessity. In the '80s, this was no longer the case. What Sasha and his fellow conspirators were plotting was a faint echo of distant thunder. The bomb and the revolver would achieve, or so they imagined, what demonstrations and café talk could not. Once they agreed that the only serious response to the situation was to assassinate the tsar, Sasha, though still unsure and suspecting that there were too many members in the group, did not falter and committed to writing a manifesto explaining the reasons for the action. A total of fifteen students were involved in the conspiracy, including two Poles (one of whom was Bronislaw Pilsudski, whose brother later became the dictator of Poland and a vigorous enemy of Sasha's younger brother). They planned to kill the tsar on 1 March 1887, the anniversary of his father's assassination.

The operation was doomed from the very start. Unlike their forebears responsible for the previous assassination, the students lacked any experience in assassination plots, a seriously considered plan of action and the necessary technical knowledge. Almost a month went by before Pilsudski managed to bring nitric acid from Vilna and the group succeeded in purchasing two secondhand revolvers. Their amateurism was further revealed when one of them wrote a lyrical letter to a comrade in Kharkov in praise of revolutionary terrorism. The letter included enough hints to alert the police, who began to follow the letter-writer and had soon tracked down all of the members of the group. Sasha's instinct about the group's scale was tragically vindicated when two students whose recruitment he had opposed betrayed him to the police. The group preparing to kill the tsar were picked up on the Nevsky Prospect. Meanwhile, the police arrived at Sasha's apartment where an unwitting Anna had dropped in to see her brother. Both of them were arrested. Sasha decided to accept total responsibility, declaring in court:

> I was one of the first who had the idea of forming a terrorist group and I played the most active part in its organisation ... As to my moral and intellectual commitment in this affair – that has been complete. I have given to it all my ability, all my knowledge, and all the force of my convictions.

When the news reached Simbirsk, Sasha's distraught mother asked a neighbour to look after the children and left immediately for the capital. For a whole month she pleaded, she fell on her knees, she did everything humanly possible to save her son. Sasha himself was not hopeful. When he finally met his mother on 30 March, he broke down and wept, asking for her forgiveness and explaining, 'Apart from the duty to one's family, one has a duty to one's country . . . I wanted to kill a man – that means I may now be killed.' The prosecutor, who had the evidence in front of him, was struck by the prisoner's speech: 'Ulyanov takes upon himself many deeds of which he is, in fact, not guilty.' The police had mislaid the manifesto he had written. He rewrote it in the prison and handed it to them; it was immediately taken to the palace at the tsar's request. Alexander III, aged thirty-three at the time, was widely regarded as a semi-literate boor. He read the manifesto and scribbled a comment: 'This is the writing not even of a madman, but a pure idiot.' Where the document said that any effort to raise the intellectual level of the population was impossible, the Father of All His People noted: 'That is reassuring.'

Sasha had few illusions about his fate. In a letter to the tsar, his mother pleaded for mercy and for a commutation of the death sentence. She was turned down. Although she was very impressed by Sasha's eloquent speech at the trial – it was a side of him that she had never seen before – she was weeping too much to sit through all of it and had to leave the court. Her son gave the court an erudite lecture on how other countries had developed and how tsarist Russia had built a roadblock to prevent any peaceful evolution of society. That is why the intelligentsia had to rise to the challenge. Terror was the tactic they used because open struggles for change were barred to them:

> Terror is that form of struggle which has been created by the nineteenth century, the only form of self-defence in which a minority, strong only through its spiritual force and the awareness of its righteousness, can resort against the majority's awareness of physical force . . . Of course terror is not the intelligentsia's weapon in organised struggle. It is only a road that some individuals take spontaneously when their discontent reaches extremity. Thus viewed, terrorism is an expression of the popular struggle and will last as long as the nation's needs are not satisfied . . . You will always find in the Russian nation a dozen people who are so devoted to their ideals and who feel their country's misfortune so deeply that for them to die for their cause is not a sacrifice.

Alexander Ulyanov was hanged on 8 May 1887. He was nineteen years old. His mother was walking to the women's prison in St Petersburg to visit her daughter when she stopped to buy a newspaper. It was here that she first read the news.

3

The Younger Brother

For a decade after the tragedy, Lenin was referred to in radical circles as Alexander Ulyanov's younger brother. As far as officialdom was concerned, the family was now beyond the pale, in total disgrace. Lenin was in his last year at the gymnasium and needed official permission to sit the exam. Kerensky defended his right to do so, pointing out to the authorities that the boy was a brilliant student, and that there was no sign whatsoever that he shared his brother's views. The headmaster's age and experience and his loyalty to the state ensured that his opinion could not be easily ignored. The younger brother sat the exam and, unsurprisingly, did extremely well. As a child he would answer parental questions with two words: 'Like Sasha'. Admiration and competition both played a part. He closely followed his elder brother's activities, learning from and comparing himself to him. His brother's death shook him to the very core. Everything changed. He was radicalised politically by the event and its aftermath. Isaac Deutscher concludes:

> The name of Alexander does not occur in any of Lenin's books, articles, speeches, or even in his letters to his mother and sisters. In all the fifty-five volumes ... of the Russian edition Alexander is mentioned almost incidentally and only twice ... So extraordinary a reticence could not be ascribed to frigidity of feeling: on the contrary, it covered an emotion too deep to be uttered and too painful ever to be recollected in tranquillity.

Sometimes, in a very relaxed mood and with friends, he mentioned Sasha's influence, as recounted in Valentinov's *Memories of Lenin*. Winston Churchill, a lifelong enemy of socialism and communism, was capable, on occasion, of rising above the fray and in his essay on Lenin five years after his death wrote perceptively:

> He was at the age to feel. His mind was a remarkable instrument. When its light shone it revealed the whole world, its history, its sorrows, its stupidities, its shams, and above all its wrongs. It revealed all facts in focus – the most unwelcome, the most inspiring – with an equal ray. The intellect was capacious and in some phases superb. It was capable of universal comprehension in a degree rarely reached among men. The execution of the elder brother deflected this broad white light through a prism: and the prism was red.[1]

After the revolution the poet Mayakovsky wrote something similar, if from a completely different point of view:

> He is earthly –
> But not of those
> Whose nose
> delves only into
> their own little sty.
> He grasped the earth
> whole,
> all at one go.

Life for the family became difficult in Simbirsk. Socially they were boycotted by their peers; people they had known for a long time crossed the street when they saw the boys' mother. This angered Lenin much more than the temporary suspension of the state pension due to his father's widow because the family had

---

1 Winston Churchill, *The World Crisis: The Aftermath*, London, 1929, p. 73.

produced a would-be regicide. It created in him a deep and pure hatred for liberals and their hypocrisies. How easily they were swayed by the changing moods of the establishment. How easy it was for them to hop from one opinion to another and express surprise when reminded of what they had said only a few months ago. This contempt for political chameleons stayed with him all his life, spreading effortlessly to include right-wing social democrats when they behaved in similar fashion.

Lenin in 1887, the year his brother was hanged.

After numerous petitions from his remarkable mother, the pension was restored. The family decided to leave Simbirsk for Kazan, where Lenin studied law at the university. His father had studied there too when the distinguished mathematician Nikolai Lobachevsky (immortalised by the Tom Lehrer song) had been rector of the university and intellectual life had flourished. It was different now. A deadening apathy enveloped the city and the university. Police spies roamed campuses throughout the country. The Ulyanov name was known to all, which meant that Lenin was watched closely from the minute he arrived at the university. His low-key participation in an orderly protest against oppressive conditions led to his first arrest. The gendarme escorting him to prison asked, 'Why are you causing trouble, young man? You're breaking your head against a wall.'

Lenin's response was spirited and prescient: 'The wall is rotten. One good shove and it will collapse.' After four months (including three days in prison), he was expelled from the university.

What would he do? Avenge Sasha? The thought must have occurred to him, but he rejected it. Not because he had become a Marxist – he was still very far from all that. The book that changed him was not *Capital*, as official hagiographers would later maintain, but Chernyshevsky's novel *What Is to Be Done?* In discussions of the book with fellow students and others, he was gradually coming to the conclusion that the sacrifice of his brother and the other five students hanged with him had been in vain. It was the last gasp of a party that was now dead. Not simply because of the repression, but also because the strategy had proved to be ineffective. No act of terror – not even the successful targeting of the tsar – had triggered any mass uprisings. A period of quiet had set in, a gloomy and melancholy time for the young and for the liberal intelligentsia. Nothing remotely progressive seeped through the long twilight of the 1880s. All the radical magazines had been suppressed. The newspapers of Moscow and St Petersburg were dull beyond belief. No critical voices could be published or heard. Time to read books. He devoured them.

Lenin had been banished to his hometown after the Kazan fracas, but since there was nobody left in Simbirsk, the authorities agreed that he could reside at his maternal grandparents' farm in Kokushino, some thirty miles from Kazan. His sister, Anna, was sent there after her release from prison in St Petersburg and the rest of the family moved in as well. Memories of Sasha must have been strong. They had spent most of their summers here and Sasha, disgust written on his face, had once pointed out to his younger brother the enslaved Jewish boys being taken through the streets to unknown places, where they would be forcibly converted to the Orthodox faith. They all thought of Sasha, but did not talk about him much.

The aunts whispered to his mother that whatever else, young Vladimir should be actively discouraged from following in his brother's footsteps. Some hope. It is not known exactly when he first came across a copy of *Capital*. The first Russian translation appeared in 1872. Sasha was reading it while on vacation in the summer of 1886, but Lenin at that time was absorbed in Turgenev and probably did not even notice the title. A dozen or so copies had been circulating in Kazan during his brief stint at the university. During the First World War, Karl Radek later claimed, Lenin told him that he had joined a circle of the People's Will in Kazan, where he first heard of Marx from another student. Infected with Marxist measles at the time, this student, Mandelshtam, later became a liberal-conservative and joined the Constitutional Democrats (Kadets). This rings true. When asked about this period, his sister Anna, the most reliable source on his early life, would reply: 'There wasn't much to say anyway. He read, he studied, he argued.'

The family had received permission to move back to Kazan and Lenin renewed contact with some friends. Fearful of involving his family in any way, he invited none of these friends home. One can presume that none of them wished to visit him either, given the regular police surveillance of the Ulyanovs. Chetvergova, a veteran member of the People's Will, lived in Kazan at the time. Lenin met her on a number of occasions and questioned her in detail about the organisation and its past. Reading Marx played a huge part in his own intellectual formation, but it did not become an immediate substitute for his People's Will affinities. He never spoke about

Sasha and was reticent when Sasha's admirers attempted to engage him. Nor did he ever write about him. The only people with whom he talked about Sasha later and in some detail were his sisters, his wife Nadya Krupskaya and his close comrade and lover Inessa Armand. The tragedy left a deep scar inside him, which never disappeared. In silent homage he avidly read most of the books on Sasha's shelves. Having ignored Chernyshevsky while Sasha was alive, he now read *What Is to Be Done?* and became extremely heated when it was criticised (which was often, because it did not work as literature). Valentinov, once a young Bolshevik, who became well acquainted with Lenin during his Swiss exile, recalled Lenin's explosive response when he criticised the book:

Chernyshevsky's novel fascinated and captivated my brother. It also captivated me. *It ploughed me over again completely* . . . It is useless to read it when your mother's milk has not yet dried on your lips. Chernyshevsky's novel is too complex, too full of thoughts and ideas, in order to be understood and valued at a young age. I myself tried to read it when I was fourteen years old . . . It was a worthless and superficial reading that did not lead to anything. But then, after the execution of my brother, knowing that Chernyshevsky's novel was one of his favourite works, I began what was a real reading and pored over the book not several days, but several weeks. Only then did I understand its full depth. It is a work which gives one a charge for a whole life . . . It is his great merit that he not only showed that any correctly thinking and truly honest person must be a revolutionary, but also something more important: what a revolutionary should be like, what rules he should follow, how he should approach his goal and what means and methods he should use to achieve it . . . Before I came to know Marx, Engels, Plekhanov, only Chernyshevsky wielded a dominant influence over me, and it all began with *What Is to Be Done?*[2]

2 Nikolay Valentinov, *Encounters with Lenin*, New York, 1968. The best personal-political biography of Lenin precisely because it lacks reverence. Valentinov was the underground pseudonym of N. V. Volsky, from a leading aristocratic family. The family estates were situated in a

It was a slow path that took him from People's Will to Social Democracy. Even when he had definitively moved on, he always retained a soft spot for the old terrorists, knew their places of residence in different parts of the country and would make time to go and see them whenever possible. More importantly, his ideas of how a revolutionary party should function in conditions of clandestinity owed something to the pre-Marxist revolutionary traditions of tsarist Russia.

Had the People's Will recovered and regrouped, Lenin might have been confronted with a serious dilemma. But it was already clear that the party was irretrievable. This had been evident in the complete failure of the 1887 plot carried out by Sasha and his comrades. The year that followed cemented the collapse. Lev Tikhimirov, the principal theoretician and strategist of the People's Will who had a few years previously argued for a seizure of power and an immediate socialist revolution, had dramatically changed his line. In March 1888 he declared his solidarity with the autocracy and published a widely distributed pamphlet entitled *Why I Have Ceased to Be a Revolutionary*. Several thousand People's Will activists followed his lead and changed sides. The anarchist poet Nadson's last lines included one addressed to his own generation: 'No, I no longer believe in your ideals.'

The suicide rate amongst young people was frighteningly high. Chekhov explained the causes thus:

> On the one hand a passionate thirst for life and truth, a dream of activity, broad as the steppes ... On the other, an endless plain, a harsh climate, a grey austere people with its heavy chilling history, savagery, bureaucracy, poverty and ignorance ... Russian life weighs upon a Russian like a thousand-ton stone.

And yet, this same decade of defeat produced the first organised Social Democratic (virtually synonymous with Marxist in those

---

town where Georgy Plekhanov's brother was the chief of police. Young Volsky recalls how nervous policeman Plekhanov used to get when questioned politely on how his brother was getting on in exile.

early years) current in Russia: Emancipation of Labour, whose founders – Georgy Plekhanov, Vera Zasulich and Deutsch – had all once been radical Populists. Zasulich had tried and failed to assassinate General Tepper, the chief of police, in St Petersburg. As far back as 1880, the Executive Committee of the People's Will (itself a recent offshoot of the Land and Freedom Group) had written to Marx: 'Citizen! The intellectual and progressive class in Russia has reacted with enthusiasm to the publication of your scholarly works. They scientifically recognise the best principles of Russian life.' They had obviously been impressed by the strong moral condemnation of exploitation, without fully grasping the central thesis of *Capital*.

A ramshackle bridge from the Populist shore to Social Democracy had been constructed. In 1893 Lenin, newly arrived in the capital, joined one of the Emancipation of Labour groups in St Petersburg, in which Peter Struve, Tugan-Baransky and Potresov were already active. Henceforth his own life was fused with this party that had recognised as their own the cause of the industrial workers, who laboured in appalling conditions in the factories mushrooming on the fringes of the city.

A different and equally tiny study circle, led by a local Marxist operating under the nom de guerre of Julius Martov and composed exclusively of students, was already meeting in the city. Martov was convinced that the stagnation of the intelligentsia was temporary and that the struggle of labour against capital would soon dominate the big cities, render Populism redundant and win over both workers and intellectuals to the cause. His main worry was whether they would be able to organise a workers' party in time:

> Whether one succeeds in realising that task before the occurrence of that revolution toward which Russia's present condition is moving, or not, is all the same. If not, then we shall take part in the revolution side by side with the other progressive parties; if so, then the organised social-democratic party will prove capable of retaining the fruits of victory in the hands of the working class.

To do what? The debates regarding the character of the revolution that adherents of all these groups sought had not yet begun. One interpretation of Marxist orthodoxy suggested a bourgeois democratic upheaval to get rid of the autocracy and start a new phase in Russian history, creating the space needed for the transition to socialism. The model, envisaged in its broadest sense, was that of the French Revolution.

Martov, slightly fed-up with café talk, decided to move temporarily to Vilna to test his theories on the Jewish workers of the city. Heartened by the results of the experiment, Martov returned to St Petersburg with something to report and a pamphlet he had written with Arkadi Kremer, a Vilna activist: *On Agitation*. This text, suggesting a way out of the intellectuals/workers dichotomy by stressing the unity of theory and practice, made an extremely strong impression on Lenin. He understood that practice was an essential component of revolutionary consciousness. The mass of workers would be radicalised through their own collective experiences, but what about the theory?

In 1895 the two circles of Social Democrats combined to form the St Petersburg Union of Struggle for the Liberation of the Working Class. Similar developments were taking place in Moscow and Kiev. The increased frequency of workers' struggles throughout the country led some participants to argue that they should be joining these fights; workers would discover through experience that the authorities always sided with the employers, which would push them towards a Marxist understanding of the system as a whole. Some Social Democrats disagreed, arguing that the workers did not need anyone else to guide them. Their industrial strength was sufficient to take them forward. The idea itself was not new. Populist groups had set up workers' circles in the factories to help them organise and fight for everyday improvements. Now it was being proposed by Kuskova (an early Social Democrat in Moscow) that a separate political party was unnecessary and that the efforts of Russian Marxists should be limited to helping the workers in the factories while participating in the liberal constitutionalist movement backed by the Russian bourgeoisie.

Both Lenin and Martov, the two dominant figures of the fledgling Social Democrats, strongly opposed these ideas. Lenin's theoretical abilities and skill in deconstructing and demolishing arguments which he considered mistaken had established his authority. In a group almost completely populated with intellectuals, it could hardly be otherwise. In *What the 'Friends of the People' Are and How They Fight the Social Democrats* (1894), he spelt out the processes at work in Russia and insisted strongly on its capitalist evolution. He did not argue that Russian capitalism had completed its work and that all that lay ahead was socialist revolution.[3] The main line of his argument, as he explained to a colleague, was that 'the disintegration of our small producers (the peasants and handicraftsmen) appears to be the basic and principal fact explaining our urban and large-scale capitalism, dispelling the myth that the peasant economy represents some special structure.'

Soon afterwards he decided to go abroad and consult various figures in exile as well as activists in European Social Democracy. He may also have wanted to get out of the country to reflect, and recover from family tragedies. His younger sister, Olga, to whom he was very attached, had died of typhoid at the age of nineteen, after which Lenin had put all else to the side and spent the summer of 1891 with his mother in Samara. In Europe in 1895, he met the elders of Russian Marxism: Plekhanov and Axelrod in Switzerland, Paul Lafargue (Marx's son-in-law) in Paris and Wilhelm Liebknecht in Berlin. The meetings with the Russians were amicable. Lenin was a diligent student and listened happily on this occasion to Plekhanov, who was equally happy to be admired by this young man and impressed by his intensity.

The strike waves of 1896–97 reinforced Lenin's view that the creation of a unified all-Russian Social Democratic Labour Party (RSDLP) could not be left to the future. In order to prepare for this

---

3 The most illuminating and meticulous study of the evolution of Lenin's ideas and the extent to which they did or did not diverge from Marx is contained in Neil Harding, *Lenin's Political Thought*, vol. 1, London, 1977. Both this and volume 2 are now available in a single paperback.

task, Social Democrats had to agree and present a coherent set of ideas and organisational plans. The tsarist police had other ideas. Martov and Lenin were arrested in 1897 and sentenced to three years of exile in Siberia. The First Congress of the RSDLP took place in Minsk in 1898. Lenin had added a brief appendix to his pamphlet *The Tasks of the Russian Social Democrats*. Haunted by the fate of his brother, who had been betrayed by two weak-minded recruits, Lenin insisted that in Russia, the Social Democrats would need to work underground, create false identities and rely on other forms of deception in order to defend the organisation:

> Without a strengthening and development of revolutionary disci-
> pline, organisation and underground activity, struggle against the
> government is impossible. And underground activity demands
> above all that groups and individuals specialise in different aspects
> of work and that the job of co-ordination be assigned to the central
> group of the League of Struggle, with as few members as possible.

Theoretically, the coming revolution would be based on the growing strength of the proletariat, aided by the quickening pace of capitalist development and therefore bourgeois democratic in character. Its main task would be the complete abolition of the landed estates on which the autocracy rested. This would clear the space for untrammelled capitalist development which would increase the size and weight of the proletariat, thus bringing it face to face with its enemy. And this enemy was not particular individuals, however repugnant their behaviour, but the entire capitalist class. A democratic revolution was crucial in order to create legal and other structures that permitted freedom of association and a press that allowed the workers and their organisations the political space to perceive their own strength.

In 1900, soon after they had served their term in Siberia, it was agreed by their colleagues that Lenin and A. N. Potresov should go abroad for a summit with Plekhanov, Axelrod and Zasulich to discuss the future plans of the movement and the launching of a Marxist newspaper – *Iskra* (Spark) – in exile to promote their views. Martov would stay on in Russia, for the time being, in order to organise Social Democratic groups. The discussions in Switzerland with the Old Guard initially went well: Lenin supported them politically against some of their younger opponents in exile, whose views on the party's programme were at loggerheads with those of Plekhanov and Axelrod. As Lenin would soon discover, Plekhanov brooked no opposition on theoretical and organisational questions and was becoming more and more cranky as time went by.

Soon after his meeting with the 'Father of Russian Marxism', Lenin wrote an unusual text: *How the 'Spark' Was Nearly Extinguished*. Unusual in the sense that it reads like a diary, a form that he usually disliked. That he was excited and slightly nervous at the thought of winning over the grandees of Russian Marxism to support *Iskra* is not a surprise, but as he listened to them in turn, his nervousness evaporated. First stop was Zurich, where he found a charming Paul Axelrod: 'The conversation was as between friends who had not seen each other for a long time; we spoke about anything and everything, in no particular order.' In Geneva he was warned by another exile to be cautious – since a split in the union of exiles abroad, Plekhanov was in a particularly paranoid state of mind. Lenin described the meeting as a disaster:

> My conversation with him did indeed show that he really was suspicious, distrustful, and . . . I tried to observe caution and avoided all 'sore' points, but the constant restraint that I had to place on myself could not but greatly affect my mood. From time to time little 'frictions' arose in the form of sharp retorts on the part of Plekhanov to any remark that might even in the least degree cool down or soothe the passions that had been aroused (by the split). There was also 'friction' over questions concerning the tactics of the magazine, Plekhanov throughout displaying complete intolerance, an inability or an unwillingness to understand other people's arguments, and, to employ the correct term, insincerity.

The meeting between the 'older' and 'younger' generations reached a crisis point when Plekhanov accused Lenin and his comrades in St Petersburg of being too conciliatory to their opponents. When Lenin suggested that the new paper should be open to debate and discussion, the older man could not control his rage and

> refused to listen to our arguments. He displayed a hatred towards 'the Union-Abroad people' that bordered on the indecent (suspecting them of espionage, accusing them of being swindlers and rogues, and asserting that he would not hesitate to 'shoot' such 'traitors', etc.) ... It became evident that he and we were becoming increasingly disgruntled on the character of a manifesto.

The first meeting of the Emancipation of Labour Group, 1879.

After a few days of cooling down and an agreement of sorts on the first editorial, the entire Emancipation of Labour Group except for Martov – the three elders, Lenin and Potresov (Arsenyev) – met as a conference. An early item on the agenda was the attitude that should be taken to the Jewish Bund, a Social Democratic organisation for Jewish workers that was far more familiar with the everyday concerns and needs of Jewish workers and their families than any other organisation in the tsarist lands. Plekhanov now threw an anti-Semitic tantrum that deeply shocked Lenin:

Georgy Plekhanov: From early anti-Semitism to national chauvinism during the First World War.

Plekhanov displayed extreme intolerance (towards the Bund) and openly declared it to be an organisation of exploiters who exploit the Russians and not a Social-Democratic organisation. He said that our aim was to eject this Bund from the Party, that the Jews are all chauvinists and nationalists, that a Russian party should be Russian and should not render itself into 'captivity' to the 'brood of vipers', etc. None of our objections to these indecent speeches had any result and Plekhanov stuck to his ideas to the full, saying that we simply did not know enough about the Jews, that we had no real experience in dealing with Jews.

It was agreed to delay a discussion on this subject till the next conference; but on other matters too, Plekhanov's attitude struck Lenin 'as being particularly repellent' and showing 'clearly enough that normal relations did not exist between him and us'. The idea for starting a new paper had originated with Lenin and Martov in St Petersburg at one of the meetings of their new organisation.

Since it would have to be published abroad, it was suggested that they try and get the veterans on board. Plekhanov refused to accept that a handful of young whippersnappers freshly arrived from Russia were going to edit the paper. His ego, always heading in a stratospheric direction, was hurt. He refused to write the 'declaration' or to collaborate in its production, but carried on sniping and 'casually threw in a venomous, malicious, remark', describing Lenin as a 'careerist' and so on. Plekhanov won the battle to maintain control, leaving behind a residue of bitterness and resentment. Lenin summarised the situation thus:

As soon as we found ourselves alone, after leaving the steamer, we broke out into a flood of angry expressions. Our pent-up feelings got the better of us; the charged atmosphere burst into a storm. Up and down our little village we paced far into the night; it was quite dark, there was a rumbling of thunder, and constant flashes of lightning rent the air. We walked along, bursting with indignation. I remember that Arsenyev began by declaring that as far as he was concerned his personal relations with Plekhanov were broken off once and for all, never to be restored. He would maintain business relations with him, but as for personal relations – *finished*. Plekhanov's behaviour had been insulting to such a degree that one could not help suspecting him of harbouring 'unclean' thoughts about us (i.e., that he regarded us as *careerists*). He trampled us underfoot, etc. I fully supported these charges. My 'infatuation' with Plekhanov disappeared as if by magic, and I felt offended and embittered to an unbelievable degree. Never, never in my life, had I regarded any other man with such sincere respect and veneration, never had I stood before any man so 'humbly' and never before had I been so brutally 'kicked'. That's what it was, we had actually been kicked. We had been scared like little children, scared by the grown-ups threatening to leave us to ourselves, and when we funked (the shame of it!) we were brushed aside with an incredible unceremoniousness. We now realised very clearly that Plekhanov had simply laid a trap for us that morning when he declined to act as a co-editor; it had been a deliberate chess move, a snare for guileless 'pigeons' . . . And since a man with whom we desired to co-operate closely and establish most intimate relations, resorted to chess moves in dealing with comrades, there could be no doubt that this man was bad, yes, bad, inspired by petty motives of personal vanity and conceit – an insincere man. This discovery – and it was indeed a discovery – struck us like a thunderbolt; for up to that moment both of us had stood in admiration of Plekhanov, and, as we do with a loved one, we had forgiven him everything; we had closed our eyes to all his shortcomings; we had tried hard to persuade ourselves that those shortcomings were really non-existent, that they were petty things that bothered only people who had no proper regard for principles. Yet we ourselves had been taught practically that those 'petty' shortcomings were capable of repelling the most devoted friends, that no appreciation of his theoretical correctness could make us forget his *repelling* traits. Our indignation knew no bounds. Our ideal had been destroyed; gloatingly we trampled it underfoot like a dethroned god. There was no end to the charges we hurled against him. It cannot go on like this, we decided. We do not wish, we will not, we *cannot* work together with him under such conditions. Good-bye, magazine!

Young comrades 'court' an elder comrade out of the great love they bear for him – and suddenly he injects into this love an atmosphere of intrigue, compelling them to feel, not as younger brothers, but as fools to be led by the nose, as pawns to be moved about at will, and, still worse, as clumsy *Streber* who must be thoroughly frightened and quashed! An enamoured youth receives from the object of his love a bitter lesson – to regard all persons 'without sentiment', to keep a stone in one's sling. Many more words of an equally bitter nature did we utter that night. The suddenness of the disaster naturally caused us to magnify it, but, in the main, the bitter words we uttered were true. Blinded by our love, we had actually behaved like *slaves*, and it is humiliating to be a slave. Our sense of having been wronged was magnified a hundredfold by the fact that 'he' himself had opened our eyes to our humiliation.

Even as all this was going on in the tiny confines of Switzerland, back at home some of the opponents of Plekhanov were putting forward ideas that were leading to an effective rapprochement with the autocracy. These included syndicalism, a blind worship of existing class consciousness and an inability to think ahead. The economistic currents of these 'legal Marxists' were all mired in presentism, arguing, 'What exists may not be permanent but we have to accompany it till there is a change. Then we will accompany that change.'

The lodestar for most Social Democrats was the German Social Democratic Party (SPD). It was seen by European socialists, including Lenin, as a model party. But he insisted that it could afford luxuries, such as an embedded and well-defined revisionist minority in its ranks, because conditions in Germany were the opposite of those in Russia. Since 1890 the group had been able to operate legally. It had a clear-cut Marxist programme, a highly developed press, well-established methods for resolving disputes and leaders with real authority. The contrast was obvious. The German model, almost perfect for democratic countries, could not be reproduced in tsarist Russia.

This was the context in which Lenin's first major *political* work was written and published in 1902. He titled it *What Is to Be Done?* as a homage to the old radical Populist. Reading the text can be disconcerting, since it is a series of polemics aimed at groups long extinct. But it is equally disconcerting to those who open its pages hoping to find prescriptions for building a conspiratorial underground party. It is not a Marxist version of Nechaev's *Catechism*. And a reader might even be shocked to find a defence of 'dreaming' in the middle of the text where Lenin is sharply critical of those who can't think beyond the concrete conditions of factory life. Suddenly the familiar figure of Pisarev makes an appearance, and Lenin quotes from his essay 'Blunders of Immature Thought':

'There are rifts and rifts,' wrote Pisarev of the rift between dreams and reality. 'My dream may run ahead of the natural march of events or may fly off at a tangent in a direction in which no natural march of events will ever proceed. In the first case my dream will not cause any harm; it may even support and augment the energy of the working men ... There is nothing in such dreams that would distort or paralyse labour-power. On the contrary, if man were completely deprived of the ability to dream in this way, if he could not from time to time run ahead and mentally conceive, in an entire and completed picture, the product to which his hands are only just beginning to lend shape, then I cannot at all imagine what stimulus there would be to induce man to undertake and complete extensive and strenuous work in the spheres of art, science, and practical endeavour ... The rift between dreams and reality causes no harm if only the person dreaming believes seriously in his dream, if he attentively observes life, compares his observations with his castles in the air, and if, generally speaking, he works conscientiously for the achievement of his fantasies. If there is some connection between dreams and life then all is well.' Of this kind of dreaming there is unfortunately too little in our movement.

As early as 1907, Lenin made it clear that the prescriptions outlined were neither universally applicable nor would they be needed forever in Russia:

Concerning the essential content of the pamphlet it is necessary to draw the attention of the modern reader to the following. The basic mistake made by those who now criticise *What Is to Be Done?* is to treat the pamphlet apart from its connection with the concrete historical situation of a definite, and now long past, period in the development of our Party.

This was true. Neither Marx nor Lenin ever generalised from specifically local experiences. What they did understand, better than most of their peers, was that the foundations of bourgeois society were not immovable and, for Lenin, this understanding was crucial in declaring the twentieth century to be an epoch of wars and revolutions.

The universal importance of *What Is to Be Done?* did not lie in its detailed rebuttals of other political currents, but in its stress on the primacy of politics and the necessity of a revolutionary party with a vigorous set of publications, as well as its careful delineation of the relationship between theory and practice that the young Lukács would later (1924) describe as encompassing the 'actuality of the revolution'.

Where would the theory come from? Here there were no doubts whatsoever. Marxist and socialist theories did not emerge spontaneously but from the intellectual labour of many, and 'out of the philosophical, historical and economic theories that were worked out by the educated representatives of the propertied classes – the intelligentsia. The founders of modern socialism, Marx and Engels, belong by social status to the bourgeois intelligentsia.' And, as mentioned earlier, the same applied to the anarcho-Populist currents that dominated the nineteenth century: Kropotkin, Bakunin, Tolstoy.

Trade union activity was the spontaneous consciousness of the newly industrialised workers but, on its own, was insufficient and often ended up being dominated by its capitalist opponent. It would not come to socialism spontaneously. Politics and parties were essential:

> Those who refrain from concerning themselves in this way … in reality leave the liberals in command, place in their hands the political education of the workers, and concede the hegemony in the political struggle to elements which, in the final analysis, are leaders of bourgeois democracy.

It soon became obvious to Lenin that the Russian bourgeoisie was not about to play a heroic role, even indirectly like the merchants in London or the French bourgeois intelligentsia had done. The latter had rapidly lost their vision and become the principal defenders of Order, lambasted by Marx for their sins in 1848 and after. Lenin described their Russian descendants as 'toadying, vile, foul and brutal' and the 'liberal pig which deems itself educated, but in fact is dirty, repulsive, overfat and smug'.

The polemical style of debate in Russia, often attributed to the left, has a much longer pedigree. Seventeenth-century debates within the Church were often harsh. In his classic *History of Russian Literature*, D. S. Mirsky informs us that Ivan the Terrible 'was a pamphleteer of genius'. His quill, dripping with 'satirical invective', was regularly in action against the boyars and the church:

> The best is the letter to the Abbot of St Cyril's Monastery where he pours out all the poison of his grim irony on the unascetic life of the boyars, shorn monks, and those exiled by his order. His picture of their luxurious life in the citadel of ascetism is a masterpiece of trenchant sarcasm.[4]

---

4 D. S. Mirsky, *A History of Russian Literature*, New York, 1964, p. 21.

Lenin was more considered when analysing shifts in bourgeois politics, which he always followed closely both at home and abroad. He analysed in great detail, for example, Stolypin's reforms of 1906 (much favoured by the Russian academy these days as the alternative to the revolution), pointing out that they were doomed to failure not because they were unintelligent from the point of view of the liberal conservatives, but because the cooperation they were proposing with the wealthier sections of the peasantry was, in fact, impossible due to the extreme degree of political polarisation in Russia. This point in particular eluded Hayek in his admiring references to the proposals in *The Road to Serfdom*, which even he admitted were a response to the 1905 revolution whose aim was 'to undercut the voices from below and ease the concerns of the landed nobility over confiscation'.

Lenin's ideas on practical questions of strategy and tactics changed in the years that lay ahead and, while he agreed with the notion of a mass political-economic strike, he strongly disputed the notion, as Plekhanov and Axelrod had done before him, that this could transmogrify of its own accord into a social and political revolution. The coming war helped clarify his ideas further. One thing, however, was clear. Terrorism as a political tactic could not be resuscitated. It simply did not work. It was an inefficient substitute for mass action. It concentrated on individuals while leaving the system intact, which was why it had long ceased to interest or attract the bulk of the intelligentsia. A different path had been opened by revolutionary Social Democracy.

SECTION TWO

Internationalism, Socialism, Empires and War

4

The Birth of Internationalism

The internationalism of capital produced the internationalism of labour. Workers of the world wanted to unite because they shared a common enemy. This instinctive reflex predated both Marx and Lenin. The propertyless worker who had nothing to lose but his chains certainly did exist, but did not and could not spontaneously move beyond a basic solidarity. Political parties were needed for this, and international organisations. Marx grasped this fairly rapidly and helped organise such a grouping. This was the international of propaganda and agitation. The German Social Democracy laid the foundations for the Second International which united the European workers' parties under a single umbrella. This worked till the umbrella was punctured by the First World War. Most of the parties opted to fight under the banner of their respective capitalist governments. They mistook the primeval outbursts of chauvinism for something permanent, and, once the war revealed itself for what it was, the parties divided into two and sometimes three currents. This was a huge turning point for Lenin, who had denounced the war from the very first day and regarded the Zimmerwald declaration against it as too weak. The European fault lines stretched back to the French Revolution.

From 1789 to 1815, continental Europe was deeply engrossed in its own wars and revolutions. Two huge American empires constructed by Britain and Spain had been or were being lost to revolutionary settler nationalism. The losses were real enough in economic terms, but there were consolations as well. Those who ruled the former colonies were, for the most part, white-skinned

Europeans. The largest factions of European religion, Protestantism and Catholicism, were dominant in North and South America respectively. Four major European languages – English, French, Spanish and Portuguese – had taken root in the New World. German would arrive a bit later. This, apart from all else, maintained links with the mother continent without the settlers needing to accept its domination. The European empires saw each other as rivals. They did not believe in unity against common enemies. General Washington had been extremely thankful for the help received from France, and Ferdinand of Spain's plea for help against Generals Miranda and Bolívar was brutally snubbed by the British. Imperialist internationalism was a contradiction in terms.

Britain was determined to find colonial replacements elsewhere in the world. All through the Napoleonic Wars, it was slowly expanding its hold on India, where it had acquired Bengal after the Battle of Plassey in 1757. It was not only capitalist greed buttressed by technical advantages in weaponry that led to the scramble for colonies. India and other parts of Asia were in desperate straits. Old empires had collapsed. The end of the centralised Mughal Empire had left India open to new adventurers. The Qing dynasty (1644–1911) was still doing well in the late eighteenth century, but the Europeans and Japanese would close in for the kill in the decades that followed, with Britain initially in the lead. Chaos in the shape of invasions, warlordism, fragmentation and famines had made the continent vulnerable. Asia seemed unable to renew itself. Europe launched the first globalisation. Trading companies from Holland and England saw easy pickings and established outposts that would soon be militarised as a prelude to full-scale colonisation. Grabbing colonies that 'belonged' to others never posed a problem for the British on any level.

France, too, had a head start, with imperial possessions in the West Indies and North Africa. Belgium captured the Congo and inaugurated the worst genocide in imperial history. The upstart industrial-capitalist powers – the United States, Germany and Japan – would have to fight for their share of empire. The ultimate results of uneven development and the competitive expansion of industrial capitalism were the two brutal world wars of the twentieth century.

With the industrial revolution in full swing in Britain, spreading rapidly to the rest of the continent and the United States, a working class was also being born, its youth portrayed for eternity in the grim depictions of Charles Dickens, Émile Zola, Upton Sinclair, Maxim Gorky and others, as well as powerful analytical essays by Engels and the Chartist intellectuals of Britain: O'Connor, Harney, Jones.

The call put out by Marx and Engels in 1848 was clear enough: workers of the world unite; you have nothing to lose but your chains and a world to gain. Would they? Could class unity from below defeat the imperialism espoused by monarchies and republics alike during the last half of the nineteenth century and the first half of its successor? Might the 'workers of the world' (i.e., those in Europe and North America) create their own international organisations to combat the wars decided upon by their rulers? Early indications were positive and, when Lenin entered the fray later, he was convinced that there was no other way forward, even in the medium term. Internationalism was given a huge boost by the radical upheavals primarily in France but also in North America and Eastern Europe. France remained the intellectual workshop of the world but, as Marx noted in his essays on developments in that country, 'the struggle against capital in its highly developed modern form – at its crucial point, the struggle of the industrial wage-labourer against the industrial bourgeois – is in France a partial phenomenon.'[1]

The 1848 revolution in France, despite its defeat and Louis Bonaparte's coup, had nonetheless reignited hope. Trade unions, political assemblies and radical newspapers were banned but the industrialisation of the country continued apace, increasing the weight of the working class in French society. The imperial dictatorship ruled the country using a combination of repression and some reforms. Protests were drowned in blood, but attempts were

---

1   Karl Marx, *Surveys from Exile*, ed. David Fernbach, London and New York, 2010.

made to effect a reconciliation with workers by improving their standard of living. The king created industrial councils and the state subsidised welfare organisations. It also allowed the creation of mutual benefit societies, kept the price of bread low and, with the help of Baron Haussman, instituted spectacular construction of public works in a number of cities, which reduced unemployment and, in the case of Paris, erected architecture that was both imposing and safe: it would no longer be as easy to construct barricades.[2] The economic crisis of 1857–58 brought these initiatives to a halt. The Franco-Prussian War, twelve years later, ended Bonaparte's regime. Taken prisoner by the Prussians at the Battle of Sedan, he was allowed to proceed to exile in Britain.

In England the Chartist rebellions demanding radical democracy had been contained by 1848, but their residue never disappeared. Their most gifted leader and publicist, Ernest Jones, who became a close friend of Marx, devoted his entire adult life to the cause of socialism and international solidarity, the seeds of which had been planted in the preceding century by Tom Paine and continued by clandestine societies and circles inspired by the French Revolution. The writings of William Godwin and his even more gifted wife, Mary Wollstonecraft, had a huge impact on the younger generation, including on the poetry and intense radicalism of their precocious son-in-law to be, Percy Bysshe Shelley. Ernest Jones, like Bakunin and Kropotkin, belonged to the aristocracy. His father, a dashing cavalry officer who fought under Wellington in the Spanish Peninsula, was wounded in the conflict and transferred to serve the Duke of Cumberland (later King of Hanover), who was also Ernest's godfather. Jones was born and educated in Germany at a school in Lüneburg created for aristocratic families. At eighteen he came to England, where he studied law, became a barrister, wed an heiress belonging to the Earl of Derby's family and was presented to Queen Victoria. Far too intelligent to

---

2 Here, in a nutshell, was the embryo of the Keynesianism that would become the core of the socioeconomic programmes defended by revisionist currents in European Social Democracy, and abandoned only in the 1990s with a reversion to tooth-and-claw capitalism.

vegetate in high society, he read voraciously and in 1846, completely fortuitously, became the owner of the Chartist paper *Northern Star*. This made him a Chartist for the rest of his life; he spent most of the wealth he inherited on the cause till he ran out of money altogether. Like others he was imprisoned in 1848, spending two years in solitary confinement in a tiny cell, barred from reading books, denied pen and paper and subjected to the uniquely English punishment of being forbidden to speak or smile. The prison, where two other Chartists died during Jones's confinement, wreaked havoc on his health, which never recovered. In the prison hospital he was offered immediate release if he abandoned politics for the rest of his life. He refused with contempt. In an arduous propaganda tour of the most important working-class cities in the country, Jones almost single-handedly attempted to revive Chartism, but the moment had passed. Most of Chartism's best-known leaders had given up, usually quietly but in some cases denouncing their own pasts. Jones died on his fiftieth birthday in January 1869 in Manchester, where several thousand workers attended his funeral.

A tide of reaction had engulfed Europe, sending Marx to the library. Jones's speeches had combined socialism and internationalism. He had proposed creating an institution of embryonic dual power: an explicitly Labour (working-class) parliament that would function as an instrument of the workers and the poor against the House of Commons, which would exclusively represent and defend the

Ernest Jones: The foremost Chartist intellectual and activist, a close friend of Marx.

ruling class. How would such a Labour Parliament function? To this Jones responded that it would be in permanent session; it would direct trade union struggles, debate tactics and strategy, finance strikes and develop cooperative societies with the savings of working people. Marx, still despondent about his and his cohort's immediate prospects, nonetheless got excited by the idea and was duly elected an honorary delegate at the opening session in 1854. Jones's letter explained the reasons for instituting a Labour Parliament (which petered out after a few weeks) and stressed its internationalist aims:

> The mere assembling of such a Parliament, marks a new epoch in the history of the world. The news of this great fact will arouse the hopes of the working classes throughout Europe and America . . . If the Labour Parliament proves true to the idea that called it into life, some future historian will have to record that there existed in the year 1854, two parliaments in England, a Parliament in London and a Parliament in Manchester – a Parliament of the rich and a Parliament of the poor.[3]

Fluent in German and French, Jones regularly read the radical press in both languages and was a staunch supporter of the Polish uprising against tsarist Russia in 1862–63, as well as an equally steadfast opponent of Louis Napoleon, the dictator of France. He loathed tsarist Russia, for the same reasons as his friend Marx, who denounced it as 'the great bastion of European reaction'. Both men supported Abraham Lincoln. Despite his failing health, Jones was a tireless agitator and played an important role in convincing the Lancashire workers that even though three-fifths of the spindles and looms in Lancashire had been switched off, leaving tens

---

3 John Saville, *Ernest Jones, Chartist*, London, 1952. Given the period, such a parliament was a utopian idea, but just over half a century later the emergence of soviets (workers' representative assemblies) after the 1905 revolution in Russia and then again in 1917 suggested that Jones was too far ahead of his time. The soviets are discussed in some detail in Section Three.

of thousands of workers unemployed, the disruption it caused to the flow of cotton from a Civil War–torn United States was just. Slavery was unacceptable and support had to be given to the Union armies. The sooner they won, the sooner factories would reopen. Jones was not alone in this and was backed strongly by a number of trade union leaders and activists. Huge mass meetings in Manchester and London warned the government against the intervention it was considering on the side of the slave-owners, largely for economic reasons. The US Civil War was finely balanced at the time and Lincoln greatly appreciated working-class support from Britain. He answered every address from British workers and was particularly affected by one from Manchester, to which he replied: 'I know and deeply regret the sufferings which the workers of Manchester are undergoing in this crisis ... Under these circumstances their conduct is an exalted example of Christian heroism, which has not been surpassed in any country in any epoch.' Methodist churches were, of course, involved in the campaign, but it was the remnants of Chartism and the socialists who were at the forefront.

In the same period, London workers and apprentices gave an enormous welcome to the Italian revolutionary nationalist leader Garibaldi when he arrived as a refugee in April 1864. The government refused to let him stay, provoking a series of angry battles between protesting demonstrators and the police.

The formation of the First International, however, was triggered by the brutal defeat inflicted by the tsar on Polish aspirations for national freedom and independence. The Polish uprising of 1863 was the third and largest of its kind. The sympathies of French and British workers lay on the Polish side and a series of huge public meetings demanded that the Palmerstone government intervene, which it refused to do: its own colonies were increasing by the month and any action in solidarity with the natives in Poland could be misunderstood in India. The official reason given was that it was unthinkable to do anything without French support. Since France was a police state and all political assemblies were banned, it was impossible to put public pressure on the government. French workers and radicals were seething with anger at the events in Poland, where it took a whole year for the tsar's armies to defeat the Poles.

But contacts between French and English trade unionists were established and the basis laid for creating an international workingman's association, that was founded at a public meeting of English and French workers in St Martin's Hall in London on 28 September 1864. The workers invited Marx to write the inaugural address and the organisation's constitution, which he did after a few discussions with them. George Odger was a shoemaker and a founder of the London Trades Council, and became the first president of the General Council of the International; William Cremer, a carpenter, was also on the General Council, as was George Howell, a mason and secretary of the London Trades Council. Henri Tolain, an engraver, became the chief representative of the International in Paris. At this public meeting Odger decided to raise the question of immigrant labour with his French colleagues, pointing out the problems that underlay the 'import of lower-paid workers to break strikes and proposed "regular and systematic communication between the industrious classes of all countries" as the solution to the problem'.[4]

Marx realised very clearly that these workers were far from being on the same wavelength as himself, or even in full agreement with each other on issues such as socialism and materialism. French Proudhonists and the supporters of Mazzini were hostile to the very idea of an independent workers' movement. Marx understood only too well the uneven development of political consciousness and decided that the best way to advance the cause was to be as helpful as possible in building the International. Cremer ended up as a Liberal MP and Tolain sat in the Assembly at Versailles during the Paris Commune. The shark-infested sea had to be navigated with great caution to preserve the newly created International. Marx informed Engels that 'it will take time before the revival of

---

4 David Fernbach, 'Introduction', in Karl Marx, *The First International and After*, ed. David Fernbach, London and New York, 2010, p. 12.

the movement allows the boldness of language to be used. We must be *fortiter in re, suaviter in modo* [strong in deed, gentle in style].' This gentleness in style was something that his Russian followers in particular – Lenin, Plekhanov, Axelrod, Martov, Trotsky – would never envisage, leave alone imitate.

The Inaugural Address is certainly a long way from the style of *The Communist Manifesto*, but another oddity is the balance struck between discussing the situation in Britain (four-fifths of the document) and analysing events in the rest of the world. It was clearly designed as an appeal to English trade unionists rather than the workers of the world. On that level it was successful. Marx knew his audience and the address was geared to its needs. The bulk of it is little more than a sober and revealing account of the growth of English capitalism that had made the rich even richer and reduced the workers to desperate levels of poverty. The workers possessed one huge advantage over their bosses. Marx might have quoted Shelley at this point ('Ye are many, they are few') but he pressed on, explaining that political power was essential if the workers were to emancipate themselves, provided that they understood that superiority of numbers 'weigh only in the balance if united by combination and led by knowledge'. Marx had deliberately and wrongly left out any reference to Ireland and India, confining world politics to the US Civil War and the oppression of Poland. This concluding paragraph, despite its insufficiencies, was the most powerful section of the address:

If the emancipation of the working classes requires their fraternal concurrence, how are they to fulfil that great mission with a foreign policy in pursuit of criminal designs, playing upon national prejudices, and squandering in piratical wars the people's blood and treasure? It was not the wisdom of the ruling classes, but the heroic resistance to their criminal folly by the working classes of England, that saved the west of Europe from plunging headlong into an infamous crusade for the perpetuation and propagation of slavery on the other side of the Atlantic. The shameless approval, mock sympathy, or idiotic indifference, with which the upper classes of Europe have witnessed the mountain fortress of the Caucasus falling prey to, and heroic Poland being assassinated by Russia; the immense and unresisted encroachment of that barbarous power, whose head is at St Petersburg, and whose hands are in every cabinet of Europe, have taught the working classes the duty to master themselves the mysteries of international politics; to watch the diplomatic acts of their respective governments; to counteract them, if necessary, by all means in their power; when unable to prevent, to combine in simultaneous denunciations, and to vindicate the simple laws of morals and justice, which ought to govern the relations of private individuals, as the rules paramount in the intercourse of nations.

The fight for such a foreign policy forms part of the general struggle for the emancipation of the working classes.

Proletarians of all countries unite.[5]

The First International remained a small organisation. Its prestige lay in the radical utterances of its leaders and its fiery proclamations. To say that its enemies and its friends grotesquely exaggerated its strength would be an understatement. On the eve of the Paris Commune, the leaders of the French section were facing their third trial. The charge sheet accused them of belonging to a secret society, and the prosecutor informed the court that the combined membership of this sinister International was 811,513. One supposes that it was his French pride that compelled him to declare that of these over half (433,785) were French. Next came Germany with 150,000 and the Austro-Hungarian empire with 100,000. England was relegated in the scheme of things – only 80,000 – and the Swiss allocated 4,500 , while the Spanish came last with a paltry 2,728. These numbers, the court heard, were large enough to pose a revolutionary threat to society. Had the figures been accurate, the conclusion might well have been justified.

---

5 Marx, *The First International and After*, p. 81.

A statue of Napoleon I brought down from the Vendôme Column by
the Communards, 1871.

A few weeks later, fourteen Austrian Social Democrats were
arrested and charged with high treason. The global figure bran-
dished in the Viennese courtroom was a membership of a million
strong. In other words, 150,000 people had joined since the farce in
Paris. And so it went. The friends of the International entered the
competition with fanatical zeal, in numbers that reached a feverish
pitch when the North American editor of the *Working Man's
Advocate* in Chicago calmly informed a Congress of the International that the National Labour Union alone, affiliated with the
International, spoke for 800,000 workers. And *L'Internationale*,
the journal of the Belgian section, reported that same year (1870)
that the International had already assembled several million workers under its aegis in Europe and the United States. The Belgian left
never completely abandoned this tradition in the century that lay
ahead, and as new Internationals big and small came into being.

Had any of this been true, the dues paid (1 shilling a year for
individuals and 3 shillings a year for members of affiliated unions)

would have drowned the International in money. In reality they were always short of funds. It was a struggle to pay even the few existing salaries on a regular basis. The actual membership was minuscule. Marx advised the General Council that since the public believed them to be more numerous than they were, it might be advisable not to publish a list of members. These were estimated at the end of 1870 as being no more than 294 in England and a few thousand in France and Switzerland. Germany was a disaster story; Marx complained bitterly to Engels that a year after the German International's founding, Wilhelm Liebknecht had not even managed to recruit six members. August Bebel had joined as late as 1867 when the organisation had only a few years left. In Italy, Mazzini's influence was so strong and his hostility to socialism and the International so pronounced that nationalism – 'All Italians should unite' – won the day. A worker's association in Naples affiliated in 1866 and was recorded in the minutes as having 600 members, a figure that seems slightly exaggerated. It was only after the Paris Commune that Italian workers began to abandon Mazzini and move leftwards, spurred on by Garibaldi, who greeted the Commune and offered his services in any capacity. Recorded membership in Italy grew to 10,000, though a more sober assessment suggested a maximum of 2,000, which itself was not bad compared to England. Who were they? A mixture of well-meaning eccentrics, poets, intellectuals and more than a few fanatics. Very few workers. 'In Italy', wrote Engels on 11 March 1872, in a despairing letter to Marx's daughter Laura Lafargue in Paris, 'journalists, lawyers and doctors have pushed themselves so much that we [the International] are unable to get in touch with the workers; now it has begun to change, and we are discovering that the workers, as everywhere, are quite different from their spokesmen.'

It could be argued that the International temporarily struck gold, or at any rate silver, mainly in the United States, where a group of first generation immigrants and refugees fleeing economic crises and reaction in Europe had found refuge. The first German sections were formed in Chicago and Milwaukee in 1868, followed soon by American, French, Czech, Irish and Scandinavian sections in New York, San Francisco, New Orleans, Newark, Minneapolis,

Springfield, Washington and Williamsburg. Unsurprisingly the Chinese and Japanese populations on the West Coast remained aloof. The International was essentially a Euro-American outfit.

The figure of 5,000 in 1871 was not exaggerated, but an unnecessary split between intellectuals and workers in the following year led to an exodus by a majority, leaving behind only 950 members. The radical impulse, however, survived and would reemerge in the International Workers of the World (IWW, a.k.a. the Wobblies) and other organisations. The Wobblies, unlike the International, did recruit Chinese and Japanese workers.

In Europe a new dividing line was drawn. Bakunin, regarding the General Council as too passive and reformist, had created his own International Alliance of Socialist Democracy and asked for affiliation. Marx was nervous. He could see that the Alliance would be an International within an International and Bakunin's real plan was to seize control. Affiliation was rejected, whereupon Bakunin dissolved the Alliance and asked that its section become part of the International. This was agreed. But the Alliance effectively continued as a secret society on which Bakunin imposed a Jesuitical discipline, arguing that 'the individual is lost in the collective will, in the life and activity of the organisation.'

Bakunin's supporters rapidly gained control of the sections in Italy and Spain, and Bakunin prepared a similar takeover in France and Switzerland – the continental European sections – leaving England and North America to Marx. Journals under Bakunin's influence had already begun to subject the activities of the General Council to scathing critiques. It was only two years previously, in 1868, that Bakunin had written to Marx: 'My fatherland is now the International, of which you are amongst the most prominent members. You see therefore, my dear friend, that I am your disciple, and proud to be one.' In April 1870, the Bakuninists had split the French section at its conference in La Chaux-de-Fonds, creating havoc inside the General Council.[6] A split

---

6   Simultaneously, the rulers of Europe, exaggerating the strength and military capacities of the International but not its propaganda, which was extremely effective, were attempting to crush it via a series of trials and imprisonment of key local figures.

was taking place and was to be the main item at the Congress scheduled for Mainz in September of that year, but this had to be postponed when the Franco-Prussian War broke out. The provocation had come from the French dictator, but Bismarck's response was a bit too eager. In its Second Address, inspired and written by Marx, the General Council of the International denounced the war as being against the interests of workers in both countries. The French Internationalists followed suit with a manifesto published in *Reveille* on 12 July 1870:

> Once more, on the pretext of the European equilibrium, of national honour, the peace of the world [i.e., Europe] is menaced by political ambitions. French, German, Spanish workmen! Let our voices unite in one cry of reprobation against war! ... War for a question of preponderance of a dynasty can, in the eyes of workmen, be nothing but a criminal absurdity. In answer to the warlike proclamations of those who exempt themselves from the impost of blood, and find in public misfortunes a source of fresh speculations, we protest, we who want peace, labour and liberty! Brothers of Germany! Our division would only result in the complete triumph of *despotism* on both sides of the Rhine.

The response from German workers in Chemnitz and Berlin was couched in similar internationalist language. Even amongst liberals in France and the local *belligeratti*, men like Thiers and his cohort, there was no stomach for a war. But Louis Bonaparte was set on suicide. He must have wanted the Second Empire to end with the thunder of foreign cannon rather than a French insurrection. Bismarck, who had his own plans for Germany, duly obliged him. It did not all go according to plan. The workers and citizens of Paris decided to defend themselves against the Prussians and their de facto French allies. Defeated at the Battle of Sedan, the French Republican successors of Louis Bonaparte linked arms with the Prussians. They left Paris undefended and fled to Versailles. Bismarck released 100,000 prisoners to help the *Versaillais* retake Paris. Versailles in 1871; Vichy in 1940.

The workers, craftsmen, huge numbers of women and radical intellectuals decided to defend their Paris against the Prussians; against Thiers and Haussman, who had taken the city away from them, and against the speculators and corrupt politicians who thought they could rule forever. This noble attempt, doomed from the start, heroic in the extreme, entered the annals of history with an aura all its own. Sometimes defeats elicit more respect than half-hearted and half-baked 'victories'. The experience resonated throughout the twentieth century and in all parts of the world. Marx wrote about it at length, as did Lenin, who was haunted by its history and studied the causes of the defeat in minute detail, as only he could. The defeat of the Jacobins in the 1790s and the Paris Commune just under a century later were subjects to which he returned time and time again, both in prison and in exile. Born almost exactly a year prior to the birth of the Commune, the political lessons of its defeat and the issues that came to the fore during its brief existence preoccupied him greatly and influenced his thinking on several key issues till the very end: foreign and civil wars, the state and workers' democracy, daring and audacity (or the lack thereof).[7]

What was this Commune that left such a deep mark on its friends and enemies? Prosper-Olivier Lissagaray, its greatest historian, a rank-and-file participant in the events, produced a work of rare quality, a political history matched by few others. Almost half the book explains the reasons for the defeat. The language is fierce, passionate, angry and uncompromising. Its only equivalent in literary France is the poetry of Rimbaud. Nine years after the defeat,

---

7   Academic fashions today are so centred on presentism that the past (history) is avoided like the plague. For some, it's best to forget the past and concentrate on individuals or buildings or monuments and find a 'new' way of looking at old events. Why not study the French Revolution via a 'feminist' reading of Marie Antoinette? Why not underplay Marx's enormous contributions by denouncing him as an 'anti-Semite'? And so forth. A retreat from politics in times of defeat is nothing new. Stendhal wrote about it well after 1815. In the twenty-first century many of the old left settlers in the academy have opted for safety by simply jumping ship.

Lissagaray publicly thanked two friends for agreeing to be his seconds in a duel with a journalist notorious for slandering the Commune and its participants:

> I thank you for having helped to shed the light of day on the ineffable cowardice of our slanderers in the *figariste* press over the past nine years. The same people who acted as Gallifet's [the general who led the repression] dogs during the sack of Paris, denouncing the survivors, finishing off the wounded, spitting on the dead . . . the same people who, for these nine years, piled filth on the deportees and the exiles . . . These are the literary scum who for all these years, in sole control of newspapers and bookstores, invented their own legend of the deeds and the men of the Commune.[8]

The 'literary scum' included Flaubert, Zola, Sand, Daudet, the Goncourt brothers and Maupassant, but not Rimbaud. The debacle of French literature would have been complete had it not been for the verses of an unrecognised young poet moving in and out of the besieged capital. Arthur Rimbaud preserved the honour of French literature with his poetry. The mood in Paris, the contempt for their rulers, the burning anger is all on display in 'Parisian War Cry':

> Spring is at hand, for lo,
> Within the city's garden plots
> The government's harvest is beginning to grow –
> But the gardeners call the shots!

---

8 Quoted in Eric Hazan's foreword to Prosper-Oliver Lissagaray, *History of the Paris Commune of 1871*, tr. Eleanor Marx, London and New York, 2012, pp. ix–x. For those who want a detailed historical account rather than well-meaning, if sometimes mystifying, academic ramblings, there can be no better book. The Commune and its impact can only be understood through a political prism. Anarchist or Marxist is a matter of choice, though both can be read and compared. Marx's own writings on the subject (e.g., *The Civil War in France*) educated many generations in Europe and other continents and still stand out as clear-headed and cogent.

O May! What bare-assed ecstasy!
Sèvres, Meudon, Bagneux, Asnières,
Hear out Farmer-Generals, busy
Planting in the empty air!

Guns and sabres glitter in parade,
Bright-mouthed weapons pointing straight ahead –
It's a treat for them to beat their feet
In the mud of a river running red!

Never, never now will we move back
From our barricades, our piles of stone:
Beneath their clubs our blonde skulls crack
In a dawn that was meant for us alone.

Like Eros, politicians hover overhead,
Their shadows withering the flowers:
Their bombs and fires paint our garden red:
Their beetle-faced forces trample ours.

. . .

The city's paving stones are hot
Despite the gasoline you shower,
And absolutely, now, right now, we've got
To find a way to break your power!

Bourgeois, bug-eyed on their balconies,
Shaking at the sound of breaking glass,
Can hear trees falling on the boulevards
And, far off, a shivering scarlet clash.[9]

---

9   Arthur Rimbaud, *Complete Works*, tr. Paul Schmidt, New York, 2000. For a fascinating cultural history of the Commune, see Kristin Ross, *The Emergence of Social Space: Rimbaud and the Paris Commune*, London and New York, 2008.

In the artistic world, too, the Commune left its mark. Courbet was elected a delegate in April and immediately proposed that artists elect two delegates from each of the twenty-two arrondissements. He also proposed that these delegates oversee the appointments of curators and directors of all public museums and rules for exhibitions, as well as abolishing the École des Beaux-Arts, the French Academy in Rome and all old awards and medals. Artists who disagreed with the majority should be allocated galleries for their own shows. Four hundred artists gathered on 15 April to discuss these proposals, which were accepted with acclamation. The meeting established a Parisian Federation of Artists on the basis of three principles:

> The free expansion of art released from all governmental control and all privilege; equal rights for all members of the federation; the independence and dignity of each artist guaranteed by all, through the creation of a committee elected by universal suffrage of all the artists.

Courbet and other artists played a major role in the decision to bring down the Vendôme Column. It had been built in 1803 with the metal of melted cannons captured by Napoleon's armies: 150,000 pounds of Austrian and Russian bronze. The original idea had been for Charlemagne to be stationed at the top, but this was replaced, after construction began and sycophants sprang into action, with a statue of Napoleon depicted as a Roman emperor. This statue was removed in 1814 after the Bourbon restoration and replaced with the white royalist flag. Under Louis-Philippe, the flag was removed and Napoleon came back, but this time attired in modern uniform. During the 1848 revolution, Comte proposed that the whole column be demolished, but there wasn't time. Napoleon III had the modern statue taken down and back went a new statue of the original Napoleon as a Roman emperor. After the defeat of Sedan, angry Republicans demanded that Citizen Courbet be charged with unbolting the columns that made France look 'ridiculous and odious'. Courbet was not in favour of destroying old monuments. He saw them as reflections of the historical phases through which a nation had passed. But he loathed the Vendôme Column.

Even so, he thought it should be unbolted and taken to the Invalides, where maimed veterans could reflect on the fruit of their sacrifices. In a strong letter to the mayor of Paris, the artist argued that

> the removal, from the proximity of a street called Rue de Paix, of a mass of melted cannon that perpetuates the tradition of conquest, pillage, and murder, and which is as absurdly out of place as a howitzer in a ladies' salon, among the shops filled with silk frocks, laces ... which adjoin the establishment of Worth, the favourite dressmaker of the Empire's courtesans ... would you preserve in your bedroom the bloodstains of a murder? ... Let the reliefs be transferred to an historical museum, let them be set up in panels on the walls of the court of the Invalides; I see no harm in that. Those brave men captured those cannons by the sacrifice of their limbs.

It was left to the Commune to complete the task. The Column was finally brought down.

The Commune was the first example of a class attempting to emancipate not only itself, but society as a whole. Paris had been abandoned by the conservative and liberal political factions who fled to Bordeaux and later settled in Versailles, hoping that the Prussian army laying siege to Paris might enter the city and drown its insurgents in blood. Bismarck refused point-blank. His message to Versailles was simple: we'll help by releasing French prisoners of war, but you must do your dirty work yourselves. Seventy years later, Hitler would be more understanding of the needs of French politicians in Vichy. Common enemies would be happily exterminated by the Wehrmacht, but the imperialist world had moved forward by then.

The politicians who had served Louis Napoleon and had been pushed into declaring a Republic by the Parisian crowds were extremely nervous. Having failed to convince the Prussians, they decided to assault the Commune. It was *they* who decided to fight fellow Frenchmen instead of the invading Germans, the French right and centre who singled out the Terror during the French Revolution as the biggest tragedy ever (the victims of the guillotine were in the 3,000 range). During the Commune, 30,000 died, of which 14,000 men and women were executed. Others were imprisoned or deported. Many fled into exile. The greatest number of refugees settled in London and Geneva; the most radical among them, including Lissagaray, gravitated in the direction of the Marx household. Others found shelter in New York, where tens of thousands had marched in solidarity with the Commune after its defeat.

Even five years later, demands for amnesty were rejected 372 to 50 in the Chamber. Lissagaray pointed out the amazing response and solidarity shown by the Irish in Ireland, the United States and New Zealand after the Fenian rebellion and the hanging of three Fenians in Manchester. They were three and had hundreds in prison, while the Communards were in the several thousands. He ended his book with this appeal to his fellow-citizens:

> Do you understand, working men, you who are free? You now know what the whole situation is and what the men are. Remember the vanquished not for a day, but at all hours. Women, you whose devotion sustains and elevates their courage, let the agony of the prisoners haunt you like an everlasting nightmare. Let all workshops every week put something aside from their wages. Let the subscriptions no longer be sent to the Versaillese committee, but made over to loyal hands. Let the Socialist Party attest to its principles of international solidarity and its power by saving those who have fallen for it.[10]

Order had been restored in France largely because the countryside had supported the dictatorship and the assault on Paris. France as a whole, however, had been weakened. Its domination of continental Europe that had started with the Sun King and continued with Napoleon was coming to an end. French and British conservative historians argue that it was the war that ended the Second Empire, underplaying the fact that France was rotting from within.

---

10 Lissagaray, *History of the Paris Commune*, p. 367.

The rurals alone had kept Louis Napoleon's dictatorship in place. The cities were in a defiant mood, as revolutionary Paris had demonstrated during the Commune. The armies of the first Napoleon were the product of the revolution as much as he was a child of the Enlightenment. Those times had gone. The French Army was in a state of advanced decay, its officer corps morally and financially corrupted, its soldiers unenthusiastic and half-starved. It was ready for surrender even before the Battle of Sedan. Its last victory in the nineteenth century was against its own people.

Speaking in exile to mark the fortieth anniversary of the Commune in 1911, Lenin stressed its spontaneous character: a reaction to military defeat, mass unemployment suffered by workers and the ruination of the petty bourgeois that led to an 'indefinable fermentation among the working class'. To this he added the total failure of a National Assembly dominated by the most reactionary segments of the bourgeoisie as well as rural conservatives to offer any lead to the nation as a whole. These were the factors that led to the revolution in Paris propelling the National Guard to power:

> This was an event unprecedented in history. Up to that time power had customarily been in the hands of landlords and capitalists, i.e., in the hands of their trusted agents who made up the so-called Government. After the revolution of March 18, when the Thiers Government fled from Paris with its troops, its police and its officials, the people remained masters of the situation and power passed into the hands of the proletariat. But in modern society, enslaved economically by capital, the proletariat cannot dominate politically unless it breaks the chains which fetter it to capital. This is why the movement of the Commune inevitably had to take on a Socialist colouring, i.e., to begin striving for the overthrow of the power of the bourgeoisie, the power of capital, to destroy the very foundations of the present social order.[11]

---

11   V. I. Lenin, 'In Memory of the Commune', 1911, available at the Marxists Internet Archive, marxists.org.

It was, he argued, its incipient socialist character, its radical reforms, its courage to challenge the established order that ensured it a glorious afterlife.

'Now we have finished with Socialism for a long time', said their leader, the bloodthirsty dwarf, Thiers, after the bloodbath . . . About 30,000 Parisians were killed by the ferocious soldiery, about 45,000 were arrested and many of these were afterwards executed, thousands were imprisoned or exiled. In all, Paris lost about 100,000 of its sons, including the best workers of all trades . . . But these bourgeois crows cawed in vain.[12]

It was because it was the most politically advanced struggle of the modern world that it had such a huge international impact.

The Prussian triumph in the 1870–71 war had also announced the birth of a new power on the continent. In vain did the artists plead for European unity. Courbet, who had spent much time in Bavaria, wrote to them:

When we've met at Frankfurt and Munich, I declared our common tendencies. Just as I demanded liberty for art, you asked as well for liberty of the people . . . We drank then to France and to the advent of the European Republic. At Munich again, last year, you swore by the most fearful oaths not to be enfeoffed with Prussia. Today you're all registered in the banks of Bismarck; you bear on your brow a *nombre d'ordre* and know how to give the military salute.

Courbet, in this regard, was both ahead of and behind his time. A confident Bismarck negotiated, bullied and bribed his way to the unification of Germany under the Hohenzollern family. This belated unity, the sudden emergence of a new state, was the material basis for an ethnic nationalism, an ideological cement that proved difficult to dislodge. It did not exist in a void. Industrialisation was transforming the country; the rapid growth of the working class had accelerated the socialism that only recently had lit the

---

12   Ibid.

horizon (or darkened it, from Bismarck's point of view). The Iron Chancellor was in a hurry to catch up with France, England, Belgium, Portugal and Austro-Hungary on other fronts as well. How come, he asked, they all have large empires and we do not? He needed this not as a surplus space for Germans, since industrialisation had brought emigration to a virtual halt, but because a self-respecting European state needed an empire too. Why should Germany not have an equal share in the world?

As a young man, Bismarck had travelled to Hull and York and caught a train for Manchester and neighbouring small towns to witness the industrial revolution first-hand. His English was excellent and he always had a healthy appetite. His favourite hotel meal was breakfast, so much better than the fish and 'atrocious fruit tart' that comprised lunch, leave alone the disgusting soups 'so strongly seasoned with white and black pepper that few foreigners can eat them'. But English breakfasts were fine because 'the most colossal pieces of every sort of meat are available and they put them before you to cut as much or as little as you choose without effect on the bill.' Bismarck would soon learn that the same could not be done with the British Empire.

In most of the discussions of the rise of internationalism, mention is usually made of the solidarity shown by Russian Social Democrats and their Populist-anarchist predecessors to the cause of Polish independence. Russian and Polish revolutionaries often fought side by side against the autocracy. There is, however, one heroic episode of internationalism that is barely mentioned. In 1877 the Russian Empire declared war on the Ottomans in Bulgaria. The propaganda was familiar. The Slavs were threatened by Islam. Turkish atrocities in the Balkans had exceeded all civilised norms. And so forth. The tsar wanted a war so he could take back Constantinople for his empire and Christianity. The British knew full well that these were the real reasons, and were opposed to a war. They were not prepared to see trade routes controlled by Russia. At home, the defeated Liberal leader Gladstone campaigned for a humanitarian intervention against the Ottomans. Disraeli refused point-blank and warned the Russians that Britain would enter the war to prevent the dismemberment of the Ottoman Empire.

The tsar went to war and the segment of the Balkans that is now Bulgaria became the battlefront. A national resistance emerged against both empires. Hundreds and hundreds of members of the radical Populist party Land and Liberty went to Bulgaria to fight against the tsarist army, as the Ottomans had already been pushed back. The war lasted for a year and a half. The British prevented the fall of Istanbul and the Russian generals returned home. Many of the young internationalists who did the same were arrested and exiled, and a few executed. It was this that sent them underground to form a new clandestine operation, the People's Will, that abandoned all public activity and, as discussed above, concentrated on assassinating the key personnel of the autocracy.

5

Socialism

The disintegration of the First International was complete by 1873. Police agents were in control of some branches in France and Switzerland, exacerbating the sharp differences between Bakunin ('It's a war of the knife against Marx and Engels') and Marx. The collapse was predictable, and the decision to shift the General Council to New York and rebuild was a failure. Nor was it a huge tragedy. Many of its members moved on to play an important part in helping to organise socialist parties in Europe and the United States. There is a similar pattern in the formation of all European socialist parties: internal conflicts, splits, programmatic disputes, unity. Russia was different mainly because of the political conditions that prevailed in the country. The combination of autocracy and late industrialisation had delayed the formation of trade unions and left the main factions of the Russian Social Democratic and Labour Party (RSDLP) no option but to operate in clandestinity. This reality left its mark on *all* oppositionist currents, from the Decembrists and the People's Will to the Bolsheviks and Mensheviks.

The formation of the Socialist International also marked the beginning of the end of decades of radical anarchist hegemony in the Euro-American left. And like all victors the socialists wrote off the contributions of those over whom they had triumphed.[1]

---

1 Militant anarchism hung on in Russia and Spain till the conclusion of the civil wars that beset both countries in the 1920s and '30s. In revolutionary Russia, the anarchist army in the Ukraine was led by

Socialist parties began to spring up throughout the continent and the United States and play an important political role both in extra-parliamentary actions (such as strikes) and, where possible, in parliament. Of these the German Social Democrats were the most advanced and the most successful. Bismarck, worried by their rapid growth, was determined to suppress the socialist and workers' movement. His government introduced the Anti-Socialist Law which banned the German Social Democratic Party (SPD). It was passed with majority support in the Reichstag on 21 October 1878 and renewed every two to three years. Only after pressure from the mass workers' movement was the 'Exceptional Law Against the Socialists' abrogated on 1 October 1890. During these twelve years the repression was unremitting, with 332 trade unions linked to the SPD dissolved, 1,300 newspapers and magazines banned, more than 1,000 activists sent underground and 1,500 members imprisoned for at least a year. It did not succeed in impeding the growth of the SPD: in 1881, a year after the draconian measures were passed, the German socialists received 310,000 votes in the elections to the Reichstag. In 1883 that figure rose to over half a million and by 1887 they were up to 763,000. In 1890, after the

---

Nestor 'Bat'ko' Makhno, an extremely gifted anarchist cavalry commander whose talents were deployed under Trotsky's command to help the Red Army on a number of critical occasions and were decisive in helping defeat the Whites in the region. Trotsky insisted, largely for administrative military reasons, that Makhno and his troops fight under the unified command of the Red Army. A foolish attempt to arrest Makhno was foiled and he fled into exile with some followers. Most of his troops were forcibly conscripted into the Red Army. Makhno himself died in Paris in 1934, two years before another civil war.

In Spain the anarchists played a major part in Catalonia during the Spanish Civil War and were the most radical current on the Republican side. They were crushed like everyone else by the right, but also by the Republican coalition under socialist and Communist control. Durutti, an anarchist military leader, was greatly admired by many non-anarchists for his integrity and military skills. A mystery still surrounds his death. Mass revolutionary anarchism was not to rise again.

law was repealed, they doubled their vote to 1.4 million. The SPD, with nineteen daily papers and forty-three weekly magazines, was the main opposition in the country. Would it succumb to 'parliamentary cretinism'? Or might it succeed in defeating Bismarck's ambitions at home and abroad?

Half a century previously, a great German poet had issued more than one warning of what lay ahead. Like the bards of ancient times, Heinrich Heine had a remarkable third eye that could peer into the future. His nightmares were unsettling. During the summer of 1840, the beginning of a decade that he would spend in exile and thirty years before German unification, Heine wrote a prescient little poem titled, simply, 'Germany':

> Germany's still a little child,
> And the sun's his nursing maid,
> She suckles him not on placid milk
> But on wild flames unstayed.
>
> On such a diet one grows fast,
> The blood runs hot in truth.
> You neighbour's kids, watch out before
> You tangle with this youth!
>
> He's a little giant, a clumsy one –
> Tears oak trees from the ground,
> To beat your backside black and blue
> Or bat your brains around.
>
> He's much like Siegfried, the noble lad
> Of song and story, who
> Right after he had forged his sword
> Cleft the anvil itself in two!
>
> – Yes, you'll be our Siegfried and you'll slay
> The ugly dragon, my boy!
> Hey ho! In heaven your nurse will laugh
> Down on the scene with joy!

You'll slay him and you'll seize his hoard,
The jewels of empire, now.
Hey ho, how bright the golden crown
Will gleam upon your brow![2]

Would Heine's young friend of that period, Karl Marx, have enough time to prepare an antidote? Would his followers? The First International, the first such attempt, had a smaller impact in Germany as compared to France, Switzerland and the United States. The thirty-year transition from the defeat of the Commune to the next century had seen the rapid growth of European colonization, accompanied by the rise of socialist parties (Britain has remained an exception in this regard) whose politics were effectively dominated by the ideas of Marx. Of these parties, the SPD was the strongest numerically and the most advanced theoretically. Created at a conference in Gotha in 1875 when the Marxists and the Lassalleans decided to merge, this organisation was seen as the model for the rest of continental Europe. Not by Marx and Engels, who wrote a stinging critique of certain aspects of the programme, especially its semi-literate discussion of labour and wages as well as its ambiguities on internationalism. The criticisms were suppressed during Marx's lifetime, and were only published by Kautsky in the party's theoretical journal *Die Neue Zeit* after strong pressure by Engels, who threatened that if they refused, the *Critique of the Gotha Programme*, as it was later known, would be published in Vienna. Angered by the publication, the German leadership of the SPD loudly and publicly rejected the criticisms.

The German socialists took the lead in preparing the Founding Conference of the Second (Socialist) International. It met on 14 July 1889, the centenary of the fall of the Bastille. Two banners dominated the Salle Petrelle where they met: 'Workers of the World Unite' and 'Political and Economic Expropriation of the Capitalist Class – Nationalisation of the Means of Production'. At the conclusion of the conference, the delegates marched to the Père Lachaise cemetery. A

---

2   Heinrich Heine, *The Complete Poems: A Modern English Version*, ed. Hal Draper, Oxford, 1982, p. 538.

gigantic wreath carried by sixteen men was laid at the graves of the Communards. The Second International had revealed the unevenness of the socialist movement. The British delegation was led by Keir Hardie, William Morris, Eleanor Marx, John Burns and R. B. Cunninghame-Graham. In his address, Hardie stuck to the facts: 10 million industrial workers, of which only a million belonged to trade unions. The latter, however, were far

Eduord Bernstein (left) and Karl Kautsky: The SPD today is well to the right of both its fathers.

removed from continental socialism and believed that class divisions needn't be conflictual; they were stuck quite happily in a coital lock with the Liberal Party, but had set up a committee to explore the 'radical' idea of pulling out to secure more direct parliamentary representation. Hardie, realising the urgent need to fill the vacuum, was the central figure behind the Bradford conference in 1893 where the Independent Labour Party was founded.

The French left was recovering from the repression unleashed during and after the Commune, but six different currents had failed to unite, despite the fact that, as Jules Guesde pointed out to the founding conference of the Second International,

> our *bourgeoisie* are more heartless and ruthless than any other, as they showed in the massacre of workers in June 1848 and May 1871. They ground the French working class to powder, smashed it to smithereens and, by suppressing trades unionism and freedom of association, deprived it of all possibility of common action.

Despite the divisions, French socialists moved up from 179,000 votes in the 1889 elections to 440,000 in 1893. In Belgium, too, the Walloon socialists (influenced by anarchism and Blanqui) and their Flemish counterparts (much closer to Marx and Engels) settled their differences and formed the Belgian Socialist Party.

The party demanded the franchise for workers; a pamphlet demanding these rights and titled *A Catechism of the People* sold over half a million copies. It was these demands that led to a huge strike in the predominantly mining district of Charleroi, spreading like fire to Liège and the Borinage and thereby transforming itself into a general strike. The army was called. In his authoritative history of Belgium published in 1932, the historian Henri Pirenne described in gory detail how

> for some days the province of Hainaut presented the dramatic spectacle of a full-scale war. Martial Law was proclaimed in the towns, town halls were occupied by the Army, soldiers were camped in the yards of factories and around the pit-heads, squadrons of cavalry patrolled the streets. The soldier's bullets crushed the workers' uprising with terror.

Killing workers at home coincided, on this occasion, with colonial atrocities abroad. These were horrendous in scale. Belgian imperialism was one of the more vicious of Europe's colonialisms.

The outcome, however, was an important, if limited, political victory for the workers. They won the right to vote, albeit with restrictions: it was not equal suffrage (one man, one vote) but plural suffrage (more than one vote allocated to certain voters according to the number of their children, the size of their property, and so forth). The main opposition to the socialists always came from the Catholic Church and its clergy. For a long period it was religion, not ethnicity, that was the main dividing line in Belgian politics, keeping both socialist atheists and neighbouring Dutch Protestants at bay.[3]

---

3 The birth of socialism and its parties was its most heroic phase, to which it is impossible to do justice in this book. For those who wish to be conversant in the past, there are many works on the subject, two of which are of particular value because of their scholarly precision: Julius Braunthal, *History of the International, 1864–1914* [vol. 1] and *1914–1943* [vol. 2], trs Henry Collins and Kenneth Mitchell, London, 1966, and Donald Sassoon, *One Hundred Years of Socialism*, London, 1996.

Before moving on to Russian Social Democracy, a brief look at why working-class turbulence in the United States only produced a short-lived socialist party unequal to its European counterparts, leave alone its Russian peers. There were, after all, many similarities between the US working class in formation and workers in Western Europe. During the late nineteenth century the bulk of

Eugene Debs: The presidential candidate of the US Socialist Party. He received just under a million votes on two occasions.

migration – barring East Asia – was from Europe. Ideas crossed the Atlantic as well, both anarchist and socialist. Publications in German predominated, but Scandinavian and Italian newssheets were also widely read. There were libraries and meeting rooms where they could be obtained and where discussions could be held with like-minded (or not) others. Factory owners strongly resisted the formation of occupational trade unions, but the Wobblies had made progress by recruiting all over the country (including Chinese, Japanese and African American workers) as well as putting together an effective section that specialised in political propaganda in different languages, with a popular repertoire of songs in which Joe Hill, in particular, excelled.

In terms of industrial militancy, the strike waves of 1877, 1885–86 and 1894 were astonishing both for their militancy and solidarity and, in some cases, developed a semi-insurrectional character. The actions of British, French, Italian and German workers in this period were relatively modest by comparison. The Belgian and Austrian strikes for universal male suffrage were the exception. And later, of course, the upheavals in Russia and Poland. But in terms of industrial working-class ferocity, the US workers were certainly not lagging behind. They were ahead.

And on the level of political consciousness? Here, too, the figures are surprising. In the first two decades of the twentieth century, the

Socialist Party of the United States (SPUSA), founded in 1901, had 125,000 members in 1912 and 100,00 at the end of the war. Only the German socialists had a larger membership: 380,000 in 1906 and 243,000 in 1917. In the US presidential elections of 1912 and 1920, the socialist presidential candidate, Eugene V. Debs, won over 900,000 votes on both occasions. There were two SPUSA congress members, over a hundred socialist mayors and numerous socialist state officials. Add to this that the SPUSA's electoral base – strong in Oklahoma, Texas, Montana, Washington, Nevada, and so forth – encompassed much more of the country than that of the Germans and Italians. With disastrous consequences, the latter virtually ignored the southern part of their country and the former, despite Engels's injunctions and Kautsky's pleas, overlooked the country-side. There is, of course, no doubt whatsoever that the factions in the SPUSA were wilfully blind to many realities, but so were their counterparts. The much vaunted 'tried and tested methods' (i.e., maturity) of the SPD could not prevent the debacle of 1914, and the vitality of the Italian socialists did not result in acceptance of the twenty-one conditions laid down by Lenin for joining the Comintern. Many other examples are available that convey American socialists' similarities to their European comrades. The reason for a lower vote tally when compared proportionately and numerically with the German, French and Italian parties was mainly the US electoral system, as all third-party candidates subsequently discovered. It was also due to the de facto disenfranchisement of African Americans in the South, after the collapse of the short Reconstruction period that followed the American Civil War. This gigantic absence only began to be remedied from below by the non-violent mass mobilisations led by Martin Luther King Jr and the threats of violent disorder levied by Malcolm X, Stokely Carmichael, the Black Panther Party and others. The victories of the 1960s were the result of mass mobilisations and mass riots in virtually every major city.

In his first major essay, *Prisoners of the American Dream*, Mike Davis suggests, with good reason, that a major difference between the United States and Europe was a campaign of sustained violence against the working class by successive US governments, vigilantes and privatised 'security' firms, such as Pinkertons. This violence was part of the system itself and its aim was not simply to crush strikes and provide the muscle for blacklegs to replace unionised or striking workers, but also to preempt the emergence of socialist groups and militant unions. True, Europe tried it too, but there success was limited. Hence fascism, the last resort of a petrified ruling class. In the United States there was no need for fascism. The existing system, via a combination of coercion and consent, succeeded in regularly pruning the system of all 'undesirables'. Davis's grim chronicle of the shootings by company vigilantes, targeted assassinations by local police and mercenaries registered as companies, beatings, lynching, surveillance, purges and FBI infiltration makes a horrendous catalogue. This was not a bourgeois-democratic norm, except in the United States for over a century, from Hayes to Nixon. The physical attacks on protesting workers were often coupled with legal restrictions. Heavy infiltration was used to immobilise socialist groups. There was blanket suppression and intimidation of black populations, largely but not exclusively in the South. US democracy, in other words, is almost a permanent state of exception. This is true as far as the African American population and militant workers are concerned, though when segments of the state apparatuses are themselves divided, an important political space is created for mass dissent.[4]

The Russian pattern was dissimilar because (in addition to the reasons already suggested) Congresses could only be held in exile. And delegates arriving from tsarist Russia did so with great

---

4 This was the case during the Vietnam conflict (1961–75), the last conscript war fought by the United States. With the State Department and the military divided, we had the spectacular sight of over a hundred veterans marching outside the Pentagon chanting, 'Ho-Ho-Ho Chi Minh, the NLF is going to win.' It took a decade or so to revert to the status quo ante and, in the process, Nixon was forced to resign. As the Vietnamese prime minister commented: 'The road to Watergate went through Vietnam.' It took a third-rate Hollywood actor to win the United States back to its pre-Vietnam 'values'. But memories of the exemplary internationalism of hundreds and thousands of American citizens never completely disappeared. Its lasting legacy has been the dumping of (or on) conscription.

difficulty. As a result the exiles dominated these gatherings. The editorial board of *Iskra* was the ideological and organisational centre of the Russian Social Democrats, and its divisions appeared to be generational. The old guard – Plekhanov, Axelrod, Zasulich – versus the new – Lenin, Martov, Potresov. Lenin's *What Is to Be Done?*, when first published, had been distributed willingly and happily by all Social Democrats (Martov was a particular enthusiast). They saw it as a simple codification of what the founders of the Social Democratic movement, Plekhanov and Axelrod, had long argued: namely, that the weaknesses of the Russian bourgeois class were so pronounced that its political tasks would have to be completed by the Russian workers. The struggle would, from the very beginning, be *political* and not simply economic. It was the powerlessness of both bourgeois and peasant that had placed this burden on the shoulders of the proletariat. Lenin took this argument further by illustrating the type of political instrument required to make such a revolution in Russia: a centralised, vanguard party of professional revolutionaries. Even on this point, there was initially little disagreement.

Matters came to a head during the course of the Second Congress of the RSDLP that opened in Brussels on 30 July 1903. A great deal of the preparatory work had been done by the *Iskra* editors, who were the functioning leadership of the party. They had agreed not to allow the Jewish Bund to affiliate because it would divide workers on the basis of ethnicity. Martov and Trotsky, socialists of Jewish origin, had very strong views on the subject. When, after the Kishinev pogrom of 1903, the Bund criticised *Iskra* for combatting Zionism harder than anti-Semitism, Martov responded in defence of the paper, arguing that Zionism posed an immediate threat to socialism by acting as a roadblock that prevented politically conscious Jewish workers from moving forward, whereas anti-Semitism attracted the most backward political groups of the population. Trotsky, in his report from the Congress, criticised the Bund for its 'militant provincialism' and 'parochial conceit', pointing out that it was the Bund's insistence on monopolising the representation of Jewish proletarians that precluded a compromise:

The Bund's organisational isolation forced the revolutionary energies of its workers into a cramped reservoir and pitilessly narrowed the political horizon of its leaders ... The Fifth Congress of the Bund that preceded our congress, put forward a new thesis: the Bund is 'the social democratic organisation of the Jewish proletariat and enters the party as the sole representative of the Jewish proletariat.' ... All that remained was to count the votes. Forty delegates against the five belonging to the Bund, with three abstentions. And the Bund left the party.

While the debate on the Bund had taken up a great deal of time, the real shock lay ahead. 'What political astrologer', asked Trotsky, 'would have forecast that Comrades Martov and Lenin would have spoken at the congress as hostile leaders of opposing sides?' Nobody had predicted that this Congress would be a parting of the ways, but that is what it became, dividing the RSDLP into majority (Bolshevik) and minority (Menshevik) factions which later solidified into two distinct parties.

The dividing line appeared to many inside and outside observers at the time to be marginal, concentrating as it did on the first paragraph of the party statutes defining who could and could not be a member. Even staunch supporters of Lenin were bemused. Lenin himself was initially surprised that the dispute had led to a permanent division. As I explained in the Introduction, he had enjoyed close and good working relations with Martov, despite many disagreements. His widow, Nadya Krupskaya, a staunch militant herself, later recalled a simile by Tolstoy that she and Lenin often used to explain the conflicts and activities of the Bolsheviks:

Once when walking, he [Tolstoy] spotted in the distance the figure of a man squatting on his haunches and moving his hands about in an absurd way: a madman, he thought, but on drawing nearer, he saw that it was a man sharpening his knife on the paving-stone. It is the same thing with theoretical controversies. Heard from aside, they do not seem worth quarrelling about, but once the gist is grasped, it is realised that the matter is of the utmost importance. It was like that with the Programme.[5]

Confronted by two critical events, the First World War and the Russian Revolution, the Mensheviks became further divided, with Martov both opposing the war and critically supporting the revolution and most of his former supporters in the leadership doing neither. Other Mensheviks supported the Whites in the civil war. As a result the division at the 1903 Congress – the first real one – that began in Brussels and had to be concluded in the East End of London was usually treated as an early sign of Lenin's prescience. This was not so, though Lenin's 'hardness' on who could be a member of the Russian party was not completely misplaced. Perhaps the fact that his brother Sasha had been betrayed by two newer members of the terrorist group whose recruitment he had strongly opposed also left its mark on Lenin. The issue was not unimportant. Despite all this, the tsarist secret police penetrated both groups fairly easily. There is a psychologically interesting report which suggests that when informers embedded in the two socialist factions were reporting back to the police generals who ran the outfit, each of them took on the colouring of the group to which they 'belonged' and became quite heated with each other, causing some merriment at headquarters but also indicating that the state apparatuses were not completely impervious to the debates in which they participated.

Though the disputes inside the RSDLP were particularly intense, every European socialist party contained two or three currents with differing opinions, as became clear in 1914. Seven years prior to that, the Russian socialists were confronted with a huge opportunity. Japan's victory over Russia in 1904 – the first act of a larger

---

5   Nadezhda Krupskaya, *Memories of Lenin*, London, 1930, p. 84. The Tolstoy story is a post-factum justification of differences that accelerated out of control, employed not just by Lenin. It was often used in the 1960s and '70s by Trotskyist and Maoist groups to justify sectarianism of the worst type, making one feel that Tolstoy's knife-sharpener was a polite version of the story – that the fellow on the pavement had actually been masturbating in an exaggerated fashion.

inter-imperialist conflict that lay ahead – was a huge blow against the autocracy and greeted as such by Bolsheviks and Mensheviks at the time. It led to a wave of strikes and demonstrations, the emergence of soviets – elected workers' councils that rapidly acquired legitimacy in the eyes of the urban masses – and armed struggle during the Moscow uprising.

Spatially and demographically, Russia, with a population of 143 million in 1904, was the stronger power. The islands of Japan had a population of only 47 million. Both countries were ultra-conservative and controlled by overcentralised states. The Meiji restoration had begun the process of modernisation, which had not, however, been accompanied by any meaningful democracy. Anarchism never emerged in Japan. The first glimmerings of socialism came after the Sino-Japanese War of 1894–95. Shakai Shugi Kenkyui-kai (the Association for the Study of Socialism) was formed in 1898 to determine whether or not socialism could be applied to Japan. Tiny groups, including a handful of intellectuals, began to translate and circulate socialist ideas from Western Europe, assembling a mixture of liberalism and Fabianism with a sprinkling of Fourier and Owen. Some argued that various Japanese institutions and religions had always contained seeds of socialism, which could now be gently cultivated and grown. This mood was best expressed by the sociologist Abe Iso, the extremely reluctant founding father of Japanese socialism:

Our industries are still young and a wide gap between the rich and the poor is not yet noticeable . . . The poor are satisfied with their condition, while the rich do not attempt to oppress them . . . Pauperism is scarcely known, because the rapid growth of industry gives a chance for everyone to earn a living; and none think of socialism except as a question of the distant future . . . We are not yet in the whirlpool; we have to prepare ourselves to escape . . . or at least know how to behave, if we should come into it later.[6]

---

6   Abe Iso, 'Social Problems and Their Solution', *Far East I* (20 July 1896). Given the arguments in the text, the title is slightly misleading. Quoted in Hyman Kublin, 'The Japanese Socialists and the Russo-Japanese War', *Journal of Modern History* 22: 4, 1950.

The Japanese socialists were the same as the RSDLP in terms of their membership's proportion to the general population, and were admitted to the Second International. Underneath its umbrella, Japanese and Russian socialists jointly published a statement denouncing the war in the Far East. The defeat went deep in Russian society as a whole. It was hardly a secret that Nicholas II and his unofficial circle of aristocratic cronies had dreamt of glory in the Far East and kept leading cabinet ministers – war, finance, foreign affairs – in the dark concerning these war aims. The tsar was not one of the brighter specimens of the Romanov family. Weak, mistrustful, unable to grasp even the most basic elements of strategy at home or abroad, Nicholas was easily swayed in policy-making by his equally incompetent and sycophantic friends. Dominic Lieven writes that 'he created a hole in the centre of decision-making that he was unable to fill ... The emperor was primarily responsible for Russia's debacle in east Asia, and his reputation never recovered.'

Setbacks in the Crimean War had forced the tsar at the time to emancipate the serfs in however botched a fashion. Defeat by Japan provoked the 1905 uprisings. And we know what lay ahead. As for the victors, they too were confronted with political shifts. Marxism, till then non-existent on the islands, made its first appearance after the Russo-Japanese War.

6

Empires at War

In 1887, Friedrich Engels described with chilling prescience what a new conflict in Europe might look like. It would, he suggested, be a world war of a kind that had not been seen before and would involve between 8 to 10 million soldiers who, he argued,

> will destroy one another and in the course of doing so will strip Europe clean in a way that a swarm of locusts could never have done . . . The devastation caused by the Thirty Years War telescoped into 3–4 years and spread over the entire continent . . . all this ending in general bankruptcy, the collapse of old states and their vaunted wisdom . . . the utter impossibility of foreseeing how all this will end and who will emerge victorious from this struggle; only one result is absolutely beyond doubt: universal exhaustion and the creation of conditions for the final victory of the working class.

In 1907, after a long debate at the Stuttgart Congress of the Second International, during which the coming war was taken for granted, a statement jointly drafted by Lenin, Luxemburg and Martov was *unanimously* passed by the Congress with, as the minutes noted, 'tumultuous, long and continuously repeated applause, with particular enthusiasm from the French delegation'. It read as follows:

> If a war threatens to break out, it is the duty of the working classes and their parliamentary representatives in the countries involved, supported by the co-ordinating activity of the International Socialist

Bureau, to exert every effort in order to prevent the outbreak of the war by the means they consider most effective, which naturally vary according to the sharpening of the class struggle and the sharpening of the general political situation.

In case war should break out anyway, it is their duty to intervene in favour of its speedy termination, and with all their powers to utilise the economic and political crisis created by the war, to rouse the masses and thereby to hasten the downfall of capitalist class rule.

The resolution was a compromise. The German SPD refused to accept the call for an immediate, Europe-wide general strike against the war. Some of Bebel's arguments were realistic, pointing out that war had a very dislocating effect on class consciousness and that a general strike was unrealistic. The bulk of his arguments, however, were related to what would happen once the war started: family life disrupted, concentration on war industries, blockade of exports, and so forth. What Lenin, Keir Hardie and Luxemburg were calling for, however, was a *preemptive* general strike to stop the war from taking place. This may have been utopian, but was never tried. Bebel officially closed the conference in order, he said, for the unity of all the delegates against the coming war to be remembered 'in golden letters' as the high point of the International. He died the following year. At the Congress he had repeatedly warned that the Balkan War was merely a prelude to a much larger conflagration.

As the years progressed, rearmament by the larger imperial states underwent a rapid acceleration. Britain had

August Bebel: German socialist leader and author.

accepted the rise of other powers, as long as British interests weren't directly challenged. When the French got too uppity (as in Africa), London threatened war. Paris retreated and an agreement between the two powers was signed in 1899. The British accepted French domination in Morocco as long as it did not affect trade agreements already in place, or the 'political status' of the country. It was also agreed 'that the post of Director-General of Antiquities in Egypt shall continue, as in the past, to be entrusted to a French *savant*'. The French were easily satisfied. The Boers in South Africa were not so lucky. When gold and diamond mines were discovered, the British went to war – an early case of colonial greed trumping racial solidarity.

For most of the nineteenth century the Industrial Revolution in Britain transformed the country, its innovations gradually benefiting the whole of Western Europe. Britain was thus in a commanding position in the early decades of the first capitalist globalisation, a 'World-Island', in the words of the imperial geographer Sir Harold Mackinder, who wrote a boastful ditty after the war mocking the Germans for overreach.[1]

At the beginning of 1914, European imperialism, with the British Empire in the lead, had occupied the whole of the Indian subcontinent that included Burma and Sri Lanka, the Indonesian archipelago, Malaysia and Indochina, and was busy carving up China. The Ottoman Empire dominated the Arab East. The Japanese were the colonial power in the Korean peninsula. Britain, France and Belgium controlled swathes of Africa and the newest member of the club (Germany) was 'civilising' Namibia and Tanganyika. The size of their colonial possessions determined the standing of individual imperial states, including not just the raw materials and precious mineral wealth and trade but also the inhabitants of the country.

Colonial subjects formed sizeable contingents in inter-imperialist wars, police operations in the colonies and wars of conquest.

---

[1] 'Who rules east Europe commands the Heartland / Who rules the Heartland commands the World-Island / Who rules the World-Island commands the World.'

The British used the Indian army; the French had (and still have) West African soldiers at their command and huge reserves in Algeria and Indochina; the Japanese created a Korean equivalent and later, after their conquest of Manchuria, a short-lived Chinese version. The importance of this imperial cannon fodder is often underestimated.[2] German magazines reported on the oppression inflicted by Britain and France in their respective colonies, but what they wanted was colonial space they could oppress in their own way. The massacre of the Hereros in Namibia provided an insight into German colonial rule.

The centenary of the First World War has been dominated by traditional assumptions, especially in the English-speaking world. British public opinion has been whipped up in favour of the war as one of democracy against tyranny, an argument not used much at the time given that the tsarist autocracy was a major ally. Shifting attitudes on this war are not unrelated to the imperial interventions currently underway in the Middle East, the Horn of Africa and South Asia. For most of the last century the First World War was perceived as an unmitigated disaster on every level.[3] The old notion being popularised again, that this was a war that pitted democracy against Prussian autocracy and the 'Wicked Hun', was always nonsensical. The franchise was limited in both countries (woman were not allowed to vote) and in terms of class representation, the German socialists were way ahead of their British counterparts. The propaganda about entering the war to defend 'plucky Belgium' was not convincing either. Belgium was the most savage

---

2   During the Second World War, the Germans had a supply of contingents from most of the European countries they had occupied. Franco refused to join in the war on the western front, but supplied the notorious Blue Division to fight against the Red Army on the eastern front.

3   The first play I ever saw on coming to the United Kingdom (in the company of Michael Beloff) was Joan Littlewood's stunning *Oh What a Lovely War* (later filmed by Sir Richard Attenborough). This attitude toward the war was regarded as common sense at the time, the affecting scene depicting fraternisation between the soldiers during a Christmas truce much appreciated.

and repressive of all European empires in Africa. Well before the war broke out, Belgians, both Walloon and Flemish, had killed between 10 and 12 million Congolese. Private libraries housing the authors of the Enlightenment often featured shrunken heads with hands and feet alongside them, a graphic illustration of Walter Benjamin's view that barbarism and civilisation were old bedfellows. Was this 'plucky' state worth defending?

History is seen differently these days, despite the best efforts of at least two major empirical historians. Niall Ferguson has refused to accept the demonisation of Germany as exclusively responsible for the conflict and insists, as a staunch ultraconservative historian, that British entry into the war 'was the worst error in modern history' and that Britain deserves equal blame for the conflict. The war, Ferguson argues, hastened the end of the British Empire rather than strengthening it. Dominic Lieven's study of the war on the eastern front is an extremely valuable account, particularly in its discussion of tsarist Russia. Both Ferguson and Lieven accept, in different ways, the fact that imperial rivalries underlay the conflict. Lieven's opening chapter is exemplary in this regard.[4]

The assassination of the Austrian crown prince by a Serbian nationalist was the trigger for the conflict, not the underlying cause, comparable in modern times to the explosions of 9/11 that provided the pretext for the war on Iraq, the destruction of Libya, Syria and the Yemen and the total destabilisation of Afghanistan and Pakistan. The post-9/11 wars have lasted longer than the First and Second World Wars put together.

The outbreak of war in August 1914 divided governments and socialist parties alike.

In Britain, as Douglas Newton has written, there were serious debates in the cabinet and four ministers resigned, but without alerting MPs as to why, leave alone mobilising public support against the conflict. Britain had the added problem of holding fast to the colony at home: Ireland. The World Island could not be seen

---

4 Niall Ferguson, *The Pity of War*, London, 2014, and Dominic Lieven, *Towards the Flame: Empire, War and the End of Tsarist Russia*, London, 2015.

to disintegrate, for fear of sparking off rebellions in other colonies. Home rule was denied the Irish and the Tories encouraged mutinous forces in the Army to disobey orders, effectively producing a united Ireland. The Ulster Protestant leaders threatened open rebellion with military support. This was a principal reason for British nervousness with regard to the European civil war.

Lenin's sober analysis, *Imperialism, the Highest Stage of Capitalism,* written two years into the war, remains a foundational text for understanding the First World War. He explained it in terms of the continuing rise of industrial capitalism and the contradiction of Germany, now the largest industrial power in Europe but with hardly any colonies. Leaving the British Empire aside, the strategists in Berlin found it irritating that pip-squeak states like Belgium, Holland and Portugal had, proportionally, more colonies than Germany did. The core of Lenin's argument, acknowledging his research debt to the liberal English historian John Hobson, is worth reading in his own words:

For Great Britain, the period of the enormous expansion of colonial conquests was that between 1860 and 1880, and it was also very considerable in the last twenty years of the nineteenth century. For France and Germany this period falls precisely in these twenty years. We saw above that the development of pre-monopoly capitalism, of capitalism in which free competition was predominant, reached its limit in the 1860s and 1870s. We now see that it is *precisely after that period* that the tremendous 'boom' in colonial conquests begins, and that the struggle for the territorial division of the world becomes extraordinarily sharp. It is beyond doubt, therefore, that capitalism's transition to the stage of monopoly capitalism, to finance capital, *is connected* with the intensification of the struggle for the partitioning of the world. Hobson, in his work on imperialism, marks the years 1884–1900 as the epoch of intensified 'expansion' of the chief European states. According to his estimate, Great Britain during these years acquired 3,700,000 square miles of territory with 57,000,000 inhabitants; France, 3,600,000 square miles with 36,500,000; Germany, 1,000,000 square miles with 14,700,000; Belgium, 900,000 square miles with 30,000,000; Portugal, 800,000 square miles with 9,000,000 inhabitants. The scramble for colonies by all the capitalist states at the end of the nineteenth century and particularly since the 1880s is a commonly known fact in the history of diplomacy and of foreign policy. In the most flourishing period of free competition in Great Britain, i.e., between 1840 and 1860, the leading British bourgeois politicians were *opposed* to colonial policy and were of the opinion that the liberation of the colonies, their complete separation from Britain, was inevitable and desirable. M. Beer, in an article, 'Modern British Imperialism',[5] published in 1898, shows that in 1852, Disraeli, a statesman who was generally inclined towards imperialism, declared: 'The colonies are millstones round our necks.' But at the end of the nineteenth century the British heroes of the hour were Cecil Rhodes and Joseph Chamberlain, who openly advocated imperialism and applied the imperialist policy in the most cynical manner!

It is not without interest to observe that even then these leading British bourgeois politicians saw the connection between what might be called the purely economic and the socio-political roots of modern imperialism. Chamberlain advocated imperialism as a 'true, wise and economical policy', and pointed particularly to the German, American and Belgian competition which Great Britain was encountering in the world market. Salvation lies in monopoly, said the capitalists as they formed cartels, syndicates and trusts. Salvation lies in monopoly, echoed the political leaders of the bourgeoisie, hastening to appropriate the parts of the world not yet shared out. And Cecil Rhodes, we are informed by his intimate friend, the journalist Stead, expressed his imperialist views to him in 1895 in the following terms: 'I was in the East End of London (a working-class quarter) yesterday and

---

5 *Die Neue Zeit*, XVI, 1, 1898, S. 302 [Lenin's note].

attended a meeting of the unemployed. I listened to the wild speeches, which were just a cry for "bread! bread!" and on my way home I pondered over the scene and I became more than ever convinced of the importance of imperialism ... My cherished idea is a solution for the social problem, i.e., in order to save the 40,000,000 inhabitants of the United Kingdom from a bloody civil war, we colonial statesmen must acquire new lands to settle the surplus population, to provide new markets for the goods produced in the factories and mines. The Empire, as I have always said, is a bread and butter question. If you want to avoid civil war, you must become imperialists.'

That was said in 1895 by Cecil Rhodes, millionaire, a king of finance, the man who was mainly responsible for the Anglo-Boer War. True, his defence of imperialism is crude and cynical, but in substance it does not differ from the 'theory' advocated by Messrs. Maslov, Südekum, Potresov, David, the founder of Russian Marxism [Plekhanov] and others. Cecil Rhodes was a somewhat more honest social-chauvinist.[6]

The last lines referring to Russian Social Democrats who supported Russia in the war are relatively mild. The angry eruptions had taken place earlier, when the German Socialists had decided on 4 August 1914 to vote for war credits in the Reichstag. The decision had been made at a heated internal meeting of the SPD parliamentary party, which voted 78 votes to 14 to support German imperialism in the war. Discipline was applied against the minority, but a public split now became inevitable. Karl Liebknecht alone defied party discipline and voted against the war, defining a patriot as 'an international blackleg'.

Lenin was stunned by Karl Kautsky's capitulation. When he first read Kautsky's text justifying the vote in *Die Neue Zeit*, he was at first convinced that it was a forgery. Rosa Luxemburg wrote to a

6 V. I. Lenin, *Imperialism: The Highest Stage of Capitalism*, available at Marxists Internet Archive, marxists.org.

friend that 'what one gets most from the party press here is – nausea'. As the truth sank in, Lenin immediately realised the scale of the disaster that had taken place. The German section of the Second International – its largest – had effectively dynamited internationalism. As far as he was concerned, there was no real dilemma as to what needed to be done. Working with such a current internationally – the French and Belgian socialists as well as most leading Mensheviks (though not Martov and Axelrod) having fallen into line as well – was now impossible.

Rosa Luxemburg, one of the most respected leaders of the German party and the Second International, was distraught. What made matters worse and aroused her anger was the endless justification with which she was presented on behalf of the softer core of SPD parliamentarians. They were 'coerced', they 'meant well', they were 'good-hearted' unlike the 'evil-hearted' right-wingers, they were 'war patriots without chauvinism' as compared to the real chauvinists. And so this endless litany of justification and self-justification went on. She did not budge: 'No judgement can be made about *motives* in cases of such world-historical significance, only about actions.' When an SPD leader, Robert Dissman, tried to argue that members of the party's right wing were 'consistently' pro-war and that those who had reluctantly voted with them were inconsistent warmongers, she responded bluntly that 'I am, under all circumstances, in favour of consistency, but I expect nothing but wretchedness from the notion of swallowing approval of the war, and may consistency be damned.'[7]

During the first year of the war, antiwar activists – mainly socialists and a few pacifists – from all over Europe assembled in the Swiss village of Zimmerwald to evaluate the situation. Bolsheviks and antiwar Mensheviks united to sign the declaration that was unanimously passed. It was a bit too weak for Lenin, who had hoped for a Europe-wide call to transform the imperialist war into a civil war against the pro-war bourgeois governments and their state. He had also hoped for a ringing denunciation of the Second

---

7 George Adler, Peter Hudis and Annelies Laschiza, eds, *The Letters of Rosa Luxemburg*, London and New York, 2011, pp. 330–1.

1919: Trotsky and Frunze explaining the latest news from the civil war to delegates attending the First Congress of the Communist International.

International for having failed so miserably to defend its own previous resolutions on the war. A separate Bolshevik resolution along these lines was defeated. Lenin was not surprised. In a pamphlet, *Socialists and War*, written soon after the gathering at Zimmerwald, his preoccupation with wars and civil wars was noticeable. He referred to Clausewitz's maxim on war being 'a continuation of politics by other means', and praised the Prussian as 'one of the profoundest writers on the problems of war ... Marxists have always rightly regarded this thesis as the theoretical basis of views concerning the significance of every given war.'

Lenin devoured Clausewitz's writings, filling an entire notebook with his own comments and questions. He had been sent *On War* by fellow Bolshevik G. I. Gusev, who had in an earlier incarnation been an editor of the Russian *Military Encyclopedia* and developed contacts with younger military officers after the Russo-Japanese War. Gusev discovered that many of them favoured drastic reforms in the army and a unified military school and doctrine, but were aware of the resistance they would encounter upon airing their views. Shades here of the never-to-be-forgotten Decembrists.

But why such a concentrated interest in Clausewitz at this time? One reason is obvious. Lenin was in the middle of a war, with politics silenced. Retreating to a library in bad times was not unusual for him, and studying Clausewitz to understand the war no doubt helped his own analysis of the real causes of the conflict. Was there another reason? Had the shock waves created by the capitulation of a large majority of European and Russian Social Democrats to their respective war machines made him think afresh about the complexities of the revolutionary process? Obviously, he believed that if the large parties had held firm they would have been able to pierce the jingoism and chauvinism that had temporarily clouded working-class consciousness. Already by the end of 1915, desertions had begun and soldiers were being executed by their own. Soon this mood would spread from the battlefields to the capital cities of various countries involved in the war. This alone would have rewarded a united international stand against the war with huge political dividends. But Lenin understood better than all his comrades that there was no going back now. Reconciliation with those parties that had backed their own rulers in the conflict was out of the question. There was no guarantee whatsoever that the workers' militias that had emerged during the Commune would rise again spontaneously in any European country. Initially the revolutionary party might be left with no option but to create its own armed militias and organise an armed insurrection. Nothing could be left to chance again. Hence the detailed readings of Clausewitz in which Lenin detected the German military philosopher's debt to Hegel's dialectic. It's clear from Lenin's marginal comments that by the time he reaches the third volume of *On War*, he is intellectually excited.

Where Clausewitz discusses changes in French military strategy after the revolution and decries the lack of understanding concerning the link between politics and war, he concludes as follows:

> To be sure, even war itself, in its essence and in its forms, has undergone significant changes, bringing it closer to its absolute aspect. But these changes did not come about because the French government, in a sense emancipated, untied the apron strings of politics, but

rather they resulted from the altered politics issuing from the French Revolution for France as well as for all of Europe. Such politics summoned different means, different forces, thereby making it possible to conduct war with an energy otherwise unthinkable.

Lenin's marginal comment: 'Exactly!'

A reflection by Clausewitz in *A Survey of Military Instruction Given by the Author to His Royal Highness the Crown Prince in the Years 1810, 1811, and 1812* concerns defensive and offensive wars. Clausewitz wrote:

> In political terms a defensive war is a war fought for one's own independence. Strategically, defensive war means a campaign limited to my fighting the enemy in a theater of war which I have prepared for that purpose. Whether in this theater of war I fight defensively or offensively does not make any difference.

Lenin comments after the last sentence: 'Right!'[8]

The tsar had needed an intelligent, ruthless and tough-minded

---

8 Interestingly, Clausewitz's ideas became a heated subject in the Soviet Union soon after the civil war in 1921 when Frunze and others tried to establish dogmatic rules for the Red Army, provoking a scathing response from Trotsky, who denounced attempts to seal off military debates by adopting a doctrinaire strategy to apply for all time. Trotsky won the debate at the Eleventh Party Congress, but Frunze's ideas were accepted soon after Trotsky left the Commissariat of War. Trotsky had argued that on the military question it was pointless appealing to Marxism, since it had nothing to offer on this front, and he annoyed the Red Army commanders by insisting that the civil war had been won by learning from both the mobile cavalry of the Ukrainian anarchists and the White general Ungern. 'Manoeuvre', he stressed, 'is a characteristic not of revolutionary armies but of civil wars as such.' Frunze was promoted as the Soviet Clausewitz and his ideas became part of an unchallengeable orthodoxy, a frozen dialectic. Where this dogma led is hardly a secret. It was applied on 22 June 1941 and found seriously wanting. Frunze died under mysterious circumstances in 1925. Mikhail Tukachevsky, the legendary military commander capable of overriding the dogma, had been executed on Stalin's orders as a 'German spy'.

prime minister. One certainly existed. The ultraconservative former interior minister, Petr Durnovo, had crushed the 1905 revolution. His order of that time was still embedded in the memory of both sides:

> Rioters to be exterminated immediately by force of arms, their dwellings to be burned down in the event of resistance. Arbitrary self-rule [the soviets] must be eradicated once and for all – now. Arrests would not serve any purpose at present and anyway it is impossible to try hundreds and thousands of persons. It is essential that the troops should fully understand the above instructions. P. Durnovo.

Could Durnovo turn the situation around, were he given effective command of the country? On the eve of war he was asked to do so but refused, explaining frankly to his sovereign that the situation now was so bad that assassinations and uprisings could not be excluded over the next few years; were he to become head of government and interior minister, he would be held responsible. Perhaps he also realised that with the army on the front, cannibalistic repression might not work this time. He did submit a short memorandum in which he displayed a strong anti-British prejudice. Britain, he opined, liked nothing more than to manoeuvre large continental allies to fight their rivals in Europe. He suggested that fighting the Germans (Russia's main trading partner) and the Habsburgs was short-sighted. He pointed out that appeasing the ultranationalist Russians by annexing Galicia – absorbing an 'extremely dangerous Little Russian separatism which in a favourable context was capable of assuming completely unexpected proportions' – might make Ukrainian nationalism unmanageable.[9]

Durnovo's main concern was revolution. Deeply reactionary though he was, as interior minister he must have read the pamphlets and books that preceded and followed the events of 1905. It's difficult to imagine that he had not read Lenin. If he had not, his warning to the tsar is all the more remarkable that if Russia were

---

9   Lieven, *Towards the Flame*, p. 305.

Russian troops on the Eastern Front: Desertions and mutinies stalled
the war effort.

to be bled dry by the coming war and Germany defeated, there
would be revolutions in both countries. His views were ignored.
Russia entered the war which, after a year and a half of huge losses
in human life on both fronts, was grinding to a stalemate. On the
western front the casualties were growing without any decisive
military successes for either side. Conditions on the eastern front
were deteriorating out of control. The Germans were advancing
and Russian soldiers, 'peasants in uniform' as Lenin described
them, were beginning to experience first-hand the uselessness of
their military leaders and the empty rhetoric of the politicians.
Two and a half years into the war, Russia was gripped by revolution and the autocracy was overthrown. A provisional government
was put into place. In the next chapter we will discuss the course
of this revolution, but a brief look across the Atlantic is necessary.
Had the United States remained neutral, as a majority of the country wanted, a ceasefire and truce between the British and German
empires would have been the only realistic solution. Whether it
would have forestalled the Russian revolution remains a moot
point. But before any such possibility could be seriously considered, a revolution erupted in Russia. The autocracy fell. The tsar

was deposed and a broad-based provisional government took the reins of power.

This made American intervention, already under serious discussion, inevitable. In an address to the World Salesmanship Conference in Detroit in 1916, Woodrow Wilson, whose rhetoric combined fake piety and hypocrisy like no other politician of the time, offered these pearls of wisdom to the gathered salesmen:

> Lift your eyes to the horizons of business and with the inspiration of the thought that you are Americans and are meant to carry liberty and justice and the principles of humanity wherever you go, go out and sell goods that will make the world more comfortable and more happy, and convert them to the principles of America.[10]

In earlier talks, Wilson had made constant use of Providence to justify the US brand of world conquest. He had sent troops to Mexico, Cuba, Haiti, Nicaragua. Bringing his country into a European war would cost lives but, given that both Germany and Britain were bleeding badly, it would be a risk-free operation. 'Divine destiny' awaited and, as he had already made clear to a Southern businessmen's gathering in Mobile, Alabama, in 2013, they were en route to the summit: 'Slowly ascending the tedious climb that leads to the final uplands, we shall get our ultimate view of the duties of mankind. We have breasted a considerable part of that climb' and are approaching the final goal, to 'come out upon those grand heights where there shines unobstructed the light of the justice of God'. In a letter to a close friend and adviser on 21 July 1917, he had boasted:

> England and France have not the same views with regards to peace that we have by any means. When the war is over we can force them to our way of thinking because by that time they will, among other things, be financially in our hands.

---

10 Quoted in Perry Anderson, *American Foreign Policy and Its Thinkers*, London and New York, 2015, pp. 8, 9.

The war was won decisively by the manpower and technology of the United States, not the World-Island. How would they operate on the global stage? Woodrow Wilson's flatulent rhetoric and his Christ complex came into play to project the United States as a world power. The Fourteen Points lauded to the skies by liberals were little more than an attempt to respond to the Bolsheviks, now in power, who had published all the secret and imperialist treaties in the tsarist archive. Attached to the notion of 'self-determination' for some European states previously under Austro-Hungarian suzerainty, the rest of the world was left to its empires. A young Vietnamese man who turned up at Versailles to demand self-determination for Indochina was brushed aside with contempt. This was Ho Chi Minh, who went on to attend the founding conference of the PCF and inflicted a memorable defeat on the United States fifty-eight years later.

In his new position as arbiter, the American president made serious mistakes from a broader imperialist point of view. He decided to go along with French and British insistence that Germany be severely punished economically (through reparations) and neutered permanently by being forbidden to build its armed forces, except insofar as they were necessary to maintain internal order and keep the Bolsheviks at bay. An additional demand from the British and French empires to the effect that German colonies should be divided amongst the victors as bonus payment for a job well done was slightly modified by Wilson. German colonies would be under mandate to the newly formed League of Nations – a toothless entity, if ever there was one, and created essentially to preserve the postwar status quo. Germany was decolonised, its rivals strengthened and their empires left intact. The Treaty of Versailles imposed on Germany was described by Woodrow Wilson as 'this incomparable consummation of the hopes of mankind'.

We are only too aware of the consequences. The economic crash of 1929 produced a sharp political polarisation in Germany. Its leaders certainly understood the importance of the United States, admired it on many levels and saw themselves as its European equivalent. A little more than a century after the Napoleonic Wars, the Third Reich, in a Faustian bid for world domination, undertook the last serious attempt to unite and homogenise Europe. The model they had in mind was the Monroe Doctrine, much admired in Berlin as the basis for US domination of South America. The doctrine was a straightforward and hugely successful assertion of imperial hegemony over a divided continent, and its principal aim was economic: to keep the European powers out of the region.

The Luddendorf–Hitler doctrine was designed as a carbon copy of its American rival. The plan was to create a new order in Europe that could both rival the United States spatially and militarily and use the new European base to destroy the Soviet Union and Bolshevism for eternity, thus gaining vital agricultural space, oil and a permanent supply of cheap Slav labour. The German leaders were confident that if civil wars were to erupt (as, for instance, in Spain) they would still have enough indigenous support to create effective auxiliaries to fight alongside their armies. With Russia under its rule, Germany would be impregnable and the British Empire would collapse under its own weight.

SECTION THREE

1917–1920: States
and Revolutions

7

February

In 1905, his detailed account of the dress rehearsal in which he played a leading part as chair of the St Petersburg Soviet, a twenty-something Trotsky can't resist citing a much hated but not stupid senior servant of the autocracy. With good reason.

'Revolution', old Suvorin, that arch-reptile of the Russian bureaucracy, wrote at the end of November 1905, 'gives an extraordinary *élan* to men and gains a multitude of devoted, fanatical adherents who are prepared to sacrifice their lives. The struggle against revolution is so difficult precisely because it has so much fervour, courage, sincere eloquence, and ardent enthusiasm to contend with. The stronger the enemy, the more resolute and courageous revolution becomes, and with every victory it attracts a swarm of admirers. Anyone who does not know this, who does not know that revolution is attractive like a young, passionate woman with arms flung wide, showering avid kisses on you with hot, feverish lips, has never been young.'[1]

In 1905, Lenin composed a text entitled *Two Tactics of Social-Democracy* that was distributed widely by the RSDLP. His similes were not exactly those of the reptile cited above, but not as far removed as one might imagine:

---

1   Leon Trotsky, *1905*, tr. Anya Bostock, London and New York, 1971, p. 197.

Revolutions are the festivals of the oppressed and the exploited. At no other time are the masses of the people in a position to come forward so actively as creators of a new social order as at a time of revolution. At such times the people are capable of performing miracles, if judged by the narrow, philistine scale of gradual progress ... We shall be traitors to and betrayers of the revolution if we do not use this festive energy of the masses and their revolutionary ardour to wage a ruthless and self-sacrificing struggle for the direct and decisive path.[2]

Twelve years later a left Menshevik participant in the revolution and a very stern critic of Lenin began to write his memoirs:

Tuesday, 21 February 1917. I was sitting in my office in the Turkestan section [of the Ministry of Agriculture]. Behind a partition two typists were gossiping about food difficulties, rows in the shopping queues, unrest among the women, an attempt to smash into some warehouse.

'D'you know,' one of these ladies suddenly declared, 'if you ask me, it's the beginning of the revolution!'

These girls didn't understand what a revolution was. Nor did I believe them.

The 'I' is N. N. Sukhanov, once an editor of the magazine *Contemporary* and later a regular contributor to Maxim Gorky's non-party magazine, *Letopis* (Chronicle). The quotation is from the first page of his memoir's opening chapter, 'Prologue'. Sukhanov's history of 1917, written as 'a personal record', is one of the finest books on the Russian Revolution, used as a reference by Trotsky and Deutscher (their disagreements notwithstanding) and appreciated also by historians of a very different hue. Read in tandem, the histories of 1917 written by participants in the revolution were, for a long time, part of the political and literary heritage

---

2 V. I. Lenin, 'Two Tactics of Social-Democracy in the Democratic Revolution', 1905, available at the Marxists Internet Archive, marxists. org.

of the broad left: Trotsky's three volumes on the revolution and Victor Serge's graphic account of the year one were supplemented by two first-hand and first-rate journalistic accounts, by the Americans John Reed and Albert Rhys Williams. Historians tend to prefer Sukhanov's work because of the amazing details it contains. It was first published in Moscow in 1922 and remained in circulation for just under a decade, despite rude references to Lenin ('anarchist and dictator'), Trotsky ('high-handed and arrogant') and Stalin ('a sort of grey blur, dimly looming up now and then and not leaving any trace. There is really nothing more to be said about him'). He got this one badly wrong and paid the price. Charged with 'sabotage' in 1940, he was executed.

The fashionable, reactionary historians of today (fashionable because they are reactionary), taking their cue from the Italian fascist Curzio Malaparte, regard the revolution as a Bolshevik coup, a triumph of technique rather than politics and a process with limited or no popular support. Its principal leader Lenin is often depicted as a born dictator. To this latest crop of historical analyses, one could add a prominent Russian vulgarian, General Dmitri Volkogonov, whose main purpose, one assumes, was to earn a quick buck.[3] Compared to this wild bunch, the biography by Robert Service (if not his addendum) and the writings of David Shub, S. E. Utechin and others appear as models of rectitude.

The literature on the Russian Revolution is overwhelming. Interested readers will, I hope, find the books they need. This chapter is not designed as a substitute. Its aim is to study how Lenin confronted the dilemmas and contradictions posed by the February upheaval and its resulting political crisis, and chart the crucial eight months that culminated in the October insurrection. In these critical months Lenin would craft and complete two texts, linked but different in character. The *April Theses* were a call to action and to order, designed for the Bolshevik Party, whose leadership was drifting. Later, on the eve of October, Lenin more or less

---

3   On a visit to London, Volkogonov called on Isaac Deutscher's widow, Tamara, bowed, kissed her hand and declared: 'Your husband was an inspiration to all of us.' She did not reply.

completed *State and Revolution*, a text begun in 1916 that represented the summit of his politico-theoretical achievements. In it he speaks uninhibitedly of what a Communist future meant and would entail. The model evoked the Paris Commune, but was focused on achieving universal social ownership based on universal democracy. The end of state, law, punishment and the social division of labour.

On a more concrete note we find something equally startling in the text. There is not a single reference in its pages to the differences between Russia and Western Europe, a theme which constantly recurs in Lenin's previous writings. This topic was omitted because of Lenin's now definitive view regarding the state machine: because it organised and orchestrated the violence of the ruling classes at home and abroad, it was essential for any revolution to seize and destroy it through violence, regardless of all other differences. Why? Because in the last instance the total complex of the state is always determined by its coercive function. Without this understanding no revolution is possible. The revolution's triumph over the state is a theme to which Lenin returned during his last years, as he prepared a mental balance sheet of its failures.

What were the material conditions, some of which have been described in detail in previous chapters, that made the revolution possible, gave form to the Bolshevik Party – the only party of its kind to emerge from the Second International – and laid an enormous footprint on the twentieth century, transforming world politics in ways hitherto unimagined? What were the historical prerequisites that made this revolution possible?

The First World War brought matters to a head. From 1914 to 1916, tsarist Russia lost as many soldiers as Britain would over the four years of conflict, and many more than Austro-Hungary or Italy would endure come the war's end. By 1916, almost a million Russians lay dead on the eastern front, a disaster multiplied by the year's bad harvests, caused largely by the mass conscription of peasants into the army. This created near-famine conditions at home, exacerbated by the dislocation of the transport system, also courtesy of the war.

The nobility, till now the bedrock of the autocracy, slowly realised that they could not rule in the same way any longer, but had no real programme for any structural reforms. The disintegration was too rapid. In their panic, they turned, with the industrial magnates, against the monarchy which was rotting from within. They waged an intemperate campaign, accusing the court of being soft on the Germans and visualising, with the encouragement of English and French diplomats in the capital, a rapid military putsch against the tsar so that the war could be prosecuted single-mindedly.

Russia choked with sobs that soon turned to anger. As the women workers in Sukhanov's office had predicted, a revolutionary rupture was fast approaching. Lenin described the war as the great 'stage-manager' of the revolution. Trotsky wrote: 'The imperialist war sharpened all the contradictions, tore the backward masses out of their immobility, and thus prepared the grandiose scale of the catastrophe.'

The struggles waged during the last half of the nineteenth century had been led by women and men who realised full well that the revolutionary dismantling of tsarism was a necessary precondition for the development of economy and culture. But the forces they mobilised to solve this problem proved insufficient. The rising bourgeois class was frightened by all talk of revolution. The intelligentsia had attempted to raise the consciousness of the peasantry, to mobilise it for the great task that lay ahead. They hoped that this appeal to the people would persuade the *muzhik* to generalise his own miseries and his aims. The response was minimal. In despair, the Russian intelligentsia replaced the peasant with dynamite. An entire generation was burnt out by this struggle.

During the 1905 revolution, the largest upheavals had been in the imperial zones of tsarist Russia. National and class oppression had combined to produce resistance that dwarfed events in Moscow and St Petersburg. The eruption of Latvian and Georgian peasants required the dispatch of well-equipped tsarist divisions before the rebellions were quelled. It was different in 1917. Russia was trying to catch up with Western Europe. Industry had grown. Huge plants now existed in Petrograd, Moscow, the Donetz basin and the Caucasus. Working conditions and wages were appalling. The size of the factories meant there was no orderly growth of either the proletariat or their masters. The former mushroomed out of control, the latter were tiny in number and hence socially and politically weak. Because of this they were incapable of differentiating themselves from the aristocracy, which excluded them from the inner circles of power till it was too late for both. Heavily dependent on state loans and contracts, aided and crippled by foreign investors (mainly French), Russia's capitalists were constantly appeasing the court, providing funds to the conservative cause (Paul Milyukov of the Constitutional Democrats, or Kadets, was a special favourite) while savagely exploiting their own workforce.

The February Revolution in motion: soldiers and workers, men and women, fraternise.

The February Revolution that demolished the edifice of tsarism was a spontaneous, elemental upsurge of the Petrograd masses, with workers and soldiers to the fore. It was a response to the crisis as a whole, triggered by the severe bread shortage in the city that was accompanied by a strike in the giant Putilov works for a 50 percent wage increase. The fatal response of the proprietors to the strike was a lockout. This released 30,000 workers to march through the proletarian districts, appealing successfully to other workers to join them. Factories were shut down. A general strike was in motion. On 25 February, the masses, like streams heading to the river, marched in different formations to the centre of the city. Within an hour, the squares were occupied.

The court reacted in the only way it knew. The tsar ordered the garrison commanders to crush the uprising, whatever the cost. Initially the soldiers complied with these orders, but the resulting massacre detonated a series of mutinies inside the army. A critical point had been reached. The masses had lost their fire and the soldiers were disobeying orders at home and deserting the front in increasing numbers. This combination is the defining feature of any prerevolutionary crisis. Agitators were demanding 'Bread and Peace', confronting the soldiers with words, pleading with them to join the revolution. The revulsion created by the shootings spread through all the barracks. A large and active minority of 160,000 soldiers joined the uprising, and most of the others followed them. As night fell, the tsar's government abandoned the city. The workers, including many women in their ranks, soldiers, students and intellectuals were masters of the capital.

Even as the soldiers of the Pavlovsky Regiment made it clear to their officers that they would neither shoot at workers nor go to the front, a lavish dinner was in progress at the palatial mansion of the millionaire Guchkov. Present were the forces of high conservatism: Milyukov, the main leader and ideologue of the right, a few shaken generals fearful of being stirred even more and sundry notables. They agreed it was no longer possible to sustain the tsar. A delegation was dispatched to inform Nicholas Romanov of this fact. After three days, he abdicated. It had taken a spontaneous mass uprising, unforeseen by *any* political group, and eight days to end feudalism and the enfeebled absolutist state in Russia.

Discredited Duma politicians attempted to salvage the situation by establishing a committee, but here the experience of the masses in 1905 proved vital. The first political act following the tsar's departure was the convening of workers' and soldiers' soviets that immediately assumed control of the situation. On 1 March 1917, the Petrograd Soviet issued Order Number 1: all military units should retain their arms, elect representatives to the Soviet and use these political rights to the full. In one blow the Soviet had sealed off any real possibility of a traditional post-feudal bourgeois state emerging. The legitimate monopoly of violence had been transferred by popular demand to the soviets. Even the most striking manifestation of spontaneity, in this case a revolution, has its limits. How would this astonishing institutional leap forward be reflected in politics?

There was no leadership with a strategy to move forward. During the crucial eight days, the Bolshevik party included a tiny sprinkling of militants led by Shlyapnikov. The Mensheviks and Social Revolutionaries (SRs) easily won control of the Petrograd Soviet but, incapable and frightened of forming a soviet government themselves, they went cap in hand to a group of bourgeois notables, clapped-out Duma politicians who had, in the main, joined the opposition solely as part of the anti-Court campaign in 1916. These gentlemen were authorised by the Soviet to form a provisional government, a weak and sickly creature from birth. Composed of unrepresentative and unaccountable politicians, it represented neither the old nor the new. The later addition of new Menshevik and SR ministers did little to alter the political balance. The latter merely prolonged the old policies: continuation of the war, no agrarian reforms and continued suppression of the nationalities. *Plus ça change.* Nothing changed.

Russian revolutionary exiles were dotted all over the Swiss cities. They had been joined by German and Italian antiwar activists. A socialist youth group in Zurich had organised a meeting on 22 January 1917 at the People's House, where Lenin delivered a lecture on the 1905 revolution. He made one essential point and one honest, though mistaken, prediction. The first was a complete break with RSDLP orthodoxy to which both factions, in their different ways, had held on, with the exception of Trotsky. Secondly, Lenin told the young people that in Russia there would not be a two-stage revolution, first bourgeois, then proletarian. He declared:

Undoubtedly this coming revolution can only be a proletarian revolution, and in the profounder sense of this word: a proletarian Socialist revolution even in its content. This coming revolution will show to an even greater degree ... that only stern battles, only civil wars, can free humanity from the yoke of capital.

He could not predict when such an event might take place, and concluded in regretful tones: 'We of the older generation may not live to see the decisive battles of this coming revolution.'[4]

A few weeks later the Polish revolutionary Bronski burst into Lenin and Krupskaya's rented room on 12 Spiegelgasse with news of the February revolution. They were stunned. Other émigrés were already knocking on the door. They all rushed to the newspaper stands by the lakeside so that Lenin could read the news for himself. Krupskaya relates that his 'mind worked intensely'. Amongst the first things he did was write to Alexandra Kollontai, a fellow member of the Bolshevik Central Committee, in Stockholm. The message was crystal clear: 'Never again along the lines of the Second International! Never again with Kautsky! By all means a more revolutionary programme and more revolutionary tactics.' And again, just in case the intensity of the first message had not made enough of an impact: 'Revolutionary propaganda, as heretofore, agitation and struggle for an international proletarian revolution and for the seizure of power by the "Soviet of Workers' Deputies" but not by the Kadet fakers.'

Kollontai cabled back asking for *concrete* instructions. This sobered Lenin. He replied that he did not want to be misread. What he had suggested was the strategic perspective, not designed for immediate action. What needed to be done together with the unifying Bolshevik demand of 'Land, Peace, Bread' was the formation of concrete plans to arm the masses. He was insistent on this and wrote Kollontai that they must 'spread out! Rouse new layers! Awaken fresh initiatives ... Prove to people that peace can only come with armed Soviet of Workers Deputies.' He was thinking of the Paris Commune again. This time they would not be easily

---

4   Nadezhda Krupskaya, *Memories of Lenin*, London, 1930, p. 286.

defeated. And he said as much at a public meeting on 18 March at a Swiss workers' centre to mark the anniversary of the Commune. The sharpness and intensity of the lecture left an impression on everyone. The Swiss saw him as a utopian visionary. The Russians understood he was talking about the present.

Meanwhile Kollontai had reached Petrograd, where she reported to the Bureau of the Central Committee. They had already received one message from Lenin indirectly: 'What a torment it is for all of us to sit here at such a time.' They insisted that Lenin return immediately, by any means necessary.

In Switzerland, Lenin convened a meeting of all the exiles to discuss how best to return. They agreed that the only priority was to reach Petrograd as soon as possible. Martov suggested appealing to the British and French governments for a safe passage. Karl Radek mocked that suggestion, arguing that pleas to those two countries would convey, effectively, 'Please let us through so we can go and end the war, thus releasing the Germans to concentrate on you.' Martov retreated and suggested Germany. Not a bad idea in Lenin's view but, he warned, they could all be arrested and shot for treason when they reached Petrograd. The others were nervous and understandably so. History might not vindicate them. But Lenin and Martov argued them out of passivity.

Ultimately it was agreed that the German route was the only realistic possibility. A formal letter was dispatched to the Executive of the Soviet requesting support for the journey. No reply came. Alexander Helphand (Parvus), a longtime German sympathiser of Russian Social Democracy who had helped to publish *Iskra* during its early years, was the only possible mediator. Could they still trust him?

Helphand had lived in the Munich suburb of Schwabing where Lenin had spent his first months in exile in 1902; at the time, the two would meet semi-regularly. Occasionally Rosa Luxemburg would drop in to share the conversation. Lenin was, at the time, editing *Iskra* with Martov and others. Later Helphand became involved in business ventures and developed a dodgy reputation. Lenin thereafter ignored him. Trotsky, who had been much closer to Helphand, also broke off relations and disowned his

'Falstaff . . . whom we have now placed on the list of politically diseased'.

Others kept in touch. When contacted, Helphand agreed to set up a meeting at the Wilhelmstrasse with an old acquaintance named Arthur Zimmermann – a senior state official at the German foreign office in Berlin. In December 1914, Zimmermann had predicted that the war would not be 'over in a few months', despite the boasts of the kaiser and high command. Upon being asked for advice, Zimmermann prepared an intelligent memorandum entitled 'Revolutionising', the aim of which was to encourage dissent in different parts of the tsarist lands and thus to weaken the centre, compelling the tsar and his generals to make a separate peace. Helphand's visit in March 1917 must have appeared as a gift from heaven. The war was at a stalemate and German casualties were rising. They needed a breakthrough.

Zimmermann was well aware of Russian Social Democracy, its splits and its foibles and he was studying reports of the February Revolution very closely. He made it clear that the key figure in the entourage of exiles was Lenin, the only one with the will to push through a revolution. This, Helphand assured him, was not a problem. Zimmermann went to the palace and apprised the kaiser of the situation, explaining in great detail what this would entail: a free passage for the Russian revolutionary exiles from Switzerland, through Germany and to the Baltic coast. The kaiser communicated a summary of the plan to the emperor in Vienna. He was strongly opposed. It was too dangerous and might backfire. But the kaiser was insistent and prepared to take the risk. Even if these madmen succeeded, he told Zimmermann, once we've won the war we'll crush them. Lenin's response to this remark was swift: a German revolution was on the way that would permanently settle accounts with the Hohenzollerns. After detailed negotiations, Lenin and the exiles began the long journey home without the left Menshevik leader Julius Martov, who characteristically, having convinced other doubters to take the risk, refused at the last moment to travel himself until the trip had been cleared by the Soviet in Petrograd. Not for nothing did Trotsky refer to him as the 'Hamlet of democratic socialism'.

En route to Moscow, travelling by 'sealed train', Lenin and other exiles receive a warm welcome from social-democrats in Stockholm.

As the 'sealed train' steamed through Germany with its cargo, in Russia itself the uselessness of the Provisional Government and its self-inflicted paralysis had become clear to the populace. Sukhanov describes a meeting with the head of the government:

I reminded Kerensky of Secret Police Headquarters. It appeared that it hadn't been taken ... Kerensky proposed that I myself undertake to seize it and secure all the archives. He spoke as if there was a detachment and some transport for this, but I saw this was not so.

What of Paul Milyukov, the great leader of the Russian bourgeoisie? Sukhanov wrote:

He too found himself inactive. His whole appearance said plainly that he had nothing to do, that he did not in the least know what to do. Various people went up to him, began to talk to him, asked him questions, gave him information. He replied with evident reluctance and vagueness. They left him, and he started walking around alone again.

Milyukov's failure to do anything was vindicating the Bolshevik press and radicalising increasing segments of the population. Above all, it was the government's failure to end the war that cost it its political life. The old tsarist army was on the verge of collapse, under assault militarily by the Reichswehr and politically by the weight of revolutionary propaganda transmitted via a stream of Bolshevik agitators (most of them in uniform). Soldiers were deserting in droves, land seizures were multiplying in the country-side and the popularity of Bolshevik demands was reflected in the growing strength of the party. From 30,000 members in early March, they were now recruiting dozens of new revolutionary activists every day. The vacuum was being filled. Lenin arrived at the Finland Station and decided that it was time to quicken the pace. It was a historic moment, described as such even by Sukhanov, an eyewitness in his official capacity as a member of the Soviet executive committee to welcome the Bolshevik leader home. Often very critical of Lenin, the chronicler of the revolution was aston-ished by and admiring of Lenin's clarity of aims the minute he stepped on Russian soil. Lenin was welcomed by Nikolai Chkheidze, the Georgian Menshevik chairman of the Soviet:

> Comrade Lenin, in the name of the Petrograd Soviet and of the whole revolution we welcome you to Russia . . . But, we think that the principal task of the revolutionary democracy is now the defence of the revolution from any encroachements from within or with-out . . . We require not disunion . . . but the closing of democratic ranks. We hope you will pursue these goals together with us.

Sukhanov felt this 'welcome' was a provocation. Lenin literally turned his back on Chkheidze and spoke to the others who had assembled in the imperial waiting room of the Finland Station. It was a speech he would repeat from the top of an armoured tank that took him from the station to the Bolshevik headquarters. He began:

> Dear comrades, soldiers, sailors and workers! I'm happy to greet in *your* persons the victorious Russian revolution and greet you as the

vanguard of the worldwide proletarian army . . . The piratical imperialist war is the beginning of civil war throughout Europe . . . The
hour is not far distant when . . . the peoples will turn their arms
against their own capitalist exploiters . . . Germany is seeding . . .
Any day now the whole of European capitalism may crash. The
Russian Revolution accomplished by you opened a new epoch.
Long live the worldwide Socialist revolution.

This was a definitive statement. The revolution had to be socialist in character, international in scope and fought across the continent. A war against all the imperialisms fought from within and
without. Listening to him, Sukhanov was stunned. He recorded in
his notebook:

> Suddenly, before the eyes of all of us, completely swallowed up by
> the routine drudgery of the revolution, there was presented a bright,
> blinding, exotic beacon, obliterating everything we 'lived by'.
> Lenin's voice, straight from the train . . . had broken in upon us in
> the revolution a note that was not, to be sure, a contradiction, but
> that was novel, harsh and somewhat deafening.

More to the point, Sukhanov considered that 'Lenin was right a
thousand times over', but it was not enough. It was too abstract
and 'we had to understand what practical use to make of this idea
in our revolutionary policy.' For that, however, a revolutionary
government was necessary. Lenin had understood this very clearly.
Sukhanov and his left Mensheviks and more than a few Bolshevik
leaders had not.
    Lenin's differences with the Mensheviks and the SRs were both
theoretical and political. He loathed their passivity. He was
contemptuous when they refused to *act* during the 1905 revolution, arguing that workers' parties had *no* role to play while the
revolution was in its democratic stage. They regarded the Bolshevik-
led Moscow insurrection as an adventure, and Trotsky's theory of
'permanent revolution' as an ultraleft deviation. Trotsky left the
Mensheviks and set up a newspaper instead. Forced by the war to
seek exile in New York, he was on his way back home when he

was arrested and held by the British in Halifax, Canada. They released him on the request of the Soviet, whose executive had no idea that Trotsky's ideas were now in tandem with Lenin's. They had hoped otherwise.

In 1917, the position of the Menshevik majority and the SRs had not changed. They were happy to dominate the Soviet and leave the state to the Provisional Government, effectively the Kadets, since what was taking place was still the 'democratic stage' of the revolution. The abject failures of this government were ignored and it was not until May 1917 that the Mensheviks, persuaded by the Kadets that their presence in the government was necessary to preserve what was left of the fighting units of the old army on the eastern front, joined the government and said farewell to their past. A handful of left Mensheviks led by Martov and including Sukhanov opposed the suicide. Forced to take part in politics, the Menshevik majority capitulated to the government.

Lenin propounds the *April Theses*.

Lenin's tactics were twofold. On the political front he called for getting rid of the Kadets and allies from the government ('Down with the Ten Capitalist Ministers') and a transfer of power to the only instrument of self-rule that had ever existed in Russia ('All Power to the Soviets'). On another level he stressed once again the changing nature of the revolution, which was 'now maturing', and consisted of 'the proletariat and the majority of peasants, more specifically, of the poor peasants, against the bourgeoisie, against its ally, Anglo-French finance capital and against its government apparatus headed by the Bonapartist Kerensky'.

This was the context in which Lenin drafted the explosive *April Theses* that pushed the Bolshevik Party down the road to a socialist revolution. Unlike all previous revolutions in history, this was a fully conscious, carefully considered call to arms. It was not easy to convince his own party leaders, a fact that proves wrong all those who regarded the Bolshevik Party during this period as being what it later became after ten years in power. The *April Theses* marked a sharp break with orthodoxies that had previously united all factions of Russian Social Democracy, chiefly the dogma that the revolution *had to be* bourgeois-democratic, as Marx had said and as the English and French revolutions had demonstrated. Marx's own views, however, were anything but dogmatic on these issues.

Lenin presented the *Theses* three times, once to his own party, once to a joint Bolshevik–Menshevik conclave and then to the All-Russian Conference of Soviets and Workers Deputies on 4 April 1917. They were a codified version of what he had been saying from the moment he stepped off the train at the Finland Station. Russia had to pull out of the imperialist war without further delay, and explain 'with thoroughness, persistence and patience' to the people who still believed it to be a defensive war to protect the country why this was not the case. Only a revolutionary, anti-capitalist government was capable of a peace 'not imposed by violence'. The character of the revolution had changed, partially as a result of the war and partially due to internal developments. February had put power in the hands of the bourgeoisie with the support of the Soviet. This had to end, and a proletarian government based on the soviets had to be formed. Since the

Bolsheviks were a minority in the main soviets, they had to wait and convince people through propaganda and agitation. But history was on their side. The soviets were the '*only possible* form of revolutionary government'. The first acts of a revolutionary government would be to confiscate the estates, create a single state bank and bring social production and the distribution of products under the control of the soviets. This did not constitute socialism, Lenin argued, but it did lay the foundations for a commune-state to create the space in which a transition to socialism could take place, a commune-state as defended by Marx and Engels. And, Lenin continued, since Rosa Luxemburg herself had, on 4 August 1914, denounced the German SPD as a 'stinking corpse', he had to insist that a new International be created.

The denunciations were deafening. He had gone mad, was 'depraved' and out of touch with Russian realities, was a 'criminal' (this gem came from Axelrod, a longtime colleague on *Iskra*), had occupied the throne vacated by Bakunin and so on. Bolshevik leaders were more restrained, but equally angry in private. Orthodoxy had all of them in thrall and to such an extent that all they could repeat like parrots or intone like monks was a well-known paragraph from Marx:

> No social order ever perishes before all the productive forces for which there is room in it have developed; and new, higher relations of production never appear before the material conditions of their existence have matured in the womb of the old society itself.

Had medical science been more advanced in Marx's time, he could just as well have added that in those exceptional cases where a normal delivery might severely damage both the organism and the maturing entity in the womb, a more forcefully induced birth via a midwife might become necessary. He could have even enjoyed playing with the word 'caesarian'.

Two days after Lenin's thunderbolt, the Menshevik paper *Workers Gazette* mimicked Marx yet again and accused any who 'disregard those limits' (set by Marx) of helping the counterrevolution:

Lenin arrived in our midst in order to render this service to reaction. After his speech, we can state that each significant success of Lenin will be a success of reaction, and all struggle against counter-revolutionary aspirations and intrigues will be hopeless until we secure our left flank, until we render politically harmless, by a decisive rebuff, the current which Lenin heads. The principal danger . . . was on the left.

What none of his opponents had understood was that Lenin had not changed his views on whether productive forces had reached the breakthrough level prescribed by Marx. The imperialist war that was still raging in and wrecking continental Europe had convinced him that the revolution could not be restricted to one country alone. Everything he said in 1917 was centred on this new reality. The enemy was finance capitalism. What use was Petrograd without Berlin and Paris? The February Revolution had to be deepened by breaking with the bourgeoisie, ending its rule, ending the war without further bloodshed and calling on German soldiers and sailors to return home and make their own revolution. Lenin had shifted, but not as his enemies thought.

When Lenin first put the *Theses* forward at a meeting of the Soviet, his only supporter was the Bolshevik feminist Alexandra Kollontai. The others were not convinced. He was alone against every faction of Russian Social Democracy, including his own. This well-known but somewhat embarrassing episode in the history of the young Bolshevik Party was erased from later official histories and, more surprisingly, from Krupskaya's memoir, though in her case it might have been due to censorship, caution or a combination of the two. Lenin was livid when he received the post-February issues of a now legal *Pravda*. Molotov had been removed as editor by Stalin and Kamenev for being too radical and hotheaded. There was nothing in the paper that was very different from the material in the Menshevik press. Stalin and Kamenev were conciliators at the time. This was not a secret. Both favoured a united Bolshevik–Menshevik conference on the war, and this at a time when the majority of Menshevik leaders (and Kamenev himself) advocated a continuation of that very same war. That was the first indication of the 'mood in the party' and the enormity of the tasks that faced Lenin on his return. He was staggered by the failures of his own party. Having lived in exile for so long, he could not appreciate in the slightest the 'mood' for unity that existed a few weeks after the revolution. To be fair, I don't think he would have been gripped by any such mood had he been in Petrograd at the time. What he couldn't understand at all was the desire on the part of moderate and rightist Bolsheviks to appease the Provisional Government, consisting of Duma notables who had been 'elected' to the tsarist parliament by a tiny minority. The large majority were not allowed to vote.

Lenin's own mood was not improved when he inspected the identities of those who composed this government. The prime minister? Prince Georgy Lvov, reliable and trusted by the liberal right, plucked from a local council and handed the task of leading the 'democratic stage' of the revolution. Pavel (Paul) Milyukov was the foreign minister and the main ideological guide dog of a blind and impotent government. He was flanked by three fellow Kadets holding minor posts. The minister for war was Alexander Guchkov, one of the richest capitalists in the land, bloated with the money he was making from the war and who had been helping direct its operations since August 1914. The minister for finance was, appropriately enough, another influential capitalist, Mikhail Tereshenko. The minister for justice was Alexander Kerensky, the son of Lenin's old headmaster in Simbirsk. That these worthy representatives of bourgeois Russia were given the ultimate seal of approval by the US consul-general in Petrograd should not come as a huge surprise to anybody. John Snodgrass was the consul-general's name. He confided his thoughts to the paper of record back home: 'Nowhere in their country could the Russian people have found better men to lead them out of the darkness of tyranny . . . Lvov and his associates are to Russia what Washington and his associates were to America when it became a nation.'[5]

The Mensheviks and the SRs who were the elected leaders of the Soviet were simply disinterested in challenging the

---

5 *New York Times*, 25 March 1917.

Provisional Government: the Mensheviks, for reasons of Marxist orthodoxy that they endlessly explained, and the SRs because they agreed on the practical issues with the Mensheviks. If they brought down the government, it would mark the end of their collaboration with generals and capitalists, which would sabotage the war. When Martov, the most respected Menshevik leader, finally reached Petrograd in May, he spoke forcefully in favour of withdrawing all support from the Provisional Government and declared that 'either the revolutionary democracy will take responsibility for the revolution upon itself or it will lose the ability to influence the revolution's fate.'[6] Lenin did not mention Kamenev and Stalin by name, but he had no inhibitions about unleashing a fierce critique of *Pravda*, which had commented editorially that Lenin's thesis was 'unacceptable in that it starts from the assumption that the bourgeois-democratic revolution has ended, and counts on an immediate transformation of the revolutions into a Socialist revolution.' As for the ideas on war still defended by the 'moderate' Bolsheviks (including the scholarly Ryazonov), he did not mince words. No conciliation with the defenders of the war: 'I think it would be better to stand alone like Liebknecht – one against a hundred and ten.' The role of individuals in history should never be underestimated.

Sukhanov's description of the scene in the former palace (now the Bolshevik headquarters) of the tsar's ballerina mistress, Kshesinskaya, when Lenin finally got there from the Finland Station, having given dozens of speeches en route, is the *only*

---

6 *Workers Gazette*, 19 July 1917, p. 3, quoted in Alexander Rabinowitch, *The Bolsheviks Come to Power*, New York, 1976 and London, 1979, p. 25. Rabinowitch's study is one of the most detailed and valuable accounts of the February and October revolutions. The information contained in it rebuts most of the nonsense written about the nature of the October Revolution and the character of the party that carried it out. He is particularly good at illustrating the dynamic of rising mass political consciousness in Petrograd and its intersection with the Bolsheviks. The combination of spontaneity and organisation led to the insurrection.

eyewitness account and, as such, has been utilised by every subsequent historian of the revolution. The left-wing journalist got into the headquarters only by clinging to the coat-tails of the Bolshevik sailor's leader and later the Red admiral Raskolnikov, 'an unusually amiable, sincere, and honest' friend of his, who was also 'an unwavering revolutionary through and through', but, alas, also 'a Bolshevik fanatic'. Lenin recognised him and shook hands, but must have wondered how he had managed to infiltrate a closed party meeting. We can be glad he did, since he left us a riveting account.

After a string of welcome speeches of little import, including one from Kamenev, whose confusion was palpable, there came Lenin's two-hour response. Sukhanov's description of the speech retains its power, even when read today:

> I shall never forget that thunder-like speech, which startled and amazed not only me, a heretic who had accidentally dropped in, but all the true believers … It seemed as though all the elements had risen from their abodes, and the spirit of universal destruction, knowing neither barriers nor doubts, neither human difficulties nor human calculations, was hovering round Kshesinskaya's reception-room above the heads of the bewitched disciples.

Lenin, for him, was never a classical orator of the 'consummate phrase … luminous image … absorbing pathos or pointed witticism', but there was no doubt that he was an 'orator of enormous impact and power, breaking down complicated systems into the simplest and most generally accessible elements, and hammering, hammering, hammering them into the heads of his audience until he took them captive'. A simpler way of stating this would be that Lenin dominated through intellect rather than emotions. He had arrived just in time, as a Bolshevik Party conference was in progress. The day after his arrival he entered the fray with the question 'Why didn't you seize power?' His astonished comrades stuttered and stumbled, giving him reasons that were no different from those of the Mensheviks. 'That's nonsense,' Lenin told them. It would be more honest to say this:

The reason is that the workers were not sufficiently conscious and not sufficiently organised. That we have to acknowledge. The material force was in the hands of the proletariat, but the bourgeoisie was conscious and ready. That is the monstrous fact. It is necessary to acknowledge it frankly.

His writing was not dissimilar. The highly respected Russian literary scholar of the time, D. S. Mirsky, noted that 'he never admitted into his writings anything that was not strictly relevant to his argument. There is no trace of fine writing in all the twenty volumes of Lenin's collected works.'[7] His dislike of rhetoric and flowery phrases was part of his dislike of overstatement, of 'left phraseology', and this was known to many of his comrades who were not spared his scorn. 'He is perhaps', continues Mirsky, 'the only revolutionary writer who never said more than he meant. If this still leaves him the most powerful of revolutionary writers, it is because he meant a great deal.' The critic goes on to compare him to Tolstoy. Both wrote 'the most adequate prose in the Russian language', but Lenin's 'intensely workmanlike' prose differed from that of the novelist in the following sense: 'Lenin was not in the least literary . . . Between the studied and aesthetic simplicity of Tolstoy and the practical simplicity of Lenin . . . [there is] as great a difference as between an elegant yacht and an efficient engine.'[8] Mirsky loved the parentheses and footnotes in Lenin's essays and advised readers that they ignored them at their peril, because 'these rapid flashlights have sometimes an extraordinary condensation of thought and unusual suggestiveness.'

It is only possible, he confesses in conclusion, to grasp Lenin's 'unliterary excellence' after spending some time with his work and reading nothing else in between. 'The shock with which one returns

---

7   I think this is generally the case, but there are exceptions, one of which is included here as an epilogue. On Tolstoy, too, Mirsky ignores the mystical and confused ramblings interspersed in *War and Peace*, which weaken the novel artistically.

8   D. S. Mirsky, *Lenin*, London, 1932, pp. 24, 25.

Lenin in disguise in the July Days.

to other authors, to find them loose, slipshod, vague and meretricious, makes one realise Lenin's uniqueness as a writer.'

These literary-political and oratorical gifts were to be deployed to the full, first to drag his reluctant party onto the new track that he had so carefully designed in the *April Theses* and, following that, to drag the country onto it as well.

During these crucial eight months, the freest in its history, Russia was speaking out on everything it had repressed out of fear and for many centuries. From February till October the entire country seethed, arguments flowing from one group to another. Bystanders joined in to listen or to heckle. Russia resembled a huge meeting hall, but the meeting was noisy and rowdy. City squares, factories, shipyards, railway stations, village markets were awash with politics. Rolling thunder. People tossed in the air. Hugs and kisses from men with scratchy, unshaven faces. Did anyone sleep in those months? Soldiers from the front line were usually heard out without interruption – including French soldiers, one of whom, Jacques Sadoul, a socialist, stayed on and participated in the October Revolution.

The army was melting away on every front. In his multi-volume memoir, the politically unattached *belle-lettriste* Konstantin Paustovsky left us with an objective assessment of Kerensky as he 'dashed about the country, trying to hold it together . . . What he lacked in strength of ideas and conviction, he tried to make up for by pompous phrases, dramatic postures, grandiloquent but ill-timed gestures . . . an incongruous figure but wholly unaware of it.' One day Paustovsky saw him 'with his puffy, sallow face, red eyelids and sparse, greying crew-cut' insulting and 'ripping off the epaulettes of an elderly, sick, soldier, who refused to fight . . . "Coward! Back to the rear! We will not shoot you, we leave that to your conscience." . . . The soldiers turned away muttering and cursing.'[9]

October was approaching. The working class was rapidly moving to the left and the millions of peasant soldiers were no longer prepared to fight. They had felt this under the tsar, and had not changed their minds because there was now a new government. If anything, they had accelerated their departure from the front, 'voting with their legs' as Lenin put it, and had compelled the new government to grant the army a charter of political rights. Order Number 1 was written by N. D. Sokolov but, as Sukhanov writes, much of it was dictated by the soldiers surrounding him. By authorising elections of rank-and-file soldiers and sailors' committees in the army and navy, Order Number 1 sounded the death knell of the old Imperial Army. Any orders issued by the military commission of the Duma (the old tsarist parliament) would be disregarded unless approved by the Soviet. The distribution of weapons would be decided *exclusively*

9 Konstantin Paustovsky, *Story of a Life: In That Dawn*, trs. Manya Harari and Michael Duncan, London, 1967, p. 12.

by the elected committees and not by officers. The 'peasants in uniform' would determine what the 'landlords in uniform' would be permitted. Saluting was abolished, as well as 'rudeness' by officers. Regarded as a provocation by the Provisional Government, it was, as the legislators would soon discover, a declaration of class war inside the armed forces. The government's attempt to reverse the decision via an Order Number 2 that restricted the measures to the Petrograd garrison was a total failure. It was too late to reverse the tide. On the eastern front, Russian soldiers were beginning to fraternise with their German peers, exchanging token gifts and shouting, '*Germani nicht Feind. Fiend hinten*,' striking fear into both the Russian and the German high commands.[10] On the western front, too, the Russian brigade sloganised 'Down with the War!' and decided to elect their own soldiers' committee that immediately declared its solidarity with the revolution. Some of the soldiers were punished with transportation to North Africa.

It was awareness of all this rather than, as the conservative-Bolsheviks at home imagined, being 'out of touch' that led Lenin to draft the *April Theses*. All the major historians of the revolution are agreed on this fact. Most of the leaders at home were heading towards a reconciliation with the Mensheviks. And poor old Molotov was sacked as editor of *Pravda* by Kamenev and Stalin for being too rash and radical.[11]

The Bolshevik 'military organisation' was designed for propaganda purposes, not armed struggle. In Trotsky's *History of the*

---

10   John Erickson, *The Soviet High Command: A Military-Political History, 1918–1941*, Oxford and New York, 1962, p. 4.

11   Some revisionist academic is bound, sooner or later, to come up with a new version, 'proving' via carefully selected documents that actually there was no real division at all and the party was on the same track as Lenin, who simply had to be corrected on one or two issues, and so forth. This would be along similar lines to Stephen Kotkin at Princeton, who claims that Lenin's last testament was forged by his widow and his secretariat staff! For a sharp, critical review of this type of 'scholarship', see Tony Wood, 'Lives of Jughashvili', *New Left Review* 95, September–October 2015.

Russian Revolution, the links between the soldiers and the Petrograd Soviet are explained as a threefold embrace: the regiments elected delegates to the soldiers' section of the Soviet; the executive committee of the Soviet sent commissars to the regiments, and the latter had its own elective committee that was a 'sort of lower nucleus of the Soviet'. Within this framework the Bolshevik agitators inside the army grew in numbers and soon became the most influential left current in the army and navy. A specialist soldiers' canteen attracting the most radical soldiers flourished in the Petrograd offices of *Pravda*. In Riga, the 436 Novoladozhki Regiment elected a largely Bolshevik committee, which started a soldiers' club titled 'The IIIrd International' two years before the real Third International was actually set up. What this suggested was that the rank and file of the Bolshevik Party were thinking ahead, just like their exiled leader heading back home on a German train. 'During a revolution', he had written, 'millions and tens of millions of people learn in a week more than they do in a year of ordinary, somnolent life.'

8

October

In times of revolution, the masses ran ahead of the party and the party ran ahead of the leadership. When Lenin arrived at the Finland Station, determined to shift the leadership leftwards, people thought he had gone mad. In the Tauride Palace, Bogdanov interrupted Lenin's reading of the *April Theses* with cries of 'Delirium, the delirium of a madman!'

'I came out on to the street', wrote Sukhanov, 'feeling as though on that night I had been flogged over the head with a flail.'

Raskolnikov remarked: 'The most respectable party workers were here. But for them too the words of Ilyich were a veritable revelation. They laid down a Rubicon between the tactics of yesterday and those of today.' The *April Theses* were published with a disclaimer in *Pravda* itself. Lenin was in the minority. The October insurrection was opposed by a larger minority: Kamenev, Zinoviev, Rykov, Frunze and others, both 'practicals' and 'theoreticals'. During the flat expanses of time before February during which no revolutionary ferment had occurred, the Bolsheviks seemed far to the left; during the months between February and October the masses ran ahead of the vanguard. Their final coincidence produced the victorious assault on the Winter Palace.

In *State and Revolution*, the unfinished theoretical text interrupted by the revolution, Lenin abandoned all references to the divide between Russia and Western Europe that had littered previous writings. This essay was his most powerful theoretical text, paralleling and surpassing *What Is to Be Done?* The First World War had compelled a strategic rethink. Without a structured internationalist strategy, the Russian Revolution would not be able to reach its pinnacle. And the ultimate task of the revolutions in other European countries, however different the paths leading to them, would be the same as in Russia. Without the capture and defeat of the state apparatuses that defended and sustained the ruling class, there would be no socialism. The last stage of the revolution in every country, regardless of geopolitical location, had to have its insurrectionary moment. That is why he defined the twentieth century as an epoch of wars (imperial and civil) and revolution. The capitalist state exercised a monopoly of legitimate violence. Both the monopoly and the legitimacy had to be broken and the old state 'smashed' in order for a revolution to be victorious.[1]

In Russia, too, from July 1917 onwards the military high command, witnessing the disintegration on the front and noting that Bolshevik antiwar propaganda was mutinies, were disgusted by the paralysis of the Provisional Government and its failure to prepare a funeral for the revolution. Military leaders seriously discussed the possibility of seizing power and installing a military dictatorship to rebuild the army and continue the war, but the essential prerequisite for these objectives was to destroy the Bolsheviks and dismantle the soviets. From their point of view, of course, they were not wrong.

The commander-in-chief of the army, General Kornilov, decided to win over or split the Provisional Government. In this he succeeded, though he failed to convince Kerensky, now prime minister, to back an effective coup against the Soviet and exterminate the Bolsheviks. Kerensky, rightly worried that he would be used and dumped, had rejected the offer but decided to implement

---

1   The state in the capitalist societies of 1917 certainly recognised and understood this fact. Coercion in France and Germany was well documented. In Britain, too, force and repression had been deployed against the Chartists and at Manchester in the 1819 massacre at Peterloo. Social Democrats across Europe, in deciding to pitch their tents in the military encampments of their respective state armies, had soiled their shirts with the blood of the First World War.

Kornilov's political programme by himself. Both men looked in the mirror and imagined themselves as the dictator of the new regime. It was pure fantasy. Kornilov *might* have been able to establish a temporary military government; Kerensky stood no chance whatsoever.

The army planned to bring frontline troops to Petrograd for the grand putsch on 26 August 1917. The Soviet would be celebrating the six-month anniversary of the revolution. The right-wing press would be stoking anti-Bolshevik fires and warning of an insurrection. The military would, if necessary, stage a fake Bolshevik uprising, crush it and seize power. This would be entrusted to the Union of Officers, the extremely anti-Semitic and staunchly tsarist faction of the army. Kornilov tried his best to get Kerensky on his side, but here the latter's personal ambition stood in the way, even though many in the Provisional Government, especially Savinkov, the deputy war minister, were already working openly with Kornilov. Prince Lvov (the Russian George Washington, in Snodgrass's appreciation) was in total agreement with Kornilov, trying hard to convince Kerensky that a 'national' government was the only solution. Lvov claimed that he had won over Kerensky, who agreed to step down as prime minister. Kerensky, however, claimed that he had only pretended to acquiesce in order to play for time, since he knew that Lvov was Kornilov's envoy.

What all this reveals is the extent of the crisis. The moderate leaders of the Soviet were not informed of any of this by Kerensky till later, when he needed their help, which was very soon. Lvov returned to the Winter Palace and suggested that if Kerensky valued his life, he would immediately resign and exit Petrograd. The response from the SR leader was semi-hysterical laughter. The next day, to his own astonishment, Kerensky relieved Kornilov of his post and appointed Lukomsky in his stead. The 'new' commander-in-chief wired his refusal of the offer and instructed Kerensky to either join Kornilov or face untold horrors for the country. Their troops were already marching on the capital. Kerensky now publicly ordered Kornilov to turn back, thus alerting all the soviet political parties. Kornilov refused, issuing his own statement that stressed his lack of personal ambition: 'I,

General Kornilov, son of a Cossack peasant want nothing for myself, except the preservation of a Great Russia.' A majority of the military high command agreed with this aim. The stock exchange in Petrograd leapt upwards. The army marched ever closer to Petrograd.

Kerensky now suggested the formation of a directory, as in the later phases of the French Revolution. The official Soviet leaders were sympathetic. Martov was heard to shout that 'all directories spawn counterrevolutions!' Lenin was in exile in Finland; Trotsky was in prison. After the failure of the spontaneous workers' insurrection in July that none of the Bolsheviks had authorised but that they had to support, Soviet leaders ordered mass arrests of Bolshevik activists. The Bolsheviks still in the Soviet were totally opposed to Kerensky and his outfit, but agreed on a united front to defend the revolution against the army's assault. From his exile Lenin raged that the moderate Mensheviks and SRs had been in bed with the Provisional Government since its inception. They defended the war. Kerensky had been in league with the coup plotters. It was hard for Lenin to believe that there were still 'fools and scoundrels' in their ranks who couldn't see through all this even now. His advice as to what they should say to the Mensheviks:

> Our workers and soldiers will fight the counterrevolutionary troops ... not to defend the government, but independently, to defend the revolution ... We shall fight, of course, but we refuse to enter into any political alliance whatsoever with you and reject any expression of the least confidence in you.

It was hardly a secret that the Bolsheviks were gaining in popularity. Sukhanov admitted that without the Bolsheviks, no serious defence of the capital against Kornilov was possible. The worker-soldier masses 'insofar as they were organised, were organised by the Bolsheviks and followed them. At that time, theirs was the only organisation that was large, welded together by an elementary discipline, and linked with the democratic lowest levels of the capital.' What the moderate soviet parties were witnessing was the implementation of the key arguments of *State and Revolution* and the *April Theses*.

Not even the largest party can 'make' or 'steal' a revolution, but the success of such an endeavour depends on the ability, lucidity, energy and single-mindedness of a revolutionary party when confronted with a prerevolutionary crisis. Lenin's break was not with 'orthodoxy' but with a reformist and mechanical conception that treated class consciousness as a natural outcome of the workers' place in society. Lenin rejected this form of vulgar sociology in favour of politics. Bolshevik slogans and demands were not particularly if at all socialist, but they were definitely revolutionary. The 'Three Whales' of the Bolshevik party over the last decade had been 'Confiscation of the Landed Estates', 'Democratic Republic' and 'The Eight-Hour Day'. These had lit the way to February. A pithier trinity of 'Land, Bread and Peace' opened the gates to October.

In the end Kornilov was defeated politically. Bolshevik soldier-agitators, Muslim and Caucasian soldiers from Petrograd loyal to the Soviet and soviet delegates approached his crack troops as they entered small towns near the capital and, watched with awe by the officers, pleaded with their brothers not to kill their own. Railway workers had sabotaged the tracks, making it impossible for troop trains to get into the capital, and calmly explained to the troops what was going on, what the tsarist generals were attempting, why they would be met with very strong resistance and so on. The agitators won. The generals were left without an army. As a desperate last-minute attempt to retrieve the situation, Kerensky organised a directory. It was a farce from beginning to end, a very short period as it happened. Under its cover Kerensky banned two radical newspapers, *The Worker* (Bolshevik) and *Novaya Zhizn* (independent, antiwar and pro-internationalist). The Bolsheviks simply ignored the ban. As Red Guards took up their positions outside, the printers carried on with their work.

Two American journalists, John Reed and Albert Rhys Williams, were observing the events in close-up and summarising the day to each other before sending their reports back to the United States. Reed had arrived in the country later than Williams and was being briefed in some detail by his colleague, who explained the impact of the *April Theses*.

'Then those who hack away at Lenin claim that the bourgeois political revolution of February isn't complete, is that it?' Reed said.

'Lenin didn't say it was complete either, as I get it,' I said. 'It's all very complicated. Nor did Lenin say at what moment the transition to a socialist government should be made – only that these first steps must be made.'

Reed was impatient and wanted to know when the Bolsheviks would strike. Williams replied that a strike would only take place when they had a majority.

By October the Bolsheviks had won a majority in the Moscow and Petrograd soviets. They were the strongest political current in factory committees in many smaller towns where they did not control the soviets. This combination was decisive, added to which peasant militancy was setting the countryside alight, with land seizures reported from throughout the country. The nationalities were flexing their muscles and from the trenches of the eastern front to the factories and city centres, the demand for peace had become unchallengeable. Military revolutionary committees under the Bolsheviks were springing up in many towns.[2]

After the Bolsheviks' electoral triumph, John Reed turned to Rhys Williams. 'And now?'

'It can't be long now.'

Leon Trotsky, recently released from prison and elected chairman

---

2 A year later, Lenin explained why the party had not called for an insurrection in July, when a spontaneous mass outbreak nonetheless took place, was repressed, put the right on the offensive and forced Lenin and other leaders to go underground: 'We not only thought, we *knew* with certainty, from the experience of the *mass* elections to the Soviets, that in September and in early October the overwhelming majority of the workers and soldiers had *already* come over to our side.' It was this new reality that 'determined the *correctness of the slogan* "for an insurrection" in October (the slogan would have been incorrect in July, when in fact we did *not* advance it).'

of the Military Revolutionary Committee (MRC) of the Soviet, now began to prepare the insurrection of 25 October.[3] The garrison was under the control of the MRC, and Red Guards from the factories were linked to strategically important regiments. Elections for new unit commissars in the military units of the garrison saw most of the Menshevik and SR commissars voted out and replaced with Bolsheviks. In reality power now lay in the hands of the Bolshevik Party. The final assault on the Winter Palace was more of a formality, a symbolic event and far less dramatic than its depiction by Eisenstein in *October*. The resistance was pitiful.[4]

The two Americans were in a reflective mood. Reed mused:

Wonder what it must feel like to be in the shoes of Lieber, Dan, or even old Martov, let alone Georgi Plekhanov ... Practically any of these leaders, anarchist, Menshevik, SR left or right as well as Bolshevik – for years they were all hunted, shipped off to Siberia, or flogged with the knout in filthy Russian prisons ... How out of step the proud old stubborn ones must feel, how virtuous, as they see their comrades switching to Lenin! One minute they admit that only Lenin can bring peace, bread and land. But that's why they can't forgive him; so they furiously try to prop up Kerensky.[5]

---

3   The final meeting to set the date had taken place on 10 October at the house of a Bolshevik activist. She had asked her Menshevik husband, Sukhanov, to sleep somewhere else that night. Having infiltrated the Bolshevik headquarters on the night of Lenin's return, he was banned from his own bed on the eve of a much more important event that he opposed but which made his name. The ten-hour meeting approved all the details. There were two votes against: Zinoviev and Kamenev. As for the rest, the boats had been burnt.

4   The death of the Provisional Government was not far off as a spontaneous assault on its headquarters was underway. It was with great difficulty that the Bolsheviks persuaded the assailants not to lynch the ministers, who were taken to safety in the tsar's favourite prison, the Peter and Paul Fortress. Kerensky fled the palace disguised as a woman. Appropriately, the 'Jefferson' of the February Revolution obtained asylum in the United States and died in New York in 1970.

5   Albert Rhys Williams, *Journey into Revolution: Petrograd 1917– 1918*, Chicago, 1969, pp. 38–9.

A few days later on 25 October, the two men set out early for the meeting of the soviet where the announcement was about to be made.

The emergency meeting of the Petrograd Soviet began at 2:35 p.m. that day. Trotsky was given the floor: 'On behalf of the Military Revolutionary Committee, I declare that the Provisional

Къ Гражданамъ Россіи.

Временное Правительство низложено. Государственная власть перешла въ руки органа Петроградскаго Совѣта Рабочихъ и Солдатскихъ Депутатовъ Военно-Революціоннаго Комитета, стоящаго во главѣ Петроградскаго пролетаріата и гарнизона.

Дѣло, за которое боролся народъ: немедленное предложеніе демократическаго мира, отмѣна помѣщичьей собственности на землю, рабочій контроль надъ производствомъ, созданіе Совѣтскаго Правительства — это дѣло обезпечено.

ДА ЗДРАВСТВУЕТЪ РЕВОЛЮЦІЯ РАБОЧИХЪ, СОЛДАТЪ И КРЕСТЬЯНЪ!

Военно-Революціонный Комитетъ
при Петроградскомъ Совѣтѣ
Рабочихъ и Солдатскихъ Депутатовъ.

25 октября 1917 г. 10 ч. утра.

The declaration of the Military Revolutionary Committee announcing the Revolution.

Government no longer exists.' He continued to give the delegates an account of what had been achieved.[6] As he spoke Lenin entered the hall to deafening applause, a standing ovation and chants of 'Long live Comrade Lenin, back with us again.' Trotsky gave him the floor. A calm Lenin, speaking for only a few minutes, declared that a new historical epoch, a new period of history had begun, ending with a pledge to construct a new socialist order and the cry 'Long live the world socialist revolution.'

The Bolsheviks had taken power. Two days of fighting in Moscow, a few clashes elsewhere, but hardly any casualties. The Menshevik/SR leaders had decided that resistance was both foolhardy and impractical. They fumed but stood aside. Even a Menshevik-Internationalist like Martov had, at an earlier meeting, lost his temper with Trotsky and walked out. He would return, but most of his pro-war colleagues knew their time was over. When they had decided to boycott all soviet institutions, an angry Sukhanov had accused them of joining the counterrevolution. Martov, hearing his old colleague Tsereteli speak at the soviet, had gone pale with anger and called him '*Versaillais*', a reference to those who had helped crush the Paris Commune. Little did they imagine that within a few months, many of their erstwhile comrades would join the Entente-backed White armies in the civil war. The

---

6 On the first anniversary of the revolution, Stalin wrote in *Pravda*: 'All practical work in connection with the organisation of the uprising was done under the immediate direction of Comrade Trotsky, the President of the Petrograd Soviet. It can be stated with certainty that the party is indebted primarily and principally to Comrade Trotsky for the rapid going over of the garrison to the side of the Soviet and the efficient manner in which the work of the Military Revolutionary Committee was organised.' Quoted in Isaac Deutscher, *Stalin: A Political Biography*, London, 1966, pp. 210–11. These lines were only removed from Stalin's collected works in 1947, presumably in time for the thirtieth anniversary of the revolution, when all mention of Trotsky and most of the Old Bolsheviks had been brutally erased from history. The late David King's documentary book, *The Commissar Vanishes*, New York, 2014, provides a detailed account of how the photographs were doctored.

stock exchange panicked, replicating the nosedive of the Kerensky government and its backers. How long could it last? The same question was being asked in the White House.

Even as Lenin was presenting the *April Theses* to the Petrograd Soviet, the war party in Washington was almost ready to move into Europe. Woodrow Wilson was in discussions with close advisers regarding US entry into the First World War. Wilson, still regarded in some circles as an ethical and liberal figure – and an internationalist, no less – was in reality a fairly typical US politician who wore the mask better than most. In private he sometimes discarded the pretence, informing his close friend and confidant Colonel House in 1913 that 'he thought lying was justified in some instances, particularly where it involved the honor of a woman . . . [and] where it related to matters of public policy.' When House suggested that it might be better to remain silent rather than lie, Wilson agreed a bit too quickly and promised he would do so in the future. Another lie. His public statements were, in the main, pure deception and contradicted actions already taking place on the ground. This was very clear in his attitude to the Russian Revolution. In public he expressed some understanding of the event. Behind the scenes he united with his fellow orthodox Presbyterian and secretary of state Robert Lansing, who saw Bolshevism as the scourge of Christianity and its attached civilisation. Wilson vetoed any recognition of the Soviet government.

Already heavily engaged in supervising US interventions in Mexico to seal off the revolution in that country, he now began to be distracted by the rapidly changing situation in Russia. All of this was masked by statements declaring that with the overthrow of the tsar, all the Entente powers were now democratic as compared to the German-led despotism. He was, as he saw it, merely 'steering our own public opinion in the right path'.

Wilson saw Mexico and Russia as similar political problems. After October this became an obsession. Backed strongly by the Gompers unions and the American Federation of Labor, he warned the Wobblies and other radical groups that Bolshevik propaganda in the United States would be dealt with severely. He kept his promise. And not just at home. Wilson believed, like most of his

European allies, that the Bolshevik government was too unstable to last more than a few months, a year at most. It could be easily destroyed. He decided to arm and fund the White Armies of Kolchak and Denikin, just as he had done with Carranza in Mexico. In public he lied once again, first declaring how passionately he supported the right of nations to self-determination, explicitly informing the American public and the world 'that every people has the right to determine its own form of government', and insisting that the Mexicans should choose their own leaders even as he was preparing to send the US Navy to occupy Veracruz in 1914. US marines were dispatched to take Haiti in 1915 and the Dominican Republic in 1916, then sent on a land expedition deep into the heart of Mexico.

In October 1918, Wilson's deceit reached a new peak: 'My policy regarding Russia is very similar to my Mexican policy. I believe in letting them work out their own salvation, even though they wallow in anarchy for a while.' Thus began a secret war against revolutionary Russia that was never sanctioned by Congress. That same year military units were sent to Vladivostok and Archangel. Unsurprisingly the Bolshevik leaders responded to this hostility, but only verbally. On reading a telegram from the Soviet commissar for foreign affairs, Wilson was outraged by its 'impudence'. Trotsky had asked, quite openly, for Soviet diplomats to be given travel documents 'to America and other countries to propose the overturning of all governments not dominated by working people'. This worried Wilson to the extent that he accepted his secretary of war's advice not to reveal Trotsky's cable to the public, lest it encourage a 'class war' and help the Wobblies and the antiwar socialists.

Right-wing trade union leaders and pro-war socialists had already expressed strong concerns to Wilson that the utopian Bolshevik experiment was encouraging dreamers in the United States; unless this pacifism and glorification of strikes was stopped, it could spread from Europe to 'Chicago, New York, San Francisco and our other foreign industrial concerns'. Mass repression against the Wobblies and 'foreign, especially Italian anarchists' commenced in 1918. In September of that same year, Socialist Party leader

Eugene V. Debs (one of the founders of the Wobblies) was arrested under the Sedition Act for having declared in public that the war was imperialist and 'our hearts are with the Bolsheviki of Russia.' He was sentenced to ten years in prison. US military officers attached to the expeditionary force in Archangel pleaded for even more intervention. Their leader, Colonel James Ruggles, suggested that 'it is far better to kill the head – here in Russia – than to run the risk of having to do it at home.'[7] On the eve of the country's decisive entry into the European civil war and world politics, US global policy could be defined simply: permanent counterrevolution. Nonetheless the Bolsheviks preferred to concentrate their ire on British and French imperialism, and attempt to drive a wedge between the latter and the United States. Chicherin, who succeeded Trotsky as commissar for foreign affairs, was more diplomatic in tone when communicating with Washington but kept a regular barrage going, warning Wilson that US money and guns were wasted on trying to help 'a doomed corpse'.

---

7 David S. Foglesong, *America's Secret War Against Bolshevism: US Intervention in the Russian Civil War, 1917–20*, North Carolina, 1995. Written after the Cold War, this is the most carefully documented account of US politico-military intervention against the new Soviet Republic, and an exemplary explanation of its origins.

9

The Aftermath

'**R**evolutions are the festivals of the oppressed and the exploited,' Lenin had written in *Two Tactics of Social-Democracy*.

He was shocked when informed a a few weeks after the revolution that sections of the oppressed had decided to celebrate their victory in more traditional fashion by organising an impromptu festival more in keeping with medieval orgies than the lofty ideas Lenin had put forward, but with the aim of polishing off all the tsarist remnants. The scene was Petrograd. The words are those of the Bolshevik leader Antonov-Ovseenko, the chief military commissar and commander of the Petrograd garrison. The description in his memoir of what took place is rarely mentioned by historians. It was a wild and out-of-control bacchanal that lasted for weeks, paralysing the revolutionary capital:

> A wild and unprecedented orgy spread over Petrograd and until now it has not been plausibly explained whether or not this was due to any surreptitious provocation . . . The cellars of the Winter Palace presented the most awkward problem . . . The Preobrazhensky regiment, which had hitherto kept its discipline, got completely drunk while it was doing guard duty at the Palace. The Pavlovsky regiment, our revolutionary rampart, did not withstand the temptation either. Mixed guards, picked from different detachments were then sent there. They, too, got drunk. Members of the regimental committees [i.e., the revolutionary leaders of the garrison] were then

assigned to guard duty. These, too, succumbed. Men of the armoured brigades were ordered to disperse the crowds – they paraded a little to and fro, and then began to sway suspiciously on their feet. At dusk the mad bacchanals would spread. 'Let us finish off these Tsarist remnants!' This merry slogan took hold of the crowd. We tried to stop them by walling up the entrances. The crowd penetrated through the windows, forced out the bars and grabbed the stocks.

Antonov-Ovseenko, now desperate, appealed to the Council of People's Commissars (the highest authority) for help. They appointed a 'special Commissar endowed with special powers' to help solve the crisis, but he too 'proved unreliable.' Pity the author did not name him. Only when a 'Finnish regiment with anarcho-syndicalist leanings' threatened to blow up the cellars and shoot the looters 'was this alcoholic lunacy overcome'.[1] It needn't have been lunacy if the Petrograd Soviet had organised it as a public event open to all citizens. The tsar's wine would then have been consumed within a day by ordinary citizens as well as the core Bolshevik regiments. The decision of the Council of People's Commissars to pump the remnants of the cellar into the Neva River was misjudged, in my opinion, and revealed a lack of imagination. The wine could have been put to much better use with proper distribution, but obviously there were more important problems to confront at home and abroad.

Lenin believed strongly that the combination of war and October 1917 would create a revolutionary firestorm across the whole of Europe, ending both the isolation of Petrograd and European capitalism. This estimate was not totally contradicted by the events that took place during the first three years after the Russian Revolution. Never before or since has Europe been shaken to its very core as it was in the years 1918–20. A wave of almost concurrent political and industrial uprisings engulfed the continent: the Berlin uprising, the Munich Soviet, the Budapest Commune, the

---

[1] Quoted in Isaac Deutscher, *The Prophet Armed*, London, 2003, pp. 266–7.

mass strike in Austria, the factory occupations in Italy, unrest in the armies and navies of a number of countries and a growing feeling on the part of rulers that they could no longer govern in the same old way.[2]

Britain alone, separated by the Channel, avoided upheavals of this character, but it was confronted by another threat: its internal colony, Ireland, ever since the defeated Easter Rising of 1916, was simmering. The long-distance impact of that uprising resulted in the largely unexamined 1919 mutiny of the Connaught Rangers in India, the first and last of its type during the long years of British imperial rule in the occupied lands of Asia and Africa.

In Petrograd itself, two days after the revolution, the new government started working to make good on its pledges. The first of these and, in some ways, the most important was to end the war. The Soviet issued a decree written by Lenin that called on 'all belligerent peoples and their governments ... to open immediate negotiations for a just and democratic peace.' It was a two-edged sword. If the governments of Britain, France and Germany did not respond, suggested Lenin, the working class in those countries had to undertake direct action. The decree praised the radical traditions in those countries. The workers had been in the leadership of most progressive struggles and, he wrote,

---

2   As we know, none of these upheavals were successful. Liebknecht and Luxemburg were assassinated in January 1919 by the proto-fascist Freikorps under the admiring gaze of right-wing SPD leaders Noske, Ebert and Scheidmann. The rulers, too, had learnt the lessons of October: in Italy they went for fascism, while in Germany a weak republic, a divided working class and a frightened bourgeoisie ensured the victory of German fascism. The decomposition of the state in Italy and Germany after the First World War was not as advanced as in tsarist Russia, but nor was it that far removed. The state was recomposed in both countries by an open and clear-cut alliance between refined bourgeois politicians and proprietors and the fascist Blackshirts and Brownshirts who demonstrated that they alone were capable of defeating the workers and the Bolsheviks.

The great example of the Chartist movement in England, the series of revolutions, of universal historic importance, made by the French proletariat and, finally the heroic struggle against the anti-Socialist laws in Germany . . . all these examples of . . . historic creative work serve as a pledge that the workers of these countries will understand the duty which now rests upon them of saving mankind from the horrors of war.

The Entente leaders ignored the appeal. The German government accepted and agreed to attend a conference to discuss a separate peace with Russia. Both Lenin and Trotsky regarded this as the worst alternative. The only way for the Bolsheviks to justify a separate peace was if there was an outbreak of revolution in Germany.[3]

Trotsky, in his capacity as foreign minister, redoubled the intensity of previous appeals by urging the British and French governments to join the peace talks. The war was no longer even in their interests, given the large-scale butchery on the western front. It was unjustifiable to carry on in this fashion. No response from

---

3   Ultimately a separate peace deal swas signed at Brest-Litovsk by a very divided Bolshevik leadership. Bukharin and his supporters favoured a 'revolutionary war', while Trotsky and his supporters moved 'for neither war nor peace' by delaying and dragging on the negotiations. Once again Lenin was almost alone in arguing that there was no alternative but to accept the brutal German terms. Any stupidity, he said, would lead to the defeat of the revolution. All the groups agreed that a German revolution was the only real solution, but it could not be manufactured out of thin air. There were, of course, hints of growing militancy in Germany. The sailors' strike in Kiel was a tremendous boost, but an armistice could not be delayed, whatever the conditions. Lenin won the battle but at a cost. The Bolsheviks' only partner in the government, the Left SRs, reverted to old tribal tactics, assassinated the German ambassador Count Mirbach and went armed to a joint conference with the Bolsheviks in Moscow. The Bolsheviks, aware of their plot, did not turn up. The Left SRs were disarmed and arrested and their party banned.

Trotsky and Joffe (right) at Brest-Litovsk in 1918, leading the Soviet delegation.

London or Paris. The Allies were confident that a new entrant waiting in the wings across the Atlantic would decisively change the balance and help them inflict a defeat on the kaiser.

On 15 December 1917, Trotsky signed the armistice with Germany, bringing the war on the eastern front to an end. In an appeal to the 'toiling, oppressed and exhausted peoples of Europe', he explained that what they had done was necessary to stop the slaughter and called on them to cast aside the governments that had refused to attend the conference and agree to immediate peace: 'The workers and soldiers must wrest the business of war and peace from the criminal hands of the bourgeoisie and take it into their own hands ... We have the right to demand this from you, because this what we have done in our own country.' This appeal did have an impact on Europe. The workers and members of the Social Democratic Party in Austria reacted angrily when they heard that the Austrian general Hoffman had threated to rain destruction on Russia unless it capitulated to the extravagant revanchist demands put on the table at Brest-Litovsk. The Social Democrats called for mass rallies in Vienna, in solidarity with the Russian Revolution. Simultaneously, a huge wave of spontaneous strikes, surprising the Social Democrats, brought industrial life to a halt in Vienna, Styria and Upper Austria, and within a day had spread to Budapest.

Elected by the factories, an Austrian workers' soviet held its first assembly on 16 January 1918. The socialists attended the council and backed the actions proposed, but put forward no programme of their own to take matters further. A delegation, including Victor Adler and Karl Seitz, went to see a frightened prime minister. The minute the delegation arrived, they were handed a statement from Count Czernin, the foreign minister. He pledged that Austria would no longer support any territorial gains at the expense of the Soviet Republic and would recognise unconditionally Poland's right to self-determination.

The Austrian Social Democrats treated this as a triumph and hurriedly declared that the workers had won their main objective. The mood in Austria was undoubtedly prerevolutionary. Even some left Social Democrats agreed that this was the case. There was no objective reason for paralysis. But neither was there an organised political party or current to propose a total break with war, capitalism and empire. On the contrary, at a key meeting of the Vienna Soviet, the Austrian Social Democrats called on the workers to break the strike. Their speech met with an uproar and angry debates arose with militant workers denouncing the politicians. Lacking a political alternative, the strike collapsed four days later. Even as workers returned to the factories, a naval mutiny erupted at Cattaro on the Dalmatian coast, the base of the imperial Austro-Hungarian fleet. Half of the fleet – over forty battleships, cruisers and gunboats – were docked there. The pattern of revolt was no different from Russia in 1905 and 1917. The sailors seized the ships, arrested two admirals, hoisted red flags from every mast and elected delegates to a sailors' soviet. They demanded improved conditions and an immediate end to the war. Once again they were stymied by the lack of political agitators attached to a revolutionary party. The military commander Von Gusseck played for time, assembled military units from Bosnia and called for help from the navy stationed at Fiume. The sailors, armed but not politically, were surrounded from land and sea and had no option but to surrender. Eight hundred sailors were court-martialed and most sentenced to death. Only four were executed, however, after Victor Adler threatened the war ministry with a mass strike. Later the left Social Democrat Otto Bauer defended his party, arguing that had they launched a revolution, the German army would have been dispatched to crush them, the southern front would have collapsed and 'the armies of the Entente advanced from the south would have clashed on Austrian soil, with the German armies breaking in from the North. Austria would have become a battlefield.' Was ever such a weak and pathetic argument presented to justify the effective sabotage of a revolution? No analysis whatsoever of the stage of the conflict, of universal war-weariness, of the possibility that German soldiers might have mutinied if ordered to open fire on their Austrian brothers. No recognition either of the fact that the shell-shocked soldiers of the Entente were also deserting. Mutinies in the French and English armies were being crushed. The cancer of social chauvinism had infected the Austrian socialists just as much as their German colleagues. Bauer was effectively arguing that turning the world war into a civil war against Austria's own rulers would have brought the larger war back home. He considered himself a Marxist, but his justifications suggested that he had not assimilated Hegel. Times had changed, but traditional Social Democratic customs had not. Twenty years later, as they organised the desperate, last-minute, tragic Schutzbund uprising on the eve of Hitler's entry into Austria, did any of the Austrian socialist leaders reflect on the possibility that they might have avoided this calamity had they shown more daring in 1918?

And what did Bauer, Adler and their colleagues think of the turnaround in Berlin? Here, too, the Bolshevik appeal to the workers of Europe bore fruit. Inspired by the Viennese mass strike, German workers attempted the same in Berlin. Even before the Russian Revolution there was growing unrest in Germany.

Lenin addresses a May Day meeting, 1919.

On May Day 1916, the Spartacusbund, the group led by Karl Liebknecht and Rosa Luxemburg that had turned its back on the SPD leadership after 4 August 1914, appealed audaciously for a huge demonstration in favor of peace and socialism. Both leaders had been imprisoned for short terms in 1915 and had just been released. The turnout exceeded all their expectations. The mood had changed. The realities of war had pricked the chauvinist bubble. In *Karl and Rosa*, the opening novel of his great trilogy, the German writer Alfred Döblin describes that May Day scene in documentary style. Not a fact is out of place. The message is clear: in times of war, every capitalist democracy, however truncated (half the population was excluded from voting because of gender), becomes a dictatorship. More visibly in some countries than others:

What a magnificent time there on Potsdammer Platz in Berlin! The police have occupied the area early that morning, but the workers come nevertheless. Their numbers grow. Thousands of them. And then Karl appears. Karl Liebknecht in the uniform of a common private. She stands next to him ... She speaks. But Karl's voice roars above everything else: 'Down with war! Down with war! Down with the government.'

Then the police, with sabres drawn, move to arrest him. Rosa and others throw themselves between them. He goes on shouting ... The cavalry gallops up, Karl is arrested. The tumult is overwhelming. He is led away. People mill about angrily in the square and in the streets leading to it for hours ... What a volcanic May 1st! ... Karl is sentenced to four years' imprisonment ... and shortly afterwards they arrest her as well ... They sentence her to indefinite preventive detention. And now prison has swallowed her up.

The following spring (1917) there were mass strikes in Berlin, Halle, Brunswick, Magdeburg and Leipzig due to food shortages. Leipzig, however, was at the time a stronghold of the Independent Social Democratic Party (USPD) – another left-wing split after August 1914 which veered between reform and revolution but ended up firmly in the camp of the former. There the workers went much further and insisted on a government 'pledging willingness to accept an immediate peace settlement, and renouncing any open or covert annexations'.

In the summer of that same year, the mutinous sailors of the German fleet in Kiel demanded peace without annexations or reparations. 'Ten ringleaders' were court-martialled, two of them executed and the others sentenced to a total of 181 years of penal servitude. The rulers of Germany had learnt the lessons of the Russian Revolution.

In January 1918, on the heels of what had happened in Vienna, the distant thunder erupted into a gigantic storm of strikes throughout Germany. The Berlin shop-stewards' committee had, on 27

January, issued a call for a general strike. The USPD supported them as, of course, did the Spartacusbunds, whose principal leaders and key activists were in prison. A million workers (half a million in Berlin alone) went on strike for ten days. The main demand was for peace, solidarity with Russia and no annexations, but the mood of the workers, who wanted a new government, was much more militant. General Luddendorf, the effective dictator of the country, refused to budge. He decided on repression and the soldiers carried out their orders.

An Austrian Social Democratic historian would later write that 'only if the troops had gone over to the strikers' side could the movement have been turned into a revolutionary struggle. But the soldiers remained unmoved and untouched.'[4] Might this have had something to do with the abject capitulation of the SPD in August 1914? Or did it predate that event? After all, a majority of the full-time trade union leadership and base, especially in southern Germany, had long been infected with Bernstein's pro-capitalist revisionism. And as Rosa Luxemburg would later remark, the centre's (Kautsky's) opposition to Bernstein was based on its own 'conservatism'. Having been the interpreter of Marxism for such a long time, Kautsky found it difficult to break with this past theoretically. Practice was another matter altogether. Nonetheless, had the war been strongly opposed by the mass party of German workers (and Bernstein's position on the war was ambiguous), it undoubtedly would have helped educate the workers in uniform who belonged to the SPD.

The most impossible task for a soldier is refusing to obey orders. Desertions are difficult enough. And many deserters in the armies that fought in the First World War were shot as 'cowards' and 'traitors' after token court-martials. The large-scale soldiers' mutinies in Russia were made possible by the fact that the Bolsheviks, as well as many rank-and-file members and some leaders of the Mensheviks and the SRs, hated their own government. This made opposition to the war much easier. The SPD's decision to vote for the war credits

---

4 Julius Braunthal, *History of the International, 1914–1945*, tr. John Clark, London, 1967.

had disarmed the workers in the factories and on the front. Frightened by the wave of chauvinism displayed by the crowd on 4 August 1914, the SPD leadership could not think beyond present-ism. Political consciousness, as Lenin insisted many times, was not linear. It changed, as the period between the defeat of 1905 and the triumph of 1917 had amply demonstrated. Which was why a party needed to remain strong in bad times. This had not happened in Germany. The soldiers were not presented with a serious alternative to Luddendorf's iron heel. And when workers and soldiers were ready to rebel, the Spartacusbund was not strong enough.

Once war began in Britain, the Trades Union Congress and a large majority of the Labour Party dropped all opposition to it, signed a no-strikes truce for the war's duration, participated in the recruitment campaign and published a pamphlet entitled *The War to End all Wars*, a weak reflection of pro-war Liberal propaganda. The ILP and the British socialist party remained hostile but ineffective. The majority of the forty Labour MPs in Parliament followed suit, with the striking exception of Ramsay MacDonald. The suffragettes, too, split on the question. Emmeline Pankhurst called off the mass movement and sent her women supporters home to knit socks for the soldiers. Her daughter Sylvia, a staunch socialist well before the war, steadfastly opposed the slaughter and became a communist.[5] Bertrand Russell was equally hostile to the war, opposed it in strong language and served a spell in prison. It was Scotland that produced the glimmerings of an opposition. A young socialist schoolteacher, John MacLean, addressed large meetings in Glasgow, explaining the imperialist nature of the war and calling on workers not to participate in a fight for greed and colonies. If they were that desperate to fight, he suggested they march to London and get rid of the monarchy. From the beginning of his political life, MacLean stressed the separateness of Scotland and argued in favour of a Scottish Workers' Republic. He loathed the British Empire and vice versa. Arrested in 1914 under the Defence of the Realm Act, he was sentenced to three years of hard labour

---

5 Lenin's pamphlet *Leftwing Communism: An Infantile Disorder* was directed at her, amongst others.

at Peterhead Prison and force-fed when he went on hunger strike. On his release he was met by tens of thousands of workers and carried in triumph through the streets of Glasgow. The Bolsheviks honoured his struggle against the war by electing him an honorary president of the First All Russian Congress of Soviets, along with Lenin, Trotsky, Liebknecht, Adler, and Spiridonova. The news was greeted joyously on the Clyde.[6] He died of pneumonia at the age of forty-four in 1923. The combination of poverty, prison and giving his only overcoat to a freezing Jamaican comrade sent him to an early grave.

In southern Europe, the Russian Revolution had its biggest impact on Italy. United as a state as late as 1860, it was demographically dominated by a Southern peasantry that did not speak Italian and a majority of whom were illiterate till 1911. Italy's decision to join the Entente in 1915 was not popular in the South or amongst workers in Northern factories, but it was a bonus for Italian industrialists. The massive growth of industry to meet war needs was reflected in the steel and engineering sector, where output and profits (including those of the Fiat company) doubled from 1914 to 1917. This striking growth of capital was paralleled by an equally dramatic increase in the size of the proletariat: the number of workers employed by Fiat, for instance, grew from 4,400 in 1914 to 41,200 in 1918. The three corners of Italy's golden triangle were Turin, Milan and Genoa.

Sporadic peasant anger against the war, triggered by brutal

---

6 Early in January 1918, Maxim Litvinov, the Soviet ambassador to Britain, wrote to MacLean: 'I am writing to their [Tsarist] Russian Consul in Glasgow informing him of your appointment and ordering him to hand over to you the Consulate. He may refuse to do so, in which case you will open up a new Consulate and make it public through the press. Your position may be difficult somehow, but you will have my support ... It is most important to keep me informed (and through me the Russian Soviets) of the Labour Movement in North Britain.' MacLean opened the new consulate at 12 South Portland Street, Gorbals, Glasgow, but he was not recognised as consul by the British government, which instructed the post office not to deliver mail to that address or title. The pettiness of world empires!

conscriptions, food shortages and requisitions, had been evident in the countryside from January 1916 onwards, usually accompanied by violent assaults on the police and village notables. Urban discontent centred in Turin was the outcome of food shortages and very high levels of exploitation in the factories. Social amenities barely existed. The social situation was not unlike that of Petrograd on the eve of the February Revolution (Fiat's profits mirrored in the growth of the Putilov arms industry). News that the tsar had been toppled and that the workers had taken power had created hope amongst the poor in Italy, in both town and countryside. In August 1917 the *carabinieri* shot two people dead for protesting against the shortages, demanding bread and an end to the war. Women and children participated in all these protests and chanted at the police to 'join your brothers, don't fire at them.' They were ignored. The response to the killings was a general strike. Once again the objective conditions for creating citywide soviets – autonomous organs of dual power – were ripe. No political force existed that could press this point home. As the First World War ended and was followed by the imposition of a calamitous peace that ensured there would be a second one, the Italian losses were proportionate to those of Russia. Over 5 million men had been conscripted to fight. Figures vary, but these were between 600,000 and a million dead. Half a million were severely disabled and a million were wounded.

A year after the armistice, young revolutionary intellectuals fired up by the Turin strikes, the Russian Revolution and the revolutionary turbulence that both signified had gained control of a newspaper. *L'Ordine Nuovo* would now be edited by Antonio Gramsci, a young Sardinian intellectual who had studied and made his home in Turin, assisted by Palmiro Togliatti. It was this journal that became the voice of the Turin workers. As a result Gramsci was greatly respected and admired in the factories. He was not yet the leader of any political party or faction. On 20 June 1919, the newspaper published an editorial entitled 'Workers' Democracy', in which Gramsci strongly urged the workers to transform their virtually toothless 'internal commissions' (a wartime concession) into democratically elected workers' councils. The soviets had reached Turin. The response to the editorial was dramatic. In December 1919, over 150,000 workers were participating in the new councils, which consisted of commissars elected by each work team in the factory. The model was a heady mixture of Petrograd and the Paris Commune. The term of any commissar could be revoked if a majority of those who had elected him willed it to be so.

The employers were preparing as well. In March 1920, they met to establish a General Confederation of Industry. Its secretary, Signor Olivetti, brought a typed-up memorandum stating that whatever the cost, the factory soviets had to be destroyed. The government agreed. Troops were deployed to encircle Turin. A trivial dispute over daylight-saving time changes was used as a provocation by Fiat employers. They announced a lockout, insisting that the only way to reach a settlement was to disband the workers' council and revert to the old 'internal commissions'. Confronted with such a crude manoeuvre to destroy working-class organisation, the engineering workers' union and the Italian Socialist Party (PSI) called a general strike. Half a million workers responded to the call and all the large factories in Piedmont fell silent. However, the leaders of the Italian Confederation of Labour (CGL) and the PSI refused to help the strike develop, hoping it would remain provincialised. After eleven days, the Turin workers had no option but to settle the dispute, while refusing to disband their soviet. It was a stalemate.

Four and a half months later the battle resumed, this time in Milan and on a larger scale. The employers had broken off negotiations with the engineering workers' union. The latter responded with a strict work-to-rule. The employers had not experienced this tactic before and were livid. They now resorted to violence. The Alfa Romeo bosses ordered a mass punishment in the shape of a lockout. The workers occupied the factory. Elsewhere in the city other workers followed suit. Two days later the large metallurgical plants in Turin were occupied. The movement rapidly spread to Italian heavy industry, presenting a generalised challenge to Italian capitalism. The occupying workers kept production going and Red Guards protected the factories against external attacks. The situation required a political party to move forward on a national level and challenge the government. The CGL, incapable of leading the struggle, passed the buck to the PSI, who returned it by suggesting a referendum. Members were asked whether they wanted further negotiations or a revolution. Unsurprisingly, a narrow majority opted for more negotiations, fearful of losing jobs and wages and incurring mass starvation. The Liberal prime minister Giolitti made economic concessions and even claimed to agree with the principle of 'workers' control'. The occupations were ended. Not far from the summit, the Italian workers, abandoned by the CGL and the PSI (some of whose leaders were secretly negotiating with Giolitti), slipped all the way back, reeling from a catastrophic defeat with even more horrific consequences.

The Italian capitalists and the political parties on their side had been unnerved by the militancy of the workers. They were not prepared for another round, and therefore opted for fascism. Did the CGL and PSI, watching Mussolini's Blackshirts burn down trade union and party headquarters throughout Italy, pause to reflect on how it might all have been different? Those who did had already left to help found the Communist Party at a congress in Livorno in 1921. Those who, like Antonio Gramsci, had believed that a partyless road to workers' democracy was possible, soon changed their minds. The defeat of September 1920 had concentrated Gramsci's mind even more than the Russian Revolution. He admitted that his programme for the Workers' Council suffered from severe limitations, and for a short time embraced a virulent Jacobinism denouncing all representative assemblies as diversions from the main task. He soon returned to a more considered view of the relationship between the party and the masses, but he never abandoned his new position that no revolution was possible without a political party. This would be the 'Modern Prince'. And a *political* revolutionary party needed a permanent 'military substratum'.[7] Gramsci had not

---

7   Even those who disagreed with this assessment then or later must surely have been glad that it was implemented during the Italian resistance against fascism. Self-disarmament after the war was Togliatti's concession.

read much of Lenin at this time but the conclusion he had reached was not so different from one of Lenin's theses (supported at the time by Plekhanov, Axelrod and most of the leaders of Russian Social Democracy) to the effect that a revolutionary party had to be 'ready for *everything*' and especially 'the preparation, timing and execution of the *national armed insurrection*'.

Watching these uprisings and defeats from afar, was Lenin wrong in thinking that what was desperately needed was a new International and new parties? The collapse of German Social Democracy still haunted him. He would have agreed with Gramsci's critique of that party written in December 1919. The Italian had argued then that the German SPD in 1919–20 had reduced the soldiers and workers' councils in that country to 'a form malleable and plastic to the leaders' will'. And furthermore it had 'created *its own* councils by fiat, with a secure majority of its own men on them; it [had] hobbled and domesticated the revolution' and its main link to workers was the 'contact of Noske's fist on the workers' backs'.

10

The Third International

For most of September and October 1917, it appeared that Lenin saw the success of the October Revolution mainly as a springboard for revolutions throughout Europe. The war was still raging and he hoped it would create prerevolutionary crises in Germany, France, Italy and the possessions of the Habsburg Empire. For him this was the most efficient way of defeating the counterrevolution. In order to do so, it was necessary to set about organising a new International that would mark a definitive break with the federalism and political cowardice of the Second International, and its social-chauvinist sections that had capitulated to and defended their respective capitalist governments in the war. For this purpose, agreement with the statutes (and with the twenty-one conditions that Lenin had instituted in 1920 for joining the Comintern) was necessary to be part of the new organisation.

Lenin strongly believed that civil wars were about to break out all over Europe and, for that reason, a Communist International was required as the general staff of the world revolution. He was particularly contemptuous of the Second International for prioritising 'white skins' and not caring about the rest of the world, including the victims of the imperialist countries. The Communist International would fight with Asian and African comrades to defeat the stranglehold of the European empires. The war had ended and the balance sheet could be seen in cemeteries, hospitals and psychiatric clinics across Europe. The figures were horrific: 30 million dead and wounded, mass starvation, huge war debts. The creation of a League of Nations by the victorious powers was

Delegates at the founding conference of the Communist International
(Comintern), Moscow, 1919.

denounced by Lenin as 'a league of bourgeois robbers' established
to rubber-stamp colonial and other crimes.

The invitation to attend the founding conference in 1919
was drafted by Trotsky. He and Lenin signed it on behalf
of the Communist Party of Russia and were joined by a
handful of other organisations in nearby countries and the
Socialist Workers' Party of the United States. The invitation
read:

> During the war and the revolution it became conclusively clear that
> not only the old socialist and social-democratic parties, and with
> them the Second International, had become completely bank-
> rupt ... and incapable of positive revolutionary action ... The
> gigantic pace of the world revolution, constantly presenting new
> problems, the danger that this revolution may be throttled by the
> alliance of capitalist States, which are banding together against the
> revolution under the hypocritical banner of the 'League of
> Nations' ... The present epoch is the epoch of disintegration and
> collapse of the entire capitalist world system, which will drag the

whole of European civilisation down with it if capitalism with its insoluble contradictions is not destroyed.

The First Congress of the Communist International (Comintern) met in Moscow from 2–6 March 1919. Since the infant Soviet Republic was virtually cut off from the rest of the world, with no diplomats posted anywhere and threatened by civil war and interventions within, it was extremely difficult to reach the Russian capital. The newly formed German Communist Party, crippled by the murder of its two key leaders, Luxemburg and Liebknecht, did manage to send a delegate, but he reflected Rosa's view that the formation of a new International was premature. Had she been present herself, there is little doubt that she would have argued strongly for postponement till a few other mass parties existed. Lenin's view, unanimously supported for once by the Bolshevik leadership, bruised and battered by the strong differences that had emerged on signing the Brest-Litovsk Treaty with the Germans, was that a new International was needed precisely to help build mass parties. That the event took place at all was a triumph, and in a set of theses that explained the confrontation between bourgeois democracy and the revolutionary dictatorship, the tiny Congress consisting of fifty-five delegates laid out its stall. The final manifesto, written by Trotsky at a time 'when Europe is covered with debris and smoking ruins' was seen as a continuation of the *Communist Manifesto*, a call for generalising the revolutionary experiences of the working class and its allies to lay the basis for a series of worldwide revolutions. It was a scathing attack on the European war leaders: 'The most infamous incendiarists are busy seeking out the criminals responsible for the war', (tense) backed as usual by a frogs' chorus of 'professors, members of parliament, journalists, social patriots and other political pimps of the bourgeoisie'. Some things never change.

The Comintern was given a temporary boost by the short-lived Hungarian and Bavarian revolutions and, for a fleeting moment, Lenin thought that this might presage the beginning of a new offensive after the defeat in Berlin. It was not to be. The first of these had little impact outside Budapest and its origins were slightly odd. The bourgeoisie literally handed over power to a combined if uneven Social Democratic and Communist alliance. The former had 700,000 members, since trade unionists were automatically assigned membership in the party. The Communists were Hungarian prisoners of war released by the Bolsheviks. Their leader, Béla Kun, had joined the Social Democrats, and the recently formed Communist Party had 1,000 members. Lenin was both suspicious and dubious. How could this have happened? Kun assured him that he was in charge of the Governing Council, despite the overwhelming weight of the socialists. Another communist leader, Tibor Szamuely, was opposed to any merger with the socialists given the difference in membership size. He argued against Kun, pointing out that they would be prisoners from the very beginning and could be dumped when the Social Democrats regarded them as redundant. There was a prevailing view among some intellectuals that the Hungarian liberals had wanted a radical government in power to frighten the Entente and prevent it from dividing Hungary at Versailles. If this was the case, the trick worked.

Béla Kun argued in a report for *Pravda* on 4 July 1918, however, that the strike in Budapest was not a local event. It was part 'of a series of strikes embracing separate industries ... It is one mass movement ... Work has ceased everywhere.' He contested the view that this was simply a strike against hunger or for electoral reform, arguing that it was against militarism and should not be underestimated:

During the war it was impossible to transform the labour organisations in accordance with the revolutionary requirements of the proletariat; but the *workers now are carrying on the struggle in spite of the trade union leaders* ... For fifteen long years the official organs of the [Socialist] Party have threatened the bourgeoisie: 'We shall begin to talk Russian.' At the present moment, the Hungarian proletariat is talking and, actually, acting Russian.

After six months the Entente sent Romanian and Czech troops into Hungary who toppled the government, creating the space for a dictatorship, and then went to join Denikin's armies in the

Russian civil war. Kun had failed to confiscate the landed estates and distribute land to the peasants. Had the countryside been won over, the outcome might well have been different.

It is difficult to understand what happened in Bavaria without a more detailed account of the debacle in Berlin. By fall 1918 it had become clear to even the most wooden-headed members of the German high command that they had lost the war. General Luddendorf, a ruthless defender of the long-term interests of Germany, did not fall into this category, but even he knew the game was up. He strongly recommended a cease-fire to the kaiser and the formation of a more 'democratic' government to please Woodrow Wilson. It would also help Luddendorf to deflect criticism from the army to a civilian outfit that could be blamed for the defeat. The kaiser agreed and the instructions were carried out, with the SPD helpfully offering two of their own to serve in the cabinet and prepared to continue with the monarchy as long as the institution's powers were clipped as, for instance, in Britain. But the victorious powers had made Kaiser Bill into such a bogeyman that they refused the compromise. The kaiser had to go. The Imperial Naval Command were outraged and prepared to go down, all guns blazing, in defence of their monarch. On 24 October 1918 (the first anniversary of the Russian Revolution), they sent the fleet out into the open seas to engage the Royal Navy. The German sailors, unconvinced by this suicide mission, decided to mutiny. From the main naval base at Wilhelmshaven the mood spread to units all over coastal Germany, infecting many soldiers as well. Attempts to crush the revolt failed. A soldiers' and workers' soviet in Bavaria forced King Ludwig III off the throne. Munich became a Commune. In early November the German revolution reached Berlin, with vast crowds of soldiers and workers carrying red flags and demanding peace and an end to the monarchy. The kaiser abdicated. It looked as if another Petrograd was in the making. Lenin was convinced that a German revolution was possible and both he and Trotsky agreed that, if necessary, they must sacrifice all in Russia to ensure success in Germany.

Once again objective conditions favoured a revolution, but unlike in Petrograd where the Mensheviks and SRs had sat back and watched events unfold in uncomprehending amazement, their German equivalents were better prepared. The SPD leadership was totally opposed to any upheaval. They had been angered by Karl Liebknecht's uncompromising speech to a welcoming crowd in Berlin immediately after his release from prison. After attacking the capitalist war that had turned 'Europe into a cemetery', he welcomed the Russian Revolution and pledged to break its isolation:

> We must not imagine that our task is ended because the past is dead. We now have to strain our strength to construct the workers' and soldiers' government and a new proletarian state, a state of peace, joy and freedom for our German brothers and our brothers throughout the whole world. We stretch out our hands to them, and call on them to carry to completion the world revolution. Those of you who want to see the free German Socialist Republic and the German Revolution, raise your hands!

All hands were raised.

The new chancellor, SPD leader Friedrich Ebert, believed that the only way to restore order was to decapitate the Spartacusbund, as workers and soldiers continued to demonstrate and Liebknecht was joined at rallies by Rosa Luxemburg and other leaders of the fledgling German Communist organisation. Earlier, soon after the establishment of a republic, Ebert had concluded an 'oral agreement' with General Wilhelm Groener, the new chief of the army, that the key task was to prevent the 'spread of Bolshevism'. Groener later wrote that the destruction of the local Bolsheviks was absolutely vital for the officer corps, and that 'Ebert had made up his mind on this . . . We made an alliance against Bolshevism . . . There existed no other party which had enough influence upon the masses to enable the re-establishment of a governmental power with the help of the army.' In 1993, the same High Command allied with a different party for similar objectives.

Ebert decided to crush the Communists, but he knew it wouldn't be easy. Liebknecht was a symbol of courage and popular largely because he had opposed the war that Ebert and his party had defended and, what is worse, had been proved right. These cadres had to be exterminated. Ebert's 'Bloody Christmas' started early, with a military offensive against the militant workers of the city throughout December that began when military units attacked a Spartacist demonstration, killing fourteen people. The party newspaper's offices were under fire and tension enveloped the city. A poster confected by the military went up all over Berlin:

Workers! Citizens!
The downfall of the Fatherland is imminent!
Save it!
It is not being threatened from without, but from within:
By the Spartacist Group.
Strike its leader dead!
Kill Liebknecht!
You will then have peace, work and bread!
Signed: Soldiers from the Front.

On 29 December 1918, Ebert authorised the mass distribution of SPD leaflets. It was a declaration of war:

The shameless doings of Karl Liebknecht and Rosa Luxemburg besmirch the revolution and endanger all its achievements. The masses cannot afford to wait a minute longer and quietly look on while these brutes and their hangers-on cripple the activity of the republican authorities, incite the people deeper and deeper into a civil war, and strangle the right of free speech with their dirty hands. With lies, slander, and violence they want to tear down everything that dares to stand in their way. With an insolence exceeding all bounds they act as though they were masters of Berlin.

Two days later a specially convened gathering of the Spartacusbund decided on an armed insurrection as the only defence possible against the Ebert–Groener bloc. Rosa Luxemburg was against the adventure. She explained patiently that they were a tiny group, and that the SPD and the USPD had the support of a huge majority of German workers. They did not have a majority in the workers' councils or anywhere else, and to launch a struggle for power in these conditions was both undemocratic and pure madness. She was outvoted, but refused to remain aloof. Without a strategy in place, half a million workers poured into the streets; after just over a week, the uprising was crushed. Its leaders now made another mistake. Instead of leaving Berlin immediately they went underground, where they were found and arrested by the police. With Ebert's approval they were handed over to the Freikorps (most of whose members later ended up as staunch Nazis), who killed Karl and Rosa and dumped their bodies. Others would soon follow. The civil war in Germany continued over the next few months despite elections to a constituent assembly where the SPD and the breakaway USPD had a combined vote of 14 million. The KPD had boycotted them. This did not halt the armed uprisings or strikes throughout the country.

The Bavarian Soviet held out the longest. It had been ahead of Berlin in getting rid of its king and installing a 'socialist republic' under USPD leadership, with Kurt Eisner presiding. There were over 5,000 councils in existence, but the SPD had won the December elections. The USPD received 2.5 percent. On 25 February 1919, as Eisner was on his way to tender his resignation, he was assassinated by an ultraright monarchist. This event resulted in general strikes in Munich and Nuremberg; workers and soldiers in the two cities formed armed militias to resist the counterrevolution. The three workers' parties – the SPD, USPD and KPD – met together to discuss the crisis. A proposal was made to establish the Soviet Republic of Bavaria. Eugen Levine, the KPD leader, was opposed to it and argued strongly against any seizure of power, using Berlin as an example. Nor was he convinced that the SPD was serious; he worried that they would withdraw at the first pretext and stab the workers in the back, since this was their tried and tested method. Despite Communist opposition, on 7 April the other parties declared a Bavarian Soviet Republic. This collapsed rapidly. Levine knew full well that the situation was hopeless, but he could not allow the workers to be crushed. A new Soviet republic was created under KPD control. It rapidly organised production and distribution networks as well as arming the councils and creating an embryonic Red Army. Levine knew that it was doomed, but felt that it was his duty to fight side by side with the workers' militias to try and prevent a complete massacre. On 1 May, army units and Gustav Noske's Freikorps, comprising 30,000 armed men, entered Munich. A thousand workers were killed. Levine was captured, tried and executed. The counterrevolution registered yet another triumph. At his trial Levine spoke these words:

> We Communists are all dead men on leave. Of this I am fully aware. I do not know if you will extend my leave or whether I shall have to join Karl Liebknecht and Rosa Luxemburg. In any case I await your verdict with composure and inner serenity. For I know that, whatever your verdict, events cannot be stopped … Pronounce your verdict if you deem it proper. I have only striven to foil your attempt to stain my political activity, the name of the Soviet Republic with which I feel myself so closely bound up, and the good name of the workers of Munich. They – and I together with them – we have all of us tried to the best of our knowledge and conscience to do our duty towards the International, the Communist World Revolution.[1]

The form taken by the German Revolution was as Lenin had predicted in *State and Revolution*. It was mostly spontaneous mass strikes and mass action that had laid the basis for autonomous soldiers' and workers' councils (soviets), and it was in these that the USPD left and the Communists had sought to concentrate all power. The councils were a form of extreme democracy even more radical than the annual parliaments demanded by the English Chartists in the previous century. They were close to the form of

---

1 Rosa Levine-Meyer, *Levine: The Life of a Revolutionary*, Glasgow, 1973. This is a moving account of those days by Eugen Levine's wife, who later settled in London. Once, after a particularly incendiary speech by me at a London anti-Vietnam War demonstration, she came up to me, introduced herself and said, 'You should be careful. They'll kill you. Come and have tea with me.' To my eternal regret I never did, but I think she had misinterpreted my words. I had spoken of the vital need to create a new front in Europe and the United States. I meant through the antiwar movement. She must have thought I meant armed struggle.

direct democracy experienced in the eight-month interval between February and October in Russia. But the Communists and their USPD allies were not strong enough politically or numerically to prepare a *conscious* plan to take power or to organise and coordinate the forces of revolution. With the exception of some Communists (and they were a tiny force), there was nobody else. The USPD was old wine in a new bottle. Despite the favourable situation on offer, it could not break overnight with the intellectual vices it had inherited after bitter experiences inside the SPD. Rosa Luxemburg herself was not immune to this virus. She sometimes underestimated the ability of the ruling class to inflict massive violence in order to save its institutions and place in society. As late as December 1918, when Ebert and General Groener were embarking on a bloodbath, she did not change her mind. She was right, of course, in opposing the insurrection and courageous in fighting for it regardless, but even if her party had been a majority in the workers' councils in Berlin and most of Germany, any attempt to seize power would have brought them into confrontation with a violent state machine. Civil war would have become inevitable.

Lenin and Trotsky saw the early Comintern as an essential school for discussions on revolutionary tactics and strategy. This it undoubtedly was, and during the first four Congresses, debates were free and forceful, though even then the weight of Moscow as the repository of the only successful revolution provided some glimpses into the future. During the course of a lengthy discussion in 1924 on the economic crisis, for instance, Trotsky predicted with startling clarity the impact it would have on the world of empires and referred specifically to the British, whose

character has been moulded in the course of centuries. Class self-esteem has entered into their blood and marrow, their nerves and bones. It will be much harder to knock the self-confidence of world rulers out of them. But the American will knock it out just the same, when he gets seriously down to business. In vain does the British bourgeois console himself that he will serve as a guide for the inexperienced American. Yes, there will be a transitional period. But the crux of the matter does not lie in the habits of diplomatic leadership

Lenin making notes to rebut an Italian delegate – as published in the *Illustrated London News*.

but in actual power, existing capital and industry. And the United States, if we take its economy, from oats to big battleships of the latest type, occupies the first place. They produce all the living necessities to the extent of one-half to two-thirds of what is produced by all mankind.

As late as 1926, at a meeting of the plenum of the executive committee of the Comintern, the Italian Communist leader, Amadeo Bordiga, isolated inside his own party, could argue against Bukharin and Stalin, albeit for the last time, and declare:

> We have in the International only one party that has achieved revolutionary victory – the Bolshevik Party. They say that we should therefore take the road which led the Russian party to success. This is perfectly true, but it remains insufficient. The fact is that the Russian party fought under special conditions, in a country where the bourgeois-liberal revolution had not yet been accomplished and the feudal aristocracy had not yet been defeated by the capitalist bourgeoisie. Between the fall of the feudal autocracy and the seizure of power by the working class lay too short a period for there to be any comparison with the development which the proletariat will have to accomplish in other countries. For there was no time to build a bourgeois State machine on the ruins of the Tsarist feudal apparatus. Russian development does not provide us with an experience of how the proletariat can overthrow a liberal-parliamentary capitalist State that has existed for many years and possesses the ability to defend itself. We, however, must know how to attack a modern bourgeois-democratic State that on the one hand has its own means of ideologically mobilizing and corrupting the proletariat, and on the other can defend itself on the terrain of armed struggle with greater efficacy than could the Tsarist autocracy. This problem never arose in the history of the Russian Communist Party.[2]

The Cold War anti-Communist notion that the 'Kremlin' was responsible for every eruption of social discontent or revolution anywhere in the world soon found its mechanical Marxist twin: the Kremlin was responsible for every suppression of social discontent and every victory of counterrevolution. The first was ridiculous, but preached with great vigour; the second completely

---

2 Quoted in Perry Anderson, 'The Antinomies of Antonio Gramsci', *New Left Review* 100: 1, November 1966.

ignored the autonomy of indigenous parties and movements. Those parties with vitality and tough-minded leaders who could and did ignore Moscow's advice were usually those with enough strength and self-confidence to win the revolution. Those that mutely accepted mistaken directives of the Comintern were unlikely to defeat the enemy.[3]

---

3 Soon afterwards all dissent in the Comintern was extinguished, as it already had been in the mother party. The Comintern became little more than an instrument of Soviet foreign policy attempting to strangle the independence of Communist parties all over the world and carrying out expulsions of those who disagreed. And sometimes pushing decisions that cost lives: the Chinese party was not allowed to terminate an alliance with the nationalist Chiang Kai Shek even as he was preparing a bloodbath of Communists in Shanghai in 1927. Chinese Communists did not make such a mistake again. They paid lip service to Stalin but did their own thing. Mao reportedly handed the Stalinist bible *A Short Course History of the CPSU* to Liu Shaoqi with this injunction: 'Read this carefully if you want to end up dead.' This was followed by a criminal policy of equating Social Democracy and fascism in Germany and rejecting the idea of a socialist–Communist–liberal united front against Hitler, which might well have prevented his electoral triumph. The German Communist leaders were too weak to ignore Moscow and paid the price, as did Europe and the Middle East.

When the Comintern was dissolved in 1943 to appease the Allies during the Second World War, few tears were shed at its demise. The Vietnamese, Yugoslav and Chinese revolutions occurred in 1945 and 1949 respectively. The Cuban triumph came ten years later in 1959. In all four cases, Moscow was presented with a fait accompli. A rubber-stamp Socialist International is still in existence.

11

Red Army, Civil War, Military Philosophers

During the first five years of the Comintern, the newly created Red Army was regarded by friends and enemies alike as a fighting force for the 'world proletariat'. Its origins and ideology promoted this notion. It was created in a hurry to fight the civil war. Its core consisted of the Red Guards attached to the soviets or their equivalents that were offshoots of the Bolshevik Party. Some of the Red Guard commanders became celebrated military leaders during the civil war and after. On the eve of the revolution there were 10,000 Red Guards in Moscow and 20,000 in Petrograd, with scatterings in other cities. The Petrograd contingent received a boost when a sizeable section of Chinese immigrant workers brought to Imperial Russia to build and expand the railways abandoned their jobs and joined the Bolshevik Party and the Red Guards. They proved to be tougher fighters than many of their Russian colleagues. Together with prisoners of war who wished to be part of the revolution, they were welded to the Red Army as the 'International Battalion', entirely proletarian, under the command of San Yu-Fan, formally joining the Red Army in May 1918.

To this core came many newly radicalised Russian soldiers who were fleeing the front. Even those who remained in the rapidly disintegrating Imperial Army were extremely reluctant to be used against the soviets. Three weeks after the revolution, General Posokhov, the chief of staff of the XIIth Army, informed his colleagues that 'the army just doesn't exist'. An Army Congress of the XIIth met to elect an executive committee: the result was a Bolshevik majority and a Bolshevik president. These politicised units became a crucial element in the new Red Army as the pattern began to be repeated elsewhere.

Lenin, as head of government, instructed the commander-in-chief of the old army, General Dukhonin, to commence peace negotiations on every front. Dukhonin refused. Lenin sacked him by telephone. To the mortification of the old order, the Bolsheviks appointed Ensign Krylenko as the new commander-in-chief, with a stern Bolshevik and former imperial officer M. D. Bonch-Bruevich as the chief of staff. The old tsarist generals were removed from all their command posts. As they stormed the High Command head-quarters (Stavka), Dukhonin, who had refused to leave earlier with his colleagues, was dragged out of a train by an angry crowd and executed on the spot. The tsarist army had been completely destroyed. The most hard-core tsarist generals and officers would move south to set up a counterrevolutionary volunteer army, backed by the Entente, to win back the country. The stage was now set for a brutal civil war. The Whites were backed by the liberal Kadets, the right SRs and the right Mensheviks.

The Bolsheviks had created the Red Army. Where the Whites had a surfeit of officers and were desperate for more soldiers, the Reds were desperately short of skilled officers. The revolutionary process had brought some new faces to the fore: Frunze, Budyonny, V. K. Blyukher, Malinovsky and Yegorov amongst others. The civil war would test them further. Blyukher proved himself an outstand-ing military commander in the field. The most gifted military leader, however, was incarcerated in a German military prison when the revolution broke. His story is not without interest. For Lenin and his comrades, now confronted with assaults on the revolution from within and without, the appearance of a Russian half-Clausewitz, half-Napoleon was a gift from heaven.[1]

---

1   I have relied for much of this material on two major sources. John Erickson's magisterial accounts of the Red Army were an indispensable guide: *The Soviet High Command*, London, 1962, and *The Road to Stalingrad*, vols. 1 and 2, London, 1975. Isaac Deutscher's first volume of the Trotsky trilogy, *The Prophet Armed*, contains the best account, to my knowledge, of the military debates. Trotsky's own military writings

Marshal Tukhachevsky, the most brilliant Red Army commander; executed by Stalin.

Mikhail Tukhachevsky's remarkable career illuminates important episodes of the military and political past of what was then the Soviet Union. Born in Penza province of tsarist Russia in 1893, he hailed from an impoverished family of aristocrats, originally of Flemish descent: a crusading ancestor had ended up near Odessa with a Turkish wife and been granted lordship of the village of Tukhachev. Entering the Imperial Army at a very early age, Tukhachevsky fought the First World War as a lieutenant in the crack Semenovsky Guards Regiment. Captured by the Germans in 1915, he was imprisoned in the fortress of Ingolstadt: a fellow prisoner was Charles de Gaulle, slightly repelled by the Russian's nihilism and radicalism.

After five attempts at escape, he finally made it to Petrograd after the Bolshevik seizure of power in October 1917. Having been inspired by the French Revolution and the Decembrists since his youth, he had no difficulty in entering the service of the revolution.

---

offer rare insights into all these themes. Erickson paid his own tribute on p. 129 of *The Soviet High Command*: 'In view of the subsequent development of "Stalinist military science", and the deadening effect this had on Soviet military development, Trotsky's arguments received a posthumous confirmation … It would be too much to inject an element of prophecy into Trotsky's statements on military matters at this time, but it is remarkable that many of the warnings he gave at this time proved themselves valid long after the so-called "debate on doctrine" had ceased.' Tukhachevsky's own politico-military philosophy is conceptualised in a remarkable text translated in 1969: 'Revolution from Without', *New Left Review* 55, May–June 1969.

Marshal Frumze: Old Bolshevik military theorist; believed Marxism provided answers to military questions.

He first joined the Bolshevik Party and was sent rapidly to Sklyansky, Trotsky's deputy at the Commissariat of War. There was no time to test him. Within weeks, he was given command of the famous First Red Army on the eastern front, facing the Czechoslovak Legion (dispatched by the Entente to fight with the Whites) near Simbirsk, the town where Lenin had been born. Tukhachevsky's brilliance in the field was responsible for the crucial breakthrough that shattered Kolchak's line near Samara in May 1919, beginning an advance which rolled the White Armies all the way to Tomsk and Krasnoyarsk within a few months. Transferred by Trotsky to the Caucasian front, then menaced by Denikin's regroupment, Tukhachevsky gave a repeat performance. His troops rapidly outflanked Denikin's, sweeping the Whites into the sea at Novocherkassk and Tuapse in March 1920.

Two months later, after a meteoric rise, Tukhachevsky was made commander-in-chief of the western front in the new war of the young Soviet Republic against Poland, which had invaded Russia. Upsetting international expectations,

Clausewitz: Strongy defended by Lenin, Trotsky and Skylansky.

Tukhachevsky rapidly reversed fortunes in Belorussia, pushing the enemy back into ethnic Poland. After eight weeks of advance, he crossed the Bug and approached the Vistula. The Polish military dictator Pilsudski (whose older brother had been part of the same terrorist group as Lenin's older brother Sasha) recalled the moment:

> This unceasing, wormlike advance of a huge enemy horde, which went on for weeks, with spasmodic interruptions here and there, gave us the impression of something irresistible rolling up like some terrible thunderclouds that brooked no opposition . . . By this march on Warsaw, Tukhachevsky gave proof that he had developed into a general far above the average commonplace commander.

At twenty-seven, the same age as Napoleon at Lodi, Tukhachevsky was at the gates of Warsaw. On 26 July 1920, Von Seeckt, the architect of the Reichswehr in postwar Germany, wrote: 'The complete victory of Russia can no longer be called into question.' He meant the 'complete victory' in most of Europe. Tukhachevsky himself later argued that if they had not suffered a military setback, the Red Army would have been on the borders of Germany helping the German revolution. It was not to be. Von Seeckt was proved wrong. A calamitous military blunder deprived the Soviet armies of the great victory that Lenin was predicting on an operations map to Comintern delegates in Moscow even as the battle raged. The South-Western Command, under Yegorov, Budyonny and Stalin, which had been placed under Tukhachevsky's jurisdiction after the crossing of the Brest-Litovsk line, refused to obey orders to drive north in order to close in on Warsaw from below. With crass idiocy, it pursued an attack on Lvov to the south, opening a vast breach in the arc of the Russian offensive. This act of insubordination, in which both stupidity and jealousy on the part of Stalin and Budyonny played a role, cost the Red Army the war. Pilsudski immediately poured troops into the gap between the two commands and turned Tukhachevsky's armies on the left. A rout followed, aggravated by Tukhachevsky's cavalier treatment of supplies and transport during his impetuous advance. The Bolshevik revolution had been contained within its borders. Lesser commissars had been executed for lesser misdemeanors. Stalin escaped without any official reprimand for the effective sabotage of a major military operation.

There was, of course, a major political problem as well that Lenin had underestimated. Polish national consciousness had received a huge boost after the Treaty of Versailles. All Russian revolutionaries had for decades supported Polish independence, and Lenin in particular had argued with great force against the tsarist oppression of the country. The Polish peasants were not willing to replace one Russian with another. The Polish working class, too, was split and though Poland might have been used as an essential bridge to Germany and Pilsudski removed, how long this would have lasted is an open question.

Lenin's death and Trotsky's fall sealed Tukhachevsky's fate. Instead of placing him in command of the Red Army and giving him a seat on the Politburo, his enemies imposed an office job on him, though not one without importance. He worked successively as director of the Military Academy, deputy chief of staff and chief of staff. Demoted by the robotic Voroshilov, who disliked him, he became chief of the operations department of the Red Army in 1931. In this period he pioneered the use of motorised columns, tank battles and parachute drops. Under his influence, the Red Army was built into a formidable modern military machine in the 1930s. Tukhachevsky was made a marshal, but he was not see the fruits of his work.

Stalin had decided to eliminate him as early as 1936, if not before; at any rate a NKVD conspiracy against him was woven in that year. The party and the army were being politically cleansed in tandem. If the bulk of Lenin's Central Committee were to be executed as 'traitors', how could Trotsky's generals be left alive? Learning of the plans afoot against Tukhachevsky, the Nazi Sicherheitsdienst was helpful. It forged documents to make it easier for the NKVD to prove Tukhachevsky's collusion with the German high command to betray the USSR and passed them into Russia, with the deliberate aim of destroying the commander whom the Wehrmacht feared most in Russia. The forgeries were promptly used as evidence by the NKVD in secret charges against

Tukhachevsky and his closest military colleagues (Yakir, Blyukher, Uborevich, Putna, Gamarnik and others) for treason. On 12 July 1937, Tukhachevsky was shot. He was 'rehabilitated' in 1956 after the twentieth party congress in the USSR: that is, the charges of treason were dropped and two books published about him. A stamp honouring him was issued in 1963, but there was to be no enquiry into the reasons for his death and no critical discussion of his historical role permitted.

Tukhachevsky's life and work raise major historical questions. The first concerns the whole character of the Russian civil war which followed the Bolshevik seizure of power. What was its military and social nature? There is a vast and rich literature on the October Revolution itself, much of it produced by Marxists and most of it of a high scientific standard (Trotsky, Sukhanov, Deutscher, Carr, Liebman and others), while there is almost nothing of value on the civil war, which was its momentous consequence. Yet the October Revolution was, as Lenin always stressed, little more than 'hurrah socialism': the conquest of power was deceptively simple and mostly painless. The real history of the life-or-death class struggles which would decide the destiny of the Russian Revolution began not in October 1917 but in March 1918, when the Czechoslovak Legion ran up the white banner of counterrevolution along the Volga. The three devastating years of war which followed determined the final shape of the revolution far more than its innocent and utopian birth, twisting it into the mould that later became Stalinism.

There are, of course, some reminiscences of this period, some high-grade journalism, Isaac Babel's compelling short stories, but all these are usually sketchy and autobiographical. In reality we know little of this decisive ordeal. The military debates of the time, in which Tukhachevsky played a prominent part, do offer, however, important clues for any consideration of the meaning of the civil war. The different contributions to this debate all throw some light on the nature of the problems confronting the revolution after October, when war broke out on the vast plains and steppelands of Russia. There were three basic positions. Trotsky, commissar for war and architect of the Red Army, did not believe in the existence of a distinct Marxist strategy of war. He regarded military affairs as a technical branch of knowledge, with no closer relation to politics than engineering or architecture. Thus he wrote:

> Historical materialism is by no means a universal method for all sciences . . . To attempt to apply it in the special domain of military affairs would be the greatest fallacy, no less a one than an attempt to move military science into the group of natural sciences . . . Even should one agree that 'military science' is a science, it is impossible to assume that this science could be built according to the method of Marxism.

Trotsky's military policy was absolutely logical and consistent with this position. Early on, he made the fundamental decision to use former tsarist officers to train and lead the proletariat in arms. Regarded as the repositories of professional military knowledge, they were renamed 'military specialists' and given command of troops: throughout the civil war they dominated the officer corps of the Red Army above the rank of captain. Trotsky defended this policy with the utmost vigour against attacks on it for opening the door to reaction and defection within the ranks of the revolutionary armies. He was backed by Lenin, who was an orthodox Clausewitzian in this regard. Both men understood, even at this stage, that Marx's ideas did not encompass every single field of thought or practice. This included military philosophy as well as literature.

Frunze, the old Bolshevik soldier and theorist who was Trotsky's successor as commissar for war after 1922 – and who was, according to some, the victim of a medical murder by Stalin in 1925, immortalised in Boris Pilnyak's courageous novel *The Tale of the Unextinguished Moon* – was Trotsky's main antagonist in the military debates, representing views much closer to those of the rank and file of the Red Army. His starting point was the polar opposite of Trotsky's. He argued for a 'unified military doctrine', by which he meant a refusal of the separation established by Trotsky between Marxism and the theory of war. Frunze was convinced that a new 'proletarian science of war' was necessary, which would express the social character of the working class as the new master of society. 'The character of the military doctrine accepted by the army of any state is determined by the character of the general political line of the social class which stands at its head,' he wrote.[2] It was therefore incorrect to entrust the formulation of strategy to members of the former ruling class in Russia – tsarist officers who necessarily reflected the military outlook of the very enemy against which the revolution was fighting for its life. Frunze and the 'Military Opposition' argued against the vertical hierarchy and iron discipline which Trotsky established in the Red Army: they wanted a democratised structure of command, with military commissars subordinated to political commissars, themselves elected from below, not appointed from above. Frunze went on to specify the strategic doctrine of any proletarian army:

> The tactics of the Red Army were and will be impregnated with activity in the spirit of bold and energetically conducted offensive operations. This flows from the class nature of the workers' and peasants' army and at the same time coincides with the requirements of military art.[3]

Frunze insisted that, henceforward, a war of manoeuvre predominated over a war of position and analysed the civil war as a historical lesson: fast moves across huge distances would in the future decide the outcome of major military conflicts and as a class, the working class was supremely fitted, by temper and morale, to such mobile offensive actions. This was the fundamental reason for the Red victory in the civil war.

Tukhachevsky occupied a distinct third position in this debate. He agreed with Trotsky on the necessity for classical military discipline and centralisation in the Red Army, and with Trotsky he attacked the cult of anarchic partisan warfare, some of whose adepts later lost the Polish campaign by their insubordination and

---

2   'Introduction to Tukhachevsky', *New Left Review* 55, May–June 1969.
3   Ibid.

incompetence. On the other hand, he sided with Frunze and Gusev in their insistence on the new role of the offensive. 'Manoeuvre is the sole means of securing victory,' he wrote. Tukhachevsky's conception of future battles reflected his experience of the fight against Kolchak and Denikin:

> Strategic reserves, the utility of which was always doubtful, we need not at all in our war. Now there is one question: how to use numbers in order to gain the maximum force of the blow. There is one answer: release all troops in the attack, not holding in reserve a single bayonet.[4]

Trotsky and Stalin were later to accuse each other of Bonapartism, a danger that was universally feared in the Bolshevik Party. In fact, the only man who was consciously inspired by the example of Napoleon at this time was Tukhachevsky, who even modelled his addresses to his troops before battle on the style of the French general. Napoleonic military strategy had favoured swift, mobile attacks of lightly equipped armies living off the land as they marched. What Frunze believed was the *differentia specifica* of proletarian warfare, Tukhachevsky, coming from a very different background, saw as the reemergence of the principles of revolutionary warfare, perfected by the armies of Napoleon in the tempestuous glory days of France's struggle against the Grand Alliance. To this, Trotsky retorted that France in the early nineteenth century was the most economically and socially advanced country on the continent of Europe, while Russia was one of the most backward. How could it possibly mimic Napoleonic military strategy, even if that were desirable? The nascent Soviet state, on the contrary, should be guided by the Clausewitzian rule of the primacy of defence.

What was the nature of the military conflict that gave rise to these debates? The three positions outlined above only become intelligible in the light of the civil war itself. The armed struggle of 1918–21 did not, contrary to popular belief, involve vast masses of

---

4   Ibid.

men. By the standards of modern warfare, it had a markedly limited and gapped structure. Enormously destructive in its impact on economy and society (clinching the catastrophic damage already wreaked by the imperialist war), it was fought between relatively small armies, neither of which ever surpassed 100,000 to 150,000 men on each front. No battle probably ever engaged a force of more than 50,000 men at one time – usually much less. Tukhachevsky himself emphasised this fundamental characteristic of the civil war in a report to Lenin written in December 1919. The civil war was defined by 'small armies', 'feeble density of units engaged', 'extended fronts', 'irregular recruitment' and a 'low technical level'. 'All these singularities', he declared, 'distinguish the Civil War from a national or imperialist war'. John Erickson's graphic description reinforced this view:

> The straggling fronts, with their chaotic rear, could be crumpled by a thunderbolt blow, smashing like a fist through stretched paper. Once the blow lost its momentum, however, and the forces became spread ever more thinly across a greater space, a counter-blow sent them reeling away in disorder.[5]

What was the social basis of this armed contest? It is here that the root of the military debates within the Red Army must be sought. The Bolsheviks seized power with a minority of the country behind them: they had a 'strategic majority' (Lenin) because the Russian working class served as an overwhelming force in the main towns during October. The peasantry, ten times more numerous than the proletariat, were neutral or benevolent. But when the civil war got under way, the Soviet regime rapidly lost most of the goodwill it had enjoyed among the peasant masses because of the ravages of the war itself, the grip of the Entente blockade and the inexorable necessities of food procurement; compulsory grain deliveries were born, not with collectivisation, but with War Communism. Trotsky expressed the truth with brutal honesty when he later said: 'We plundered all Russia to conquer the Whites.'

---

5 Erickson, *The Soviet High Command*, p. 50.

The result was expectable. Henceforward, the revolution fought for its existence in a countryside largely hostile to it. The Whites, of course, were even more feared and hated by the mass of the middle and poor peasants: enough to ensure final military victory, but not enough to alter the political consequences of such a victory for socialism. There was no organic bond in most areas between the Red Army and the civilian population. Spontaneous guerrilla actions in Siberia at the beginning of the conflict, Trotsky remarked, played a positive role in harassing the White rear. In the Ukraine later on, where the kulak element was much more important, the peasants disrupted both sides and acted as a 'disintegrating force' (Tukhachevsky) on the Red Army. For the Red Army itself, the 'proletarian' force which Frunze postulated for his theory was not working-class in composition. By the very end of the war, after strenuous efforts, proletarian soldiers made up only 15 to 18 percent. The rest were peasants, mostly conscripted, confronting enemy armies also composed (much more exclusively) of peasant conscripts. Desertions from the Red Army were massive and uncontrollable throughout the conflict, a cruel index of the nature of the civil war. In 1919 alone, there were no less than 2,846,000 deserters. Fedotoff-White, a sympathetic historian, comments: 'The fantastic number of deserters from the Red Army was beyond doubt a symptom of a deep and acute conflict between the will of the Communist-controlled state and the masses of the Russian peasantry.'[6] Both the strategic and the social character of the Russian civil war thus separated it profoundly from the revolutionary wars of liberation that occurred later in the century.

Projected against this background, the essential flaw of Frunze's

---

6 This was the exact opposite of what later happened in China, when the Chinese Communists, driven out of the towns via repression and massacres by the Nationalists and Japanese occupation, rebuilt their strength in the countryside. Based on the overwhelming support they mustered there, this breach of Marxist orthodoxy enabled the Chinese Red armies to win back the cities, culminating in the march to Beijing in October 1949. In this fashion, Mao Zedong transcended the Russian military debates of the 1920s.

theories is evident: they presupposed political forces which did not exist. A 'proletarian' military doctrine could not emerge in Russia in 1920 because there was no proletarian army to apply it. By contrast, Trotsky's great historical merit was his unflinching awareness of the fragile social base of the war. Precisely because it was not in this sense a people's war, it could and had to be officered by tsarist technicians and fought on staff school lines. A 'proletarian' strategy was utopian in the desperate circumstances of 1919. Trotsky's rejection of the supremacy of manoeuvre was equally well-founded; he had no difficulty in seeing how it was common to both sides in the conflict, and reflected the ruined and improvised circumstances of backward Russia. Trotsky was a true successor of Engels, who had written: 'Nothing depends upon economic conditions so much as the army and the fleet. Aims, composition, organisation, tactics and strategy are in direct dependence on the given degree of production development and the means of communication.'[7] Anyone accepting this formulation needed to place overwhelming emphasis on the importance of technology and organisation. By doing so with unmatched energy and efficiency, Trotsky led the Soviet armies to victory in the civil war.

Tukhachevsky's role in the military debates, still secondary during the civil war, came to the fore immediately after it with the Polish campaign. True to his Napoleonic inspiration, he now openly advocated 'revolution from without' – the offensive proletarian war against neighbouring bourgeois states – to overthrow capitalism and install the local working class in power. Wherever a socialist revolution succeeded, it had 'as a matter of course, a natural right to expand'. The notion of a defensive militia rather than an offensive army was an 'antiquated superstitition of the Second International', which had always confined the workers to a 'passive half-battle'. 'The Second International had inoculated the conception, that such an attack (of the proletariat against the bourgeoisie) is permissible within the frontiers of the State only.'[8] What was needed now, Tukhachevsky argued, was an International General

---

7   'Introduction to Tukhachevsky'.
8   Ibid.

Staff of the proletarian revolution, coordinating external operations all over the continent.

There was no mystery as to the ancestry of these ideas. Napoleon's military genius had been displayed in a wave of external campaigns that carried the ideas of the bourgeois revolution across Europe, transforming political institutions and state frontiers wherever they went. In Italy, Germany and the Low Countries, French invasion was widely welcomed as liberation: Hegel and Beethoven were representative in regarding the new regimes as indications of historical progress. It was only when the French armies entered social terrain too dismally backward to assimilate any of the ideas of the bourgeois revolution except nationalism – Spain and Russia – that they were greeted as oppressors and defeated. Viewed from within France, Bonaparte was, as Marx always emphasised, the personification of a stable and sated bourgeois class. Viewed outside France, he was still a subversive and heroic force to many Europeans.

This ambiguity is reflected in later and even contemporary Bolshevik attitudes. It was not Robespierre or Babeuf but Napoleon who was quoted by Lenin during his last years to justify his actions in bringing about the October Revolution against perennial Menshevik accusations that it had been premature: '*On s'engage et puis on voit.*' And Trotsky, with a few hours to kill on his train during the civil war, meditated on new international possibilities. On 6 August 1919, he dispatched a memorandum marked 'Top Secret' to Lenin and the Central Committee. Its central thrust was this: the Red Army might not be a decisive force in Europe if Anglo-French militarism retained 'a measure of vitality', but might it not transform the relationship of forces in Asia by defeating the British Empire? He argued that there was a possibility of bypassing the lengthy interval that awaited them before the European revolution resumed with a forward policy in Asia:

> The road to India may prove at the given moment to be more readably passable and shorter for us than the road to Soviet Hungary. The sort of army which at the moment can be of no great significance in the European scales can upset the unstable balance of

Asian relationships of colonial dependence, give a direct push to an uprising on the part of the oppressed masses and assure the triumph of such a rising in Asia.[9]

There were a few precedents, after all, for Tukhachevsky's position.

The Bolshevik Party had legitimised offensive wars by a proletarian state against a neighbouring bourgeois state for the purpose of helping a fraternal working class in its revolution. Lenin had written in 1914:

Uneven economic and political development is an absolute law of capitalism. Hence, the victory of socialism is possible first in several or even in one capitalist country alone. After expropriating the capitalists and organising their own socialist production, the victorious proletariat of that country will arise *against* the rest of the world – the capitalist world – attracting to its cause the oppressed classes of other countries, stirring uprisings in those countries against the capitalists, and in case of need using even armed force against the exploiting classes and their states.[10]

Trotsky reiterated these principles in 1921: 'In principle, the Soviet government would always be for an offensive revolutionary war under conditions when such a war could lead to the liberation of the toiling classes in other countries.'

There was thus a certain canonical background to Tukhachevsky's doctrine. There was also a powerful counterrevolutionary foreground, as will be seen. Besides intervening in Russia itself, imperialism had after the October Revolution swiftly moved to crush further uprisings with foreign armies, and had succeeded in three important cases. The beleaguered Hungarian Commune had been destroyed by an invading Romanian army; bourgeois power was stabilised in Budapest for twenty-five years. The Finnish Revolution,

---

9   Leon Trotsky, *The Trotsky Papers, 1917–1922*, ed. and ann. Jan M. Meijer, London and The Hague, 1964, p. 622.

10   'Introduction to Tukhachevsky'.

holding off the White Guards in the north, had been caught in the rear by the landing of the German army of Von der Goltz and crushed. In the east, the Gilan Republic on the Caspian was overthrown by a British-controlled and -officered army of Persian mercenaries. In each case, the Soviet state was unable to come to the aid of a fraternal revolution and had helplessly watched its defeat not by internal forces, but by external intervention. Lenin, in particular, had bitterly lamented the failure to aid the Hungarian Commune in 1919. In this context, Tukhachevsky's ideas could be seen as a logical riposte to 'counterrevolution from without', in the new situation created by the end of the civil war in Russia.

Pilsudski's annexationist aggression of 1920 provided a natural springboard for a counterattack. When the Red Army crossed the Bug into Poland, the immediate objective was the liberation of Warsaw and of the Polish working class. The Bolsheviks had reasonable grounds for believing that the Polish proletariat was revolutionary and socialist, and would unite with them to fight the colonels' clique of Pilsudski and Śmigły-Rydz. The general strike of 1905 had lasted longer in Warsaw than anywhere else in the Russian Empire; soviets had sprung up in 1918 and Luxemburg and Tyszka's legacy endured there. Beyond Poland, moreover, lay Germany – the 'key to the international situation' as Trotsky would later call it. Gripped by insurrection and civil war, it was in a quasirevolutionary situation. The Spartacist uprising had been suppressed by the Freikorps from the Baltic; perhaps its successor could be saved by another army from the East, the Red cavalry? In 1920, every Bolshevik believed that the future of the Russian Revolution depended on revolution in the West – so motives both of international solidarity and of self-defence seemed to justify the advance of the Red Army beyond Russian borders. Lenin summed them up when he said that the Polish campaign would be a blow against the whole Versailles system – the internationally coordinated blockade of socialism in Russia, and suppression of it in Western and Central Europe.

Trotsky alone opposed the march into Poland, and warned of its dangers. Here again, he showed his clairvoyant appreciation of the limits of the Russian Revolution. Polish nationalism, he argued, was an elemental force which would be aroused by a Russian army, no matter what its colours, on Polish soil – just as Russian chauvinism had been by the invasion of Polish armies a few months before. Not only this. More fundamentally, Trotsky reminded the Bolsheviks, the Red Army was overwhelmingly a peasant force with a low level of political education which could not be used at will for dashes across Europe. The peasant soldiers who composed it would not fight with any enthusiasm outside their own frontiers. 'With such tactics', Trotsky wrote, 'we shall not be able to capture the peasant's soul.' The Red Army was not designed to conquer Brussels or Galicia. On the contrary, only a defensive military policy was possible for Russia, with its retrograde economy and non-socialist peasantry.

Trotsky was proved right. The German working class, which had no revolutionary traditions before the First World War, was radicalised by defeat and made repeated insurrectionary bids after the war. The Polish working class followed the inverse evolution. After a long history of revolutionary upsurges, it was demobilised by the war and the emergence of a Polish state under the protection of the Versailles Treaty. There was *no* popular response to the call of the Soviet armies to rise up against Pilsudski. The military defeat of the Polish campaign was avoidable: the political defeat of the conception behind it was not. Tukhachevsky's later theorisation of this was quite explicit:

> The working class may not always be ready for the helping hand extended towards it. It may still need time to look around and realise where its salvation lies. In short, a socialist offensive will not always turn out to be concerted with a revolutionary uprising of the nation concerned.

In other words, the role of the Red Army was no longer that of merely assisting an indigenous insurrection under attack. It was to initiate and, if necessary, replace it. Trotsky saw the distinction very clearly. He emphasised that 'in the great class war now taking place, military intervention from without can play but a *concomitant, cooperative, secondary part*. Military intervention may hasten the dénouement and make the victory easier, but only when the political consciousness and the social conditions are ripe for revolution.' This principle, as Deutscher points out in his classic analysis of the campaign, was precisely what Tukhachevsky had ignored. Frunze had tried to escape from the constraining limits of the civil war experience by imagining a Marxist strategy of the future. Tukhachevsky also tried to escape from them, but by returning to the past. What he did not grasp, of course, was the fundamental *difference in nature* between the bourgeois and socialist revolutions. Napoleon could for a time successfully export the ideas of 1789 on his bayonets, because the political transformations of society implied by the bourgeois revolution do not *ipso facto* demand mass participation from below. They can – as later events in Germany, Japan or Italy would amply testify – be implanted bureaucratically and repressively from above by a small oligarchy. By contrast, the socialist revolution is by definition only socialist if it involves the masses of the population taking their lives into their own hands and overthrowing existing society from top to bottom themselves. No proletarian version of the Italian campaign was ever possible in the twentieth century.

After the Second World War, Stalin imposed a bureaucratic 'revolution from without' – now historically divorced from its origins in the Leninist period – throughout Eastern Europe, with notorious results. These unnatural creations were at least the by-products of victory over Nazi aggression and defence against the threat of Anglo-American encroachments. The ultimate debasement of the once generous traditions of the Red Army was the return of a Soviet kommandatura in Prague twenty years later, no longer to drive out the Germans but simply to suppress the Czechs: reaction from without. It was a big nail in the coffin of the Soviet Union.

To situate the triangular military and political debates at the birth of the Red Army historically, a comparison may be fruitful. Engels, it will be remembered, had emphasised: 'Aims, composition, organisation, tactics and strategy are in direct dependence on the given degree of production development and the means of communication.' The defect of Engels's formulation, obviously, is its reduction of the material determinants of war to the forces of production, conceived as technology. What is missing are the *relations* of production. Hence his famous misjudgment that artillery and shrapnel had rendered barricades outdated and urban insurrections henceforward impossible. The social relations for a new kind of war were absent in Russia after October; there was nothing to do but fall back on traditional schemes.

The second great historical question raised by the enigmatic ellipse of Tukhachevsky's life concerns the performance of the Soviet armies during the Second World War. From the late 1920s onwards, Tukhachevsky devoted himself to the construction of a mechanised and industrialised army: the danger of a second imperialist intervention was by now obvious, with the rise of fascism in Europe. In the latter half of his life, Tukhachevsky abandoned the preconceptions of his civil war experience – the priority of attack over defence, and the supersession of position by manoeuvre. The technical changes introduced by the rise of mechanised units – absent from the civil war, apart from the now anachronistic use of armoured trains – had transformed the strategic problems of conventional warfare. In his article 'War as a Problem of Armed Struggle' (1928), Tukhachevsky laid down with extraordinary precision the main lines of the pattern of the Second World War. He emphasised the importance of diplomatic initiatives to divide the capitalist enemy; he predicted that trench warfare would play no role in future conflicts: he criticised unilateral insistence on attack/manoeuvre and argued that positional and defensive warfare would be equally important; finally, he attributed great importance to the skilful use of tanks, but made it clear that they should not be fetishised in isolation from other elements in a general strategy (Fullerism/Blitzkrieg), and must be combined with infantry units for optimum effect.

Two years later, Tukhachevsky was chief of the operations department of the Red Army. He swiftly formed the first mechanised brigade in 1930 (tanks and armoured cars), and then experimented with the first parachute units in 1931. According to one source, he envisaged assistance to a possible proletarian uprising in Germany in the form of dropping parachutists behind enemy lines into the Ruhr, Lower Saxony and Prussia. This idea was a return to a genuinely Leninist conception, and in fact was realised by both Allied and Soviet armies during the Second World War in their liaisons with resistance movements in the Balkans. Tukhachevsky's next innovation was the development of what he called 'concentric manoeuvre' or double envelopment, which involved breaking through enemy lines using mobile formations and which he practised in vast military exercises in 1933. The foreign military attachés who watched these exercises noticed that their tactical conception was in advance of the ability of the troops to execute them. Eight years later, it was 'concentric manoeuvre' that trapped Von Paulus at Stalingrad. As *New Left Review* put it:

> It is by no means far-fetched to claim that many of the great encir-clement operations of the Second World War, such as the battles of Stalingrad and Korsun-Shevchenkovski in 1944, owed their concep-tion to the experiments which Tukhachevsky and his group carried out on the plains of Belorussia and the Ukraine from 1931 onwards.[11]

Within the framework of untransformed social relations of war, Tukhachevsky in the 1930s developed perhaps the most advanced tactical conceptions in the world. If any one man was responsible for the eventual field victory of the Red Army over the Wehrmacht, it was, without a doubt, him.

The final question mark of his career concerns the events that led up to the Russo–German war of 1941. Since the Rapallo Pact of 1922, the armies of the two countries had trained together in special bases inside the USSR, which included a tank and aviation school. Tukhachevsky visited Germany in 1932, the year before Hitler came to power. Some reports claim that he and Gamarnik asked Stalin to close down the training stations immediately after Hitler became chancellor. Others imply that he regretted the end of technical cooperation between the two armies. At all events, the bases were shut down in October 1933. Thereafter, Tukhachevsky

---

11 'Introduction to Tukhachevsky'.

made only one major public utterance on international affairs – a long military article in *Pravda* on 31 March 1935, whose dire warnings of the dangers of Nazi aggression were prophetic.

A year later, already in partial eclipse and under suspicion, Tukhachevsky agreed to answer questions from General Isserson, the director of the newly established General Staff Academy and his colleague, Pavel Vakulich, chair of operational art, with only senior officers present. He spoke to them for two hours on what needed to be done. The first question was simple: when asked which potential enemy they should be preparing to fight, he replied without hesitation: 'Germany'. The second question was related to the operational conduct of the war to come. Here the marshal warned his interlocutors to beware of dogma. The international situation would determine the 'concrete strategic situation'. However, Tukhachevsky pointed out that the strategy deployed during the First World War was now moribund. In the coming war the enemy would strike suddenly and deploy everything available on land, sea and air to take the Red Army by surprise. To preempt this, the Soviet Union must be in permanent readiness, with hidden operational formations on the alert and capable of going on the offensive as soon as the enemy had been halted. He elaborated further:

As for the Blitzkrieg which is so propagandised by the Germans, this is directed towards an enemy who doesn't want to and won't fight it out. If the Germans meet an opponent who stands up and fights and takes the offensive himself, that would give a different aspect to things. The struggle will be bitter and protracted; by its very nature it would induce great fluctuations in the front on this or that side and in great depth. In the final resort all would depend on who had the greater moral fibre and who at the close of operations disposed of operational reserves in depth.

Shortly thereafter he was shot. Stalin had already decided to remove Tukhachevsky, along with other senior military figures who had contested him in the past and who he refused to trust. The cynical collusion between the NKVD and the Sicherheitsdienst that was responsible for Tukhachevsky's death, with the former acting as the dupes of the latter, further strengthened their 'case' and anticipated the Nazi–Soviet Pact signed two years later.

The purge of the generals proved to be, exactly as the SD hoped, a crippling blow to the fighting capabilities of the Red Army. The catastrophe of June–October 1941, in which the USSR was caught completely unawares by the German invasion, losing millions of men and the results of years of industrial construction, must be overwhelmingly attributed to the disappearance of any experienced military command after 1937. It was more than a blunder; it was a crime, and its responsibility for the disaster was so great that it remained a forbidden topic in the Soviet Union till the expiry of the state. The enormity of Stalin's blindness and incapacity was never revealed. The dubious anecdotes of Khrushchev's secret speech merely served to obscure the true gravamen against the 'Generalissimo'.

Contrary to popular legend, the Wehrmacht at no time had military superiority over the Soviet armies on the frontier. The exact opposite was the case. Not only did the Red Army deployed in forward positions outnumber the German forces on the eastern front by thirty divisions in June 1941. The Red Army had a staggering *seven to one* superiority in tanks, supposedly the decisive weapon of the Wehrmacht: its tank park numbered 24,600 to approximately 3,500 Panzers ranged against it. Even in the air, the USSR had a four to one superiority in planes over the Luftwaffe. There is thus no basis for the myth that German armoured might was initially able to smash through the Russian defences, at crushing odds, and was only finally stopped when total popular mobilisation was able to redress the balance at Moscow and Stalingrad. The German conquests of 1941 were strictly *military* victories, won by skill and surprise over a larger opponent ruined by an incompetent and demoralised command, committing blunder after blunder. Stalin's personal responsibility for this debacle was manifold: he had, over a two-year period, destroyed the officer corps of the Red Army, dismantled the 1939 defence positions, refused to believe in a German attack after repeated warnings and neglected to place Soviet industry on a war footing.

The Second World War was eventually won, not by superior military skill – after Tukhachevsky, the Red Army produced merely average, not outstanding generals – nor by the bond between a revolutionary army and its mass base – desertions to the Germans numbered in the tens of thousands – but by the economic and social weight of the USSR after the Five Year Plans, which was fatally underestimated by German intelligence. The Wehrmacht went on winning until this enormous machine was finally organised for war with reasonable rationality; it was then slowly pushed back, under the banner of nationalism. The delayed victory saved Europe from fascism: the cost was colossal. How much of it was unnecessary has yet to be computed.

In a 2001 preface to the third edition of his classic work on the Soviet high command, written several months before his death, John Erickson concluded thus:

> The system lived perpetually on a narrow knife-edge. How frighteningly narrow was brought home to me in a singular exchange with Chief Marshal of Artillery N. N. Voronov. He asked me if I was satisfied with the assistance I had received in investigating the events of June 1941 ... Knowing he was present at the very centre of events during the early hours of Sunday 22 June, I asked him for his interpretation. He said that at about 7.30 a.m. the High Command had received encouraging news: the Red Army was fighting back. The worst nightmare had been overcome. Red Army soldiers had gone to war, 'the system' had responded and would respond.[12]

They did much more than that, and it is worth restating the fact (acknowledged at the time by Churchill and his generals as well as Roosevelt and General Marshall) that without the Russian resistance and the capacities revealed by the Soviet state, the Third Reich would have taken Europe. The sufferings inflicted on the Slav *untermensch* were on a much higher level if not as clinical as the Judeocide. The triumphalist political culture that dominates the West today constantly underestimates the Soviet contribution to

---

12 Erickson, *The Soviet High Command*, p. xx.

'Private Ryan's war'. The bulk of the damage to the fascist regimes was inflicted by the Red Army. Von Paulus's surrender of the Sixth Army in Stalingrad and the effectiveness of Soviet armour in Kursk broke the spine of the Third Reich. The deliberate delay by the United States and Britain in opening a new front cost more than a million Soviet lives. The clash of war machines led to huge losses to both sides on Soviet territory. The Red Army claimed the destruction of 48,000 German tanks, 167,000 guns and 77,000 aircraft. All in all, the armies mobilised by the German fascist state lost 13.6 million soldiers. Of these, no less than 10 million met the grim reaper on the battlefields of the Soviet Union. On the eastern front, 506.5 German divisions were lost 'while Germany's sullen satellites lost a further 100 divisions as the price of participating in the war against the Soviet Union.'[13] That those who fought with the Third Reich and their successors are currently being celebrated in Croatia, NATO-Ukraine, Hungary and Serbia tells us a great deal about the times in which we live.

The victory boosted Soviet military prestige throughout the world and undoubtedly gave a fillip to the revolutionary armies in China and Vietnam. At home, once the war was over, nothing changed. The Red Army, which had now broken with its past on most levels, used its newfound nationalist popularity to demand more and more funding. Out-of-control military spending, foreign adventures in Ethiopia and Afghanistan, attempts to mimic US foreign policy, and a failure to deal with an obsolescence-racked economy finally brought the system to an end. Nobody in the leadership of the Communist Party or the army had foreseen such a rapid collapse.

Lenin himself, as well as Trotsky, Skylansky, Tukhachevsky and Blyukher, would not have been totally surprised.

---

13   Erickson, *The Road to Berlin*, p. xx.

SECTION FOUR

The Question of Women

12

The First Wave

Socialism was the first political current to understand the oppression of women and to discuss it seriously within the movement. The two key texts were written by Friedrich Engels and August Bebel, and their initial impact should not be underestimated. In an aside, Engels regretted that he had not paid more attention to the work of Charles Fourier. The Frenchman's text 'Degradation of Women in Civilisation', written in 1808, anticipated much of what was to be written later. Fourier believed deeply that the progressive or regressive nature of a society could be judged by a single criterion: how it treated women.[1] Lenin had imbibed all these texts and

---

[1] 'Is there a shadow of justice to be seen in the fate that has befallen women? Is not a young woman a mere piece of merchandise displayed for sale to the highest bidder as exclusive property? Is not the consent she gives to the conjugal bond derisory and forced on her by the tyranny of the prejudices that obsess her from childhood on? People try to persuade her that her chains are woven only of flowers; but can she really have any doubt about her degradation, even in those regions that are bloated by philosophy such as England, where a man has the right to take his wife to market with a rope around her neck, and sell her like a beast of burden to anyone who will pay his asking price? Is our public opinion on this point much more advanced than in that crude era when the Council of Mâcon, a true council of vandals, debated whether or not women had a soul and decided in the affirmative by a margin of only three votes? English legislation, which the moralists praise so highly, grants men various rights that are no less degrading for the sex [women], such as the right of a husband to sue his wife's recognised lover for monetary indemnification. The

in his speeches would often repeat Fourier's litmus test for evaluating a society.

In *The Origins of the Family, Private Property and the State* (1874), Engels mapped out a rough history of early human society, based largely on Henry Lewis Morgan's anthropological study of the customs and practices of the Iroquois tribes in the New York area. To this Engels added his own analysis of the emergence of private property and the links between it and gender practices. He shocked contemporaries by referring to marriage as 'legalised prostitution' and was scathing in his criticisms of the Church and bourgeois society at large, who propagated the idea that monogamy was God-given and eternal. Engels responded, in *The Origin of the Family, Private Property and the State*, by entering the animal kingdom, suggesting:

> If strict monogamy is the height of all virtue, then the palm must go to the tapeworm, which has a complete set of male and female sexual organs in each of its 50–200 proglottides, or sections, and spends its whole life copulating in all its sections with itself. Confining ourselves to mammals, however, we find all forms of sexual life – promiscuity, indications of group marriage, polygyny, monogamy. Polyandry alone is lacking – it took human beings to achieve that.

Engels wrote very little on the specific forms of gender oppression under capitalism. August Bebel's study titled *Woman under Socialism* (1879) attempted to remedy this defect. It was more sociological in character, mapping present-day realities and

French forms are less gross, but at bottom the slavery is always the same ... As a general thesis: social progress and historic changes occur by virtue of the progress of women toward liberty, and decadence of the social order occurs as the result of a decrease in the liberty of women.' Charles Fourier, 'Degradation of Women in Civilisation', in *Théorie des Quatre Mouvements et des Destinées Générales*, 3rd ed., Paris, 1808. This last sentence remains a valid measure (if not the only one) for assessing societies throughout the world today.

providing statistical evidence of gender discrimination on every level. The book was designed to push Social Democracy towards incorporating women's needs and demands into their political programmes. Bebel was particularly angered by the denial of education rights to half the population in England, Germany and elsewhere. In a detailed and affecting chapter on prostitution ('a supplement to monogamy'), its causes and consequences and what was necessary for it to disappear voluntarily, he strongly condemns the mistreatment and persecution of prostitutes, considering the institution to be as legitimate as 'the police, standing army, Church and capitalism'.

Neither Bebel nor Engels had much to say about homosexuality. Engels ignored it. His friend Bebel saw it as an 'aberration', even in ancient Greece, and left readers with garbled and ridiculous assumptions of no real value. To argue that the 'male population of Greece having become addicted to pederasty, the female population fell into the opposite extreme: it took to the love of members of its own sex' reveals a total failure of comprehension. Homosexuality remained a blind spot for virtually all the different factions of the European left till the middle of the twentieth century. It's not that gays were invisible to the state. They were subject to criminal laws, especially brutal in Prussia and later extended to Bismarck's unified Germany.[2] Demanding or implementing decriminalisation, a straightforward democratic demand, had to wait till the Russian Revolution.

---

2 It was left to another German of the same period, Karl Heinrich Ulrichs (born in 1825 in East Friesland in a staunchly Lutheran household) to attempt a more refined explanation. Ulrichs's own sexual experience with an older boy at school whom he came to love opened him to studying ancient Greece and learning both Greek and Latin. He wrote twelve notebooks on Urning, his word for male same-sex love. It was the first serious attempt to understand male homosexuality and inaugurated a debate that continues to this day. Ulrichs couldn't tolerate the new Germany and went to live in Italy, as Hubert Kennedy, his biographer, relates in *Karl Heinrich Ulrichs: Pioneer of the Modern Gay Movement*, San Francisco, 2002 (available at hubertkennedy. angelfire.com).

The condition of women in tsarist Russia, like everything else, was determined by the autocracy. The limited Petrine reforms of the eighteenth century were intended for a small minority of women from the nobility and the merchant classes. These were mainly concentrated on the right of women to own property, a step forward that weakened patriarchal domination. The dual exploitation of peasant women under serfdom and afterwards went unchallenged. Further reforms in the nineteenth century loosened the straitjacket in regard to education and the professions. By 1900, there were more women in tsarist Russia who were teachers, doctors and lawyers than in Western Europe and North America: if Fourier's definition of a society were to be strictly applied, tsarist Russia would need to be classified as much more progressive at the turn of the century than Germany, Britain, France or the United States, which was patently not the case.

The same applied to politics. Russian women were more engaged in politics than is recognised by current historians. Pushkin and Nekrasov's poems in praise of the Decembrist women who accompanied their husbands to Siberian exile popularised the experience for many Russians. The memoirs, diaries and letters written by the women themselves did the rest. They were read by or read to others for generations to come.

The French revolutions that ended with the Commune of 1871 had a huge impact on different sections of the Russian intelligentsia, starting with the Decembrists and ending with the two major factions of the RSDLP. When accused of being a Robespierre by the Mensheviks, Lenin used to insist that he had no particular affection for the Jacobins as such. It was their removal from power that preoccupied him. And he would add, accurately, that it was Paul Axelrod (the Menshevik leader) who identified completely with Robespierre, as did Martov with the Jacobins.

For Russian women, in particular, the French events left a pleasant aftertaste. They had read of women playing an active role on many levels. The feminist manifestos of Olympe de Gouges were translated into Russian. A butcher's daughter and a playwright, de Gouges argued for equal rights and produced a text to counter or supplement the 'Declaration of the Rights of Man'. Entitled 'Declaration of the Rights of Woman', she demanded the same rights for all women, namely, 'liberty, property, security and especially resistance to oppression'. The nation was sovereign but only if it 'reunited' men and women. Of the fourteen points in her feminist charter, a few deserve to be singled out. She stresses that there is only a single barrier to women's advancement and 'hence the exercise of the natural rights of woman has no other limits than those that the perpetual tyranny of man opposes to them.' She demands equal taxation for women and equal forced labour, but in return women 'must therefore have the same proportion in the distribution of places, employments, offices, dignities and industry.' Since women already have the right 'to climb the scaffold', she argues, they must be given the right to mount the rostrum so that they can speak their minds. The fact that she dedicated the Declaration to Marie Antoinette somewhat muted its impact. Politically a monarchist-Girondin, she was despised by the Jacobins, but not only by them. On 3 November 1793, amidst the Terror, she was tried and sentenced to death. The guillotine was stationed at the Place de la Concorde.

The main intellectual influences on educated women from the upper and middle reaches of Russian society were no different from the thinkers and poets revered by young men in the second half of the nineteenth century. Pushkin, Lermontov and Gogol were great favourites, but as far as most students, populists and terrorists were concerned, they could not compete with Chernyshevsky's didactic fiction, Dobryulov's critical reviews or Pisarev's polemics. As discussed in Chapter 1, Chernyshevsky's novel *What Is to Be Done?* defined the politics of at least two generations of Russians. The long spells that two of these writers spent in tsarist prisons gave them a special aura, an added attraction for the radical segments of society. Chernyshevsky was loathed by the more traditional liberal and conservative critics and writers. Nabokov's last Russian novel, *The Gift*, is derisive in the extreme, provoking the question of why, if the novel is so bad, spend fifty pages mocking its author and his colleagues? Though even Nabokov admits that there 'was quite definitively a smack of class arrogance about the attitudes of contemporary well-born writers towards the plebeian Chernyshevsky', and that when at home amongst like-minded friends, 'Tolstoy and Turgenev called him the "bed-bug stinking gentleman" . . . and jeered at him in all kinds of ways.' The criticisms clearly were not confined to the literary merits or demerits of the work.

For women, the novel offered a heroine in the character of Vera Pavlovna with whom they could easily identify. She was independent, radical, lived in a housing commune and had organised a bookbinding collective. The feminist Bolshevik Alexandra Kollontai found the novel hypnotic when she first read it at the age of sixteen, pleading with her mother to get in a bookbinder who could teach her how it was done and somewhat disappointed when a scruffily dressed and not very attractive middle-aged man showed up. It was the same for many other literate women, who discovered in it the ideas of emancipation, women's equality, communal living and free union. These ideas pushed men, too, away from the dominant patriarchal views in Russia and elsewhere. Lenin's own views on women were informed not only by Engels and Bebel, but by radical Russian literature. Chernyshevsky stressed gender equality, but was not a great believer in the nonmonogamous road to women's liberation. Even churchless unions, he thought, could and should be monogamous, and chaste cohabitation was an important test of revolutionary discipline, a manifestation of true equality.

Russian women from the intelligentsia were much more advanced politically than their European contemporaries. The number of women who joined the narodniks and participated in the move to the countryside to work with the peasants was surprisingly high. This was a few decades prior to the birth of the suffragette movement in Britain and the United States which, in the main, restricted itself to a single issue: women's right to vote. Elsewhere, on the question of women, many European societies were lagging behind.

In Russia nobody had the right to vote and, as a result, women and men fought together against the autocracy. When the old narodnik 'Land and Liberty' party split on the issue of terrorism

Vera Figner (1852–1942): Imprisoned for twenty years for her part in
the assassination of Alexander II.

Sophia Perovskaya (1853–81): Organised Alexander II's assassination
and was hanged. Shostakovich composed a waltz in her memory.

Anna Korba (1849–1939): Schoolfriend of Perovskaya, radicalised by
the Russo-Turkish war. Joined the Bolsheviks and remained a member
till her death.

and violence and an offshoot was formed to carry on the tradition of terror, some of the most gifted women intellectuals joined the new People's Will organisation, whose principal aim was to assassinate Alexander II. A unanimous decision by the twenty-eight-member executive committee to carry out this task was warmly applauded in different parts of the country. Ten of these members, a bit over one-third of the total, were women, a much higher proportion than that achieved later by the leading committees of either of the two factions that made up the RSDLP.

The women were Vera Figner, Sofiya Ivanova, Anna Korba, Tatiana Lebedeva, Olga Lyubatovich, the sisters Natalya Olennikova and Mariya Oshanina, Sofiya Perovskaya, Elizaveta Sergeeva and Anna Yakimova. The latter was the daughter of a monk. All the others came from landed gentry or military families. And all, bar three, ended up in prison or climbing the scaffold.

Vera Figner left behind a vivid impression of those times in her memoir. Like many others, including Vera Zasulich (the first woman to fire a revolver at a target, later a member of the *Iskra* editorial board and later still a Menshevik), she was torn by the decision to split the party and fought hard for some time to keep it united. She had spent years in the countryside. The fact that she was a doctor helped establish links with many peasant women who had never experienced medical help of any sort and, as Gorky memorably described, were used to giving birth in fields and ditches and biting off the umbilical cord. Figner was frustrated by the inability of her group's propaganda to penetrate the country-side. She returned to St Petersburg and finally joined the terrorist faction, becoming one of its central organisers and helping prepare the executions of the most hated members of the autocracy. After Alexander II's assassination, she did not panic but devoted herself to protecting party members against the swathe of police agents and informers roaming the country. They finally caught up with her in 1883. The new tsar was relieved: 'Glory be to God, that depraved woman has been arrested.' Sentenced to life, she served twenty-two years in solitary confinement at the Schusselburg Fortress. She was released in 1905 as Russia was getting ready for a revolution. In prison, Figner had realised that the propaganda of the deed was as useless as the other sort that consisted of empty talk. It never led to mass uprisings. In her affecting memoirs she renounced violence altogether, arguing that both the party and the autocracy, in resorting to 'hand-to-hand combat', corrupted everything around them. 'On its side', she wrote, 'the party proclaimed that all methods were permissible in the struggle against the enemy and that the ends justified the means.' She denounced the 'cult of the bomb and the revolver and the sanctification of the terrorist'. Burnt by the experience herself, she understood only too well how 'murder and the gibbet captivated the attention of our young people; and the weaker their nerves and the more oppressive their surroundings, the greater was their sense of exaltation at the thought of revolutionary terror.'

Sofiya Perovskaya was the main organiser of the plan to assassinate Alexander II. Each and every detail – the stationing of lookouts and bomb-throwers, the final signal that she gave – was her responsibility. Arrested soon after and questioned by von Plehve, the notorious chief of police, she admitted her role without any qualms.

Later, during her trial, she raised her voice only once: when the chief prosecutor (M. N. Muraviev), one of her childhood friends, accused her and others of being brutal, immoral killers. She responded by reprimanding him sharply. She had admitted the facts concerning the tsar of her own volition. There was no need for slander, for

> when it comes to charges against me and others of immorality, brutality, and disregard for public opinion, I should like to object and point to the fact that anyone familiar with our life and the conditions under which we had to work would not hurl charges of immorality and brutality at us.

Perovskaya fought till the bitter end. Her triumphant smile on the scaffold was accompanied by placing her feet firmly underneath a swelling on the platform so that it required two men to yank her off violently before they could hang her.[3] She was the first

---

3 In July 1904, Vyacheslav von Plehve was interior minister when members of the 'fighting unit' of the Social-Revolutionary (SR) Party

woman revolutionary to be hanged. The tsar rejected a huge number of letters pleading for mercy toward her, for apart from everything else, her father was the governor-general of St Petersburg.

Perovskaya had thought long and hard before joining the People's Will. Her courage and tactical skills rapidly propelled her to the leadership. On one question she was adamant. Their actions had nothing to do with revenge. 'Vengeance', she insisted, 'is a personal affair, something that might, by stretching a point, explain those acts of terror carried out by the personal will and initiative of separate individuals – but not those of an organised party.' And it was ludicrous to imagine that a political party could 'be formed around the banner of revenge, especially if it attracts personal sympathy that ours undoubtedly enjoys. The first shot – Zasulich's – was fired not in revenge, but as retribution for an insult to human dignity.'[4]

---

assassinated him for crimes past and present. Two years earlier a similar sentence had been carried out by the same organisation against von Plehve's predecessor. The SR leaflet explained that 'we sentenced this villain on behalf of the people.' Their reasoning was that 'von Plehve was one of the pillars which held up the wall of autocracy, a wall which blocked the people's path to freedom and happiness. If you chop down the pillars, the wall will fall.' It never quite worked like that, however, as many propagandists of the deed would discover. Even in this case it was von Plehve's vicious anti-Semitism that led to his death. Yevno Azef, the police informer of Jewish origin who headed the SR 'fighting group', didn't bother to inform the Okhrana of this particular planned assassination.

4   Vera Zasulich and another comrade, Kolenkina, both members of the hard-core terrorist group Kiev Rebels, had decided to assassinate the governor and chief prosecutor of the collective trial of dozens of party members. Zasulich was enraged by the governor's decision to flog prisoners. She confronted him and fired a number of bullets into his body. He barely survived. Charged as a criminal she was greeted in court as a heroine and acquitted, after which she fled to Western Europe. It was in this period that she realised that acts of individual terror were useless, and joined the Emancipation of Labour group in Switzerland where Plekhanov and Axelrod were already ensconced. This was where Lenin met her during his first trip to Western Europe.

In August 1918, Lenin had written and signed a decree on the list of revolutionaries and public figures who deserved to be honoured with individual monuments. The eclectic list of revolutionaries was composed of the following names:

1. Spartacus	12. Marat	22. Khalturin
2. Tiberius Gracchus	13. Robespierre	23. Plekhanov
3. Brutus	14. Danton	24. Kaleyev
4. Babeuf	15. Garibaldi	25. Volodarsky
5. Marx	16. Stepan Razin	26. Fourier
6. Engels	17. Pestel	27. Saint-Simon
7. Bebel	18. Ryleyev	28. Robert Owen
8. Lasalle	19. Herzen	29. Zhelyabov
9. Jaures	20. Bakunin	30. Sofiya Perovskaya
10. Lafargue	21. Lavrov	31. Kibalchich[5]
11. Vaillant		

In 1918, the Soviet sculptor Vladimir Tatlin unveiled a monument to Perovskaya sculpted by Rakhmanov. Most critics thought it was unacceptable; Rakhmanov's sculpture was replaced by a new depiction by the Italian futurist Orlando Grizelli. According to rumours at the time, Lenin intensely disliked the new sculpture. A third was commissioned, more traditional and staid, but with the civil war raging it was never completed. Streets were successfully named after her in Leningrad and other cities, however.[6]

The last two decades of the nineteenth century were the years of

---

5 The old man was clearly in a hurry. He missed, among others, the Europeans James Connolly, John MacLean and Thomas Münzer, and the non-Europeans Simón Bolívar, the Rani of Jhansi and Toussaint Louverture.

6 Most of the other names on the list did not even reach that status. Their monuments were not even started, much to Lenin's irritation. He was simply informed that there were more pressing priorities. The exception was a statue of Marx and Engels that Lenin unveiled himself. A constructivist critic of this very traditional monument remarked: 'It looks as if they've both got out of a bath fully dressed and together.'

defeat and despair for women. The mildest of letters written by a feminist to the ultra-reactionary Tsar Alexander III, appealing for reforms that might ease the sufferings of women, was punished with exile. Russian society was decomposing. The tsar and his ministers were convinced that a permanent state of repression was the only way to preserve order. The autocracy rested on four foundational pillars – private property, monarchy, Church and the military – supported by bureaucratic sections of the state apparatus. Alexander III had strengthened the Church and given it an unofficial armed wing in the shape of the Black Hundreds, who carried out anti-Jewish pogroms on a regular basis. But it was when the state apparatus was shaken that the court resorted to reforms. The Crimean War setbacks had laid the basis for the legal end of serfdom. Defeat at the hands of Japan had been the backdrop to 1905 and the 'great war' had accelerated in 1917. The tsar was pushed off his perch altogether, along with his regime.

But few could foresee this during 1880–90. Reactionary triumphs often induce a temporary political quietism and passivity on the part of the defeated. The political topography resembles a desert; mirages appear, but not the oasis. With the anarcho-Populist groups decimated, no sign of any other political opposition and the absence of any serious reforms from the top, the country vegetated silently. The tsar and his straitlaced Danish consort, Princess Maria Dagmar, were allergic to any form of women's emancipation.

Irina in Chekhov's *Three Sisters* (1900) sums up the prevalent mood in middle-class circles at the time:

> Oh I am unhappy . . . I can't work, I shan't work . . . I used to be a telegraphist, now I work in the town council offices, and I have nothing but hate and contempt for all they give me to do . . . I am already twenty-three, I have already been at work for a long while, and my brain has dried up . . . I'm in despair and I can't understand how it is that I am still alive, that I haven't killed myself.

Chekhov's plays concentrated on his own milieu. The conditions of peasant women and those entering industry for the first time were indescribable. Viewed as an encumbrance by their own families, young girls in the countryside were married off at puberty or soon afterwards. Unless they were very lucky, the shift from parents to in-laws was simply a transfer from one layer of hell to its lowest depths. In some areas there was a nuptial custom for the bride to bring not just her bed but also a whip as a present for her groom; in extended families it was not uncommon for the father-in-law to insist on sexual intercourse while his son was out working or travelling. Heavy labour, non-stop pregnancies, brutal mothers-in-law led to premature aging and death. Unlike Chekhov's Irina, these young peasant women were sentenced to an early death the minute they were married. How long they would survive depended on their own will to live. Some were fatalistic, and succumbed.

But others resisted and survived, displaying both courage and entrepreneurial skills that their husbands lacked. These women often demanded a separate household free of in-laws. Some avoided the marriage trap altogether by seeking refuge in a nunnery. A sensational example in this regard was set by the tsarina's sister Ella, who became a nun after the murder of her husband, Grand Duke Sergei. The turn to the nunneries, however, never became a mass movement. There was a rise in the number of nuns from 7,000 in 1855 to 47,000 in 1911, but this was trifling when compared to the women and children flocking to the factories. Perhaps the stories sent back to the villages from the nunneries were not that encouraging after all. The lives of those women who became factory workers recalled the worst days of the Industrial Revolution in Britain.

Russia's radical women were the most advanced socially and politically after the defeat of the Paris Commune. They fought not just for themselves but for the emancipation of the whole country, an exceptional phenomenon in the social history of the world at that time. In 1918, Lenin, recalling Fourier, was thinking mainly of his own country when he wrote: 'From the experience of all liberation movements, it can be noted that the success of a revolution can be measured by the extent of the involvement of women in it.'

After Perovskaya's hanging, the autocracy abandoned all restraint. Many other women were hanged and shot. Several hundred languished in prison, where they were often raped, beaten and driven to suicide. The flame flickered, but was never extinguished. Most important of all, a precedent had been established for those women who came afterwards. Terrorism as an ideology had more or less disappeared like cotton in the wind, but the entry of women into radical politics could not be reversed, as would be seen in the 1905 and 1917 revolutions that lay ahead.

Sexual equality was limited to the revolutionary movement of Russia throughout the nineteenth century. And what of sexuality itself? Monogamy and free love were hotly discussed, but the narodnik women and men were fairly restrained on these issues. Usually their discussions centred on revolution. Anything that distracted from that path was a diversion. No moral stigmas were attached to chaste cohabitation, uninhibited sex or monogamous couples, as long as there was no breach of revolutionary discipline. Engels had written that free love was a corollary to all revolutionary movements.

The Middle Ages produced heretical sects large and small in both Christianity and Islam that paid a great deal of attention to love and sexuality, occasionally in more disguised form within the mainstream. The seventeenth-century Carmelite mystic nun, St Teresa of Avila, left little room for the imagination during a 'spiritual' trance that she described in her writing as follows:

> I saw in his hand a long spear of gold, and at the iron's point there seemed to be a little fire. He appeared to me to be thrusting it at times into my heart, and to pierce my very entrails; when he drew it out, he seemed to draw them out also, and to leave me all on fire with a great love of God. The pain was so great, that it made me moan; and yet so surpassing was the sweetness of this excessive pain, that I could not wish to be rid of it.

Bernini depicted this spiritual orgasm exquisitely in his sculpture 'The Ecstasy of Saint Theresa' for the Cornaro chapel of Santa Maria della Vittoria in Rome. Various pre-Sufi and Sufi sects in the Islamic world preached the joys of ecstasy and union, usually, but not always, with the creator. The Prophet, according to a memorable *hadith*, was insistent that believers indulge in foreplay with women before closing in on the final act. The pleasure principle was important to him. Judaism, in turn, gave the world the delicious Song of Solomon.

The Catholic Church was constantly in pursuit of libertine sects. The Brethren of the Free Spirit were twelfth-century utopians who believed that as world history approached its end, God himself would arrive to personally tutor and pleasure them. Three centuries later, the Bohemian sexual radical and gay 'heretic' Martin Húska was burnt at the stake for beginning his prayers with 'Our father who art in us'. His disciples, the Adamites, were punished for cultivating an Edenite innocence: they went everywhere naked, preaching sinlessness and engaging in sexual relations openly with each other. There are no statistics as to their numbers or recruitment figures, but interestingly enough, most of these libertine sects tended towards a primitive communism and publicly expressed their loathing for the Church, its dignitaries and the wealth that they had accumulated. Karl Kautsky wrote of them as precursors of socialism, while he himself remained much more conservative than they on these and other matters.

In regard to revolutions, even the most puritanical of these sects produced an explosion of free thought and sectaries who broke with all orthodoxies. The most politically radical current during the English Revolution were the Levellers and their Digger offspring; the most socially and sexually advanced were the Ranters. This latter were hostile to organised religion and churches, did not believe in the devil or Hell, insisted that all human life ended on earth and angrily rejected any notion of original sin. Ranter intellectuals such as Abiezer Coppe in Oxford were in favour of free love and free choice, and agitated publicly for the abolition of the family and in favour of 'sexual relations with a variety of partners', for both men and women. Everything was up for grabs. Unsurprisingly, they drew large public audiences. The English slogan 'Hurrah, hurrah, the First of May, outdoor sex begins today' has its origins in seventeenth-century Ranter circles. Possibly the climate was more reliable in those times.

Christopher Hill, one of the principal authorities on this period, wrote that the Ranters were a large group and included Cromwell's chaplain, Peter Sterry, as well as the son of the mayor of London, Isaac Pennington. Hill argues that they were rarely prosecuted because most of them, not believing in the afterlife, the sanctity of the Bible or, for that matter, God, had no desire whatsoever to become martyrs and happily recanted when asked to do so by the authorities. The Puritan revolution, for its part, encouraged 'companionate marriage', whereby the wife would not be an exact equal but more of a 'helpmeet' and free to divorce. From 1653 to 1660 civil marriages were permitted as well, extending the Reformation to its logical conclusion.

The Populist-terrorists of Russia were not so free and easy with bodily favours as the Ranters or the Adamites.[7] Their bible, Chernyshevsky's much-read novel, was a savage attack on the traditional family and on the use of women as slaves and an endorsement of the right of women to choose their own partners. However, it was not a particularly adventurous tome when it came to sexual pleasure; even in his radicalism there was something monkish in Chernyshevsky. The book provided the 1860s generation with an alternative morality – a spirit of self-discipline and sacrifice that captured the ethos of that time.[8] Vera Figner, in her

---

7 Lenin was a firm supporter of nudism and nude bathing, pointing out that apart from being an opportunity to receive the health benefits of sun and water, it was the one time when a person's class origin was completely obscured.

8 A confession may be in order at this point. My attempts to read Chernyshevsky at the ages of seventeen, thirty-two and seventy-two were miserable failures. This last time I managed to read over a hundred or so pages and could grasp his appeal, which lay in the truths he recounted and elements of utopia he included, rather than the book's effectiveness as fiction. Who could read this when *A Thousand and One Nights*, Boccaccio's *Decameron* and other gems were available? It was a substitute for more direct political texts. As they grew up, most radicals simply switched to Marx.

Vera Zasulich once scolded a Chernyshevsky doubter: 'He was hampered by censorship ... He had to write in allusions and hieroglyphs. We were able to decipher them, but you, the generation of the

remarkable and affecting memoirs, describes her own need in prison for some aspects of Christianity and later a utopian dream of peasant life that came straight from Chernyshevsky. The activists read the novel in tandem with the essays, in which Chernyshevsky revealed himself to be an uncompromising and dedicated revolutionist. In his diaries he described himself as a 'Montagnard', a 'Jacobin' and 'a supporter of socialists and communists', and wrote that he felt 'an irrepressible longing for the imminent revolution'. In a pseudonymous letter to Herzen's London-based journal *Kolokol* (The Bell), Chernyshevsky demanded the most extreme solution to cure the ills of tsarist Russia: 'Only the axe can save us, and nothing but the axe! Change your tune and let your Bell not call to prayer, but sound the tocsin! Summon Russia to take up the axe!' Herzen did no such thing, but Russian radical Populists took up the call, accusing the Jacobins of inconsistency for not finishing the job they had started so well in 1792. That, argued some, was why Robespierre and Saint-Just had perished.

In our own times it seems difficult for many to accept that the violence and terrorism unleashed by the People's Will in tsarist Russia was motivated by liberal ideas and solutions. It was not for nothing that Lenin referred to them as 'liberals with bombs'. He was merely summarising their own self-description. When the US president James Garfield was shot by a deranged Charles Guiteau in 1881, the leadership of the People's Will issued a public declaration, making clear

> its profound sympathy for the American people ... The Executive Committee regards it as its duty to declare in the name of Russian revolutionists its protest against such acts of violence ... In a land

---

1900s, don't have this knack ... You find him dull and empty ... Even after Chernyshevsky had been exiled to Siberia and could no longer explain his articles, there circulated a sort of key ... You haven't got such a key today and without it, you can't know him ... You can't understand that he was not what in your ignorance ... you imagine him to be.' There is no other Russian writer, with the possible exception of Tolstoy, who excited such devotion and loyalty.

where personal freedom gives an opportunity for an honest battle of ideas, where the free will of the people determines not only the law, but the personality of its ruler, in such a land political murder as a means of struggle presents a manifestation of that despotic spirit we aim to destroy in Russia ... Violence may be justified only when it is directed against violence.

Vera Figner, Vera Zasulich, Sofiya Perovskaya and numerous other women terrorists who had run away from their aristocratic and bourgeois families, often faking fictitious marriages with their male comrades, were far more concerned with destroying the pillars of the autocracy and reforming society than setting up utopian communes or workplace crèches and the like. They were undoubtedly pioneers of gender equality, but articulating a sexually liberated feminism or bringing about a revolutionary transformation in the conditions of the women being recruited in large numbers to work in factories did not interest them a great deal.

For that, it is to their Octobrist successors that we must now turn, for it was they (and some of their male comrades) who would renew the ideas of the Ranters, the dissidents fleeing the tyranny of the Church and the women of the Paris Commune.

13

The Octobrist Women

Women played a major part in both of the revolutions of 1917, and to a much greater extent than they had in 1905. The February uprising was, in fact, triggered by the strike of women in the textile industry in their dual roles as workers and, in many cases, the wives of soldiers at the front. They sent appeals to the metal workers to join them and, by the end of the day, over 50,000 workers were marching in the streets of the capital. They were joined by housewives marching to the Duma demanding bread. It was International Women's Day (8 March by the Gregorian calendar), that the Bolshevik activist Konkordia Samoilova had made known to Russians in 1913 and that had been celebrated, observed and marked from that year onwards. It was usually a smallish public event in a few cities. Celebrating it with a mass strike led by women workers was unprecedented. There was a special irony involved: Russia's capitalists had assumed that since women were the most oppressed, docile and socially backward (in the sense that unlike the terrorist women of previous decades, a large majority were illiterate) group in Russian society, they would, according to capitalist logic, make the most obedient and trouble-free members of the workforce. This was a miscalculation. As the First World War continued, so did the need for more labour. The percentage of women in the factories doubled and trebled. The Putilov arms industry was also producing the most militant workers and Bolshevik organisers, female and male.

In Moscow, too, women workers were becoming radicalised. One of them, Anna Litveiko, eighteen years old in 1917, later described the process in a brief memoir. She and two friends roughly the same age were working in the Elektrolampa factory in Moscow's industrial belt. She recalled her father returning home in 1905 from the last barricade left in the city 'all beaten up, his clothes torn and his pockets full of cartridges'. This time it was different. Many soldiers and Cossacks were on their side. In October, choices had to be made. Which side were they on? Menshevik or Bolshevik? Anna admired the two Bolshevik organisers who worked with her. In this factory the Mensheviks sent intellectuals to address them from the outside, 'but then I was told that it was often the other way round – Mensheviks were the workers and Bolsheviks the intellectuals. How could I figure it out?'

One day she waited for one of the Bolsheviks and asked: 'What is the difference between the Bolsheviks and Mensheviks?' He replied:

> You see, the tsar has been kicked out, but the burzhuis [bourgeois] have stayed and grabbed all the power. The Bolsheviks are the ones who want to fight the burzhuis to the end. The Mensheviks are neither one thing nor the other.

Anna decided that 'if it was to the end, then I was going to sign up with the Bolsheviks.' Her two friends soon followed suit.[1]

None of the participants or the leaders of the clandestine political parties embedded in the capital had any idea that it was the first day of a revolution, except for the women office workers overheard by Sukhanov soon after he arrived at work that morning. The women came out the next day as well and this time, so did the men. And the parties of the left were now wide awake, writing, printing and distributing leaflets, most of which were similar in

---

1 Anna Litveiko, 'In 1917', in Sheila Fitzpatrick and Yuri Slezkine, eds, *In the Shadow of Revolution: Life Stories of Russian Women*, tr. Yuri Slezkine, Princeton, 2000, pp. 49–53. This fascinating book includes the memoirs of SR women and those who sided with the Whites in the civil war.

tone except for those of the Bolsheviks, who also demanded peace and an immediate end to the imperialist war. By that weekend the soft breeze had turned into a storm. Sukhanov, now out on the streets taking notes and savouring the situation, overheard two unsympathetic bystanders. 'What do they want?' said one grim-looking fellow. Back came the reply from his lookalike: 'They want bread, peace with the Germans, and equality for the Yids.' Bull's-eye, thought the future historian, expressing his delight at this 'brilliant formulation of the programme of the great revolution'.

There were only two women members of the Bolshevik Central Committee in 1917: Alexandra Kollontai and Elena Stasova. Varvara Yakovleva joined a year later and was minister for education in 1922, later becoming minister for finance. The Mensheviks were not much better. The numerical contrast with the terrorist People's Will could not have been more striking, but even their successor, the Social Revolutionary (SR) Party, showed how much had changed in the new century. The proportion of women in their leading bodies, too, had registered a very sharp decline, though marginally less so in their secret terrorist wing, the Combat organisation.[2]

The reasons for this were varied. Women workers were being recruited in huge numbers to the industrial combines. A political comparison is equally revealing. Those men and women from the old groups who wanted to maintain their allegiances in different times might have joined the SRs. The majority of them now appeared in public without the mask of terrorism.[3]

---

2   This was disbanded in 1903 when it was revealed that its commander was working for the Okhrana, the tsarist secret police.

3   Two SRs, Alexander Kerensky and Victor Chernov, became leading members of the Provisional Government. Kerensky had always been a moderate and pro-war; Chernov had attended the Zimmerwald Conference and was fond of telling the peasants that once the revolution came, every single landlord and his heirs had to be physically exterminated for any reform to succeed. As an ineffective minister for agriculture in Kerensky's government, the policies he tried to implement were slightly different. Another SR, Fanny Kaplan, tried to assassinate Lenin in August 1918 and almost succeeded.

Alexandre Kollantai (1872–1952): Veteran Bolshevik, only supporter of the *April Theses*; first woman to be appointed ambassador (to Norway).

Elena Stasova (1873–1966): Another veteran Bolshevik and very close to Lenin. She was the party secretary in Petrograd in 1917 and later a Comintern functionary.

Alexandra Kollontai was not the only woman to play an important role in the early Soviet Union, but she was undoubtedly one of the more gifted, and possessed a fiercely independent mind and spirit. It is in her work that we can see the synthesis of revolutionary (socialist, not radical) feminism. She understood better than most the social, political and sexual needs of women's liberation. She could be harsh sometimes in her estimates of women from different class backgrounds, but these views were not shared by many of her comrades, male or female. She was deliberately misinterpreted and painted as a defender of permanent libertinage; in the countryside small landlords used her name to warn poor peasants that if they went along with the plan for collective farming they would have to share the younger women of their families with all other men, while the older women would be reduced to soap.

Kollontai was only too aware of the absurd nature of most of the propaganda and became especially irritated when accused of prioritising sex above love. In her short autobiographical essay 'The Autobiography of a Sexually Emancipated Communist Woman', she explained that love had always played a large part in her life, but that it was a transient experience. More important was the need to 'understand that love was not the main goal of our life and that we knew how to place work at its centre'. She could have added, '... like men do'. She wanted love to be harmoniously combined with work, but 'over and over again, things turned out differently, since the man always tried to impose his ego on us and adapt us fully to his purposes.' The choice was either to accept this position for the sake of life or, by opposing, end it. She explained that since 'love had become a fetter', the only way out was through 'an inevitable inner rebellion ... We felt enslaved and tried to loosen the love-bond.' She claimed not that there was an absence of contradictions in the rush 'toward freedom', but the contrary: 'We were again alone, unhappy, lonesome, but free – free to pursue our beloved chosen ideal work.' It was one of the early core statements of modern feminist values, and one from which the twenty-first century has retreated, despite endless hosannas honouring 'gay marriage'.

Lenin wrote in 1918 that 'from the experience of all liberation movements, it can be noted that the success of a revolution can be measured by the extent of the involvement of women in it.' Virtually all Russian revolutionaries, regardless of faction or party, had always agreed on this. As I discussed in Chapter 12, from the 1860s onwards Russian women played an exemplary role, much more advanced than their sisters in the rest of Europe and on all other continents.

Debates on the role of the nuclear family in town and country and on the function of marriage were more advanced and real in Russia than anywhere else during the late nineteenth and early twentieth centuries. The 1917 revolutions further accelerated this process, since these issues were now no longer abstractions. Concrete measures needed to be taken. Marx, Engels and Bebel had all insisted that capitalism was negating the traditional uses and needs of the family. In peasant societies the family acted as a collective unit of production. Everyone worked, though women did so harder. Clara Zetkin, a leader of the German SPD, using the work of the three elders as a starting point, analysed the differences between a peasant and a proletarian family. The latter, she argued, was a unit of consumption, not production. This was taken further by Soviet theorists after the revolution. For Nikolai Bukharin, the development of capitalism had sown all the seeds necessary for the disintegration of the family: the unit of production shifting to the factory, waged labour for women as well as men and, of course, the peripatetic nature of city life and work. Kollontai agreed that the family was on the edge of extinction. What was crucial for the Bolshevik government was to make the transition to new forms as painless as possible, with the state providing high-quality nurseries, schools, communal eating facilities and help with housework. Lenin strongly supported this point of view. His strictures on the family were characteristically acerbic. He denounced 'the decay, putrescence, and filth of bourgeois marriage with its difficult dissolution, its license for the husband and bondage for the wife, and its disgustingly false sex morality and relations'.

The enemy was always the male partner, who avoided housework and childcare altogether. 'Petty housework', Lenin raged in

1919, 'crushes, strangles, stultifies and degrades, chains her to the kitchen and the nursery, and she wastes her labour on barbarously unproductive, petty, nerve-racking, stultifying and crushing drudgery.' His solutions were the same as those of other revolutionary leaders at the time: collective kitchens, laundries, repair shops, crèches, kindergartens and so forth. But for Lenin, the abolition of domestic slavery did *not* mean the disappearance of individual households or families.

These views were reflected in the architecture of the Constructivists. Moisei Ginzburg's apartment buildings, both large and small, expressed the new epoch. The communal laundries and dining rooms were considered a huge success. The playground for children was visible from every apartment kitchen, and the size of the space could be modified by moving huge hardwood walls on wheels. Ginzburg's vision was, as he explains in his masterwork *Epoch and Style*, greatly inspired by his five years in the Crimea where he had time, despite the civil war, to visit old mosques and other buildings from which he learnt much more than he had ever done in the classical academy in Milan. He described the spontaneous, impulsive architecture of the Tatar people as 'rushing along a natural course, following its bends and irregularities, adding one motif to another with a picturesque spontaneity that conceals a distinct creative order'. The Pravda building in Leningrad, constructed in 1924, on which he happily worked with two other architects, established his reputation as one of the finest exponents of the new culture.[4] His work was soon eclipsed by the time-servers

---

4 In 1986, on one of my last visits to old, pre-oligarch Moscow, I was asked by my hosts at the Writers' Union (then housed in an old nobleman's mansion, close family friends of Tolstoy on whom he had based Natasha's family in *War and Peace*) what I wanted to do on my free day. I asked if I could see Constructivist Moscow. A Tatar architect agreed to be my guide and it turned out to be a truly memorable tour. The buildings were still there, but almost invisible until they were pointed out; I spent a long time in each, with my knowledgeable guide pointing out all the special features. That was when I first heard the name Ginzburg. The special treat was a few miles from the city centre, in what had once been the first new industrial zone after the revolution.

of the Stalin epoch, but mercifully Ginzburg was left alone. He died comfortably in bed in 1946.

The Bolsheviks were extremely proud of their first decrees, most of which were drafted by Lenin. To mark the first anniversary of the revolution in October 1918, the Central Executive Committee of the Soviet unanimously endorsed the new Code on Marriage, the Family and Guardianship. It was drafted by the radical jurist Alexander Goikhbarg, thirty-four years old at the time, who explained that its aim was to propel the 'withering away' of the traditional family. 'Proletarian power', he wrote, at a time when hopes such as his were fairly common, 'constructs its codes and all its laws dialectically, so that every day of their existence undermines the need for their existence.' The aim was a law to 'make law superfluous'. Goikhbarg, a former Menshevik, was basing his ideas on the political philosophy that underlay Lenin's *State and Revolution*. A number of historians have remarked that during the first year of the revolution, it seemed as if the Paris Commune were being rerun.

The new family law was without precedent in history.[5] Tsarist family laws were framed by the needs of the Orthodox Church and other religions when necessary. A comparison with contemporary Saudi Arabia and Wahhabi prescriptions is instructive.

The factories had long disappeared but a medium-sized apartment block for working-class families was still in place. It was truly amazing. A communal laundry was functioning. I was shown a typical apartment. All kitchens had windows from where the children's playground was permanently visible. The hardwood walls on wheels varied the layout according to need. I couldn't help comparing this Jerusalem, with its green space, to most of the brutalist housing blocks in postwar Britain. The lack of imagination in Britain was shocking. Epochs and styles.

5   For a more detailed discussion on this and related issues, I strongly recommend the classic work by Richard Stites, *The Women's Liberation Movement in Russia: Feminism, Nihilism and Bolshevism, 1860–1930*, Princeton, 1978. Equally useful are two more recent studies: Wendy Z. Goldman, *Women, the State and Revolution*, Cambridge, 1993, and Jane McDermid and Anna Hillyar, *Midwives of the Revolution*, London, 1999.

Patriarchal brutality was enforced by the Church with the same vigour. Women needed the permission of men for virtually everything, including a passport. Total obedience was enforced and women had no rights except with regard to property. Western European family laws originating in feudalism proper had instituted 'joint' property, which effectively meant male ownership and domination. The Russian church permitted separate property rights as far as dowries, inheritance, gifts and land were concerned. This is also the case in Saudi Arabia. Women are denied political rights and equality but can own property; businesswomen function perfectly well.

A few months after October 1917, a decree abolished all tsarist laws concerning the family and the criminalisation of sodomy. Women were no longer legally inferior, they had equal rights with men; the religious marriage was invalid and only civil marriages were recognised by law; divorce was to be granted when requested by either partner, and no grounds were considered necessary. Likewise alimony: the same guarantees for both partners. The property laws stretching back centuries were abolished, ending male privileges and removing the stigma of illegitimacy. All children were entitled to equal rights, regardless of parental wedlock. This constituted a radical restructuring of European law by unlinking family obligations from the marriage contract or certificate. Interestingly, private adoptions were disallowed on the grounds that the new state would be a better parent than individual families. Given the preponderance of the peasantry, it was feared that they would facilitate the use of child labour in the countryside. More utopian educators argued that abolishing private adoption was a transitional step towards the state providing childcare for all.

Critics of the new code denounced the measures as a capitulation to bourgeois norms. Goikhbarg wrote, 'They screamed at us: "Registration of marriage, formal marriage, what kind of socialism is this?" ' And N. A. Roslavets, a female Ukrainian delegate to the 1918 Central Executive Committee of the Soviet where the new code was being discussed, was livid at the state having anything to do with marriage at all. It was an individual decision and should be left at that. She denounced the code as 'a bourgeois survival': 'the interference of the state in the business of marriage, even in the form of registration which the Code suggests, is completely incomprehensible, not only in a socialist system, but in the transition', and concluded angrily, 'I cannot understand why this Code establishes compulsory monogamy.' In response Goikhbarg pleaded that she and others must understand that the main reason for having a desacralised code was to provide people who did wish to register a marriage with an alternative to the Church. If the state did not do this, many people, especially in the countryside, would have clandestine church weddings. He won the argument, but after considerable debate.[6]

Meanwhile, in 1919, the revolutionary government set up Zhenotdel (the Department for Work among Women Workers and Peasants), whose aim was the emancipation of women. Its leadership consisted of women who had been active in this field during the crucial prerevolutionary years – Inessa Armand, Alexandra Kollontai, Sofia Smidovich, Konkordia Samoilovna and Klavdiya Nikolaeva – and understood the special needs of women. This women's liberation was not a goal for the majority of women. Social Democrats and both Vera Zasulich and Rosa Luxemburg regarded it as a diversion at a time when humanity as a whole confronted gigantic tasks. The Zhenotdel women did not see themselves as utopians. They simply believed that women's emancipation was one of the tasks that confronted the revolution. None of them thought it could be achieved quickly or even in their lifetimes, but a start had to be made *now* or the issue would simply fade to the background. And immediate action needed to be taken regarding the transfer of household chores and childcare to state institutions. By this they did not mean huge phalansteries, as visualised by Fourier, Chernyshevsky and Bukharin. The women wanted city administrations to provide local institutions, such as free daycare centres, public dining rooms and laundries. This became the subject of a heated debate. Addressing a women's conference in September that year, Lenin

---

6 Goldman, *Women, the State and Revolution*, pp. 55–6.

argued that Zhenotdel's demands and work 'cannot show any rapid results . . . and will not produce a scintillating effect.' Trotsky argued the same in several newspaper articles, citing many examples from working-class life that suggested that caution was necessary, while also defending the idea that abstract propaganda was not enough to transform gender relations. There had to be some deeds, some experiments to show the advantages to all concerned.

In reality it was, alas, the old Bolsheviks (men and women) who turned out to be the utopians. The abolition of private ownership was not enough. The victory of conservatism in the Soviet Union after 1930 led to a 'sexual Thermidor' and the reassertion of 'traditional' women's roles even without changing the laws, except to re-criminalise homosexuality in 1934. In polar contrast, the practical ideas put forward by Zhenotdel were implemented after the end of the civil war by architects designing new housing estates for workers, as explained above.

On a national level Zhenotdel members were extremely active in ensuring that women were not passed over when it came to serving on military revolutionary committees, local party and trade union apparatuses and the political department of the Red Army. Again, the involvement of Russian women in partisan wars and underground terrorism served as an example. Peasant women in 1812 had often dispatched the French soldiers who had been cut off from Napoleon's army using scythes or pitchforks, or simply by burning them alive.

During the civil war many women served as political commissars and nurses in the field hospitals. Partisan life was rough, but women liked the equality they enjoyed with the men, a tradition that would be highlighted once again during the Second World War. Richard Stites describes how 'captured nurses were often treated with special brutality by the Whites. Near Petrograd in 1919, three nurses were hanged in bandages from the beams of their field hospital with their Komsomol [Young Communist] pins stuck through their tongues.' And thousands of women served in the Red Army and 'fought on every front and with every weapon, serving as riflewomen, armoured train commanders, gunners'.[7] They also became spies. Lenin was extremely impressed by reports from Odessa and Baku that the more educated Red Army women had effectively confronted French and British soldiers fighting alongside the Whites and argued in the soldier's own languages against foreign interventionism. He ordered the creation of a special school for espionage and disorganisation. This was situated in a large Moscow house under the command of the legendary Georgian revolutionary Kamo, whose exploits in the anti-tsarist underground were legion. Those who passed through the school (many of whom were women, including the gifted Larissa Reisner) formed the First Partisan Special Purpose Detachment.[8]

It was on other emancipatory fronts that the Bolshevik feminists encountered serious resistance. There were huge problems when they set up modest headquarters in the Caucasus and Central Asia or, for that matter, in the Ukraine. Local women were frightened and shy. The men threatened the feminists with violence, even if their wives were simply being taught to read in one of the Zhenotdel 'reading cabins'.

After a trip to the Caucasus in 1920, Clara Zetkin reported to Zhenotdel headquarters what women had told her after weeks spent convincing them to speak:

> We were silent slaves. We had to hide in our rooms and cringe before our husbands, who were our lords.
>
> Our fathers sold us at the age of ten, even younger. Our husband would beat us with a stick and whip us when he felt like it. If he wanted to freeze us, we froze. Our daughters, a joy to us and a help around the house, he sold, just as we had been sold.

The work done by lower-echelon Zhenotdel women throughout the country undoubtedly bore fruit. It laid the foundations for

---

7 Stites, *The Women's Liberation Movement in Russia*, p. 318.

8 Cathy Porter, *Larissa Reisner: A Biography*, London, 1988. Porter is also the author of another riveting biography of a Soviet revolutionary feminist: *Alexandra Kollontai*, London, 2013.

imposing a strict system of gender equality in even the most socially backward regions of the young Soviet Union.[9] These courageous and self-confident women confronted the men head-on without any weapons or guards. Three Zhenotdel cadres were killed 'by bandits'. In the heart of a Muslim city, they showed a film depicting a Muslim heroine who refused to wed an old man who had bought her. In Baku, women coming out of a Zhenotdel club were attacked by men with wild dogs (there was not much difference between the two) and defaced with boiling water. A twenty-year-old Muslim woman, proud that she had liberated herself, went to bathe in a swimsuit. She was sliced to pieces by her father and brothers because it 'insulted their dignity'. There were 300 similar murders ('counterrevolutionary offences', as far as the state was concerned) over three months in 1929 alone. But despite patriarchal terror, the women won in the end. Hundreds of Muslim and other women in these regions began to volunteer as translators and office workers in the Zhenotdel offices. And there are extremely affecting reports of how on every May Day and International Women's Day, thousands of women would *voluntarily* and insolently cast off their veils. Nor did they ever look back. Self-emancipation was the model suggested by Zhenotdel, not state imposition. And it happened.

A number of leading Bolsheviks had been opposed to Zhenotdel. Rykov, heavily engaged with the predominantly male trade unions, demanded that Zhenotdel be disbanded because it was divisive. Zinoviev opposed even summoning the Women's Congress of 1919. Others wanted to use it as a way of sidelining Bolshevik women and leaving the 'real' party to the men, which was more or less the case anyway. Elena Stasova, the party secretary in October 1917, was removed from her position when the capital moved to

---

9   Muslim women from the old Soviet Republics are amongst the best-educated in the entire world of Islam and completely integrated as doctors, professors, teachers, pilots, lawyers and so forth. I met two of them at a conference on Islam some years ago, where they were spiritedly defending modernity against some relativists. I asked who they were and one of them replied: 'We're old Soviet women.'

Moscow. She was angry (even though her successor Jacob Sverdlov was the most gifted organiser available) and refused to be shunted to Zhenotdel, becoming one of the political secretaries in Lenin's office. Lenin himself vigorously defended Zhenotdel against all forms of reductionism. In what was probably his last interview on the subject (his interlocutor was Clara Zetkin), he responded angrily when she informed him that many 'good comrades' were hostile to any notion of the party creating special bodies for 'systematic work among women'. They argued that everyone needed to be emancipated, not just women, and that Lenin had surrendered to opportunism on this question. Zetkin writes:

> 'That is neither new nor proof,' said Lenin. 'You must not be misled by that. Why have we never had as many women as men in the party – not at any time in Soviet Russia? Why is the number of women organised in trade unions so small? Facts give food for thought ... That is why it is right for us to put forward demands favourable to women ... Our demands are practical conclusions which we have drawn from the burning needs, the shameful humili-ation of women in bourgeois society, defenceless and without rights ... We recognise these needs and are sensible to the humilia-tion of women, the privileges of the man. That we hate, yes, hate everything, and will abolish everything which tortures and oppresses the woman worker, the housewife, the peasant woman, the wife of the petty trader, yes, and in many cases the women from the possess-ing classes.'[10]

Sexuality was another battleground. But this was not a new debate. From the 1860s onwards there had been strong differ-ences of opinion amongst liberals, Populists, terrorists and social-ists. Chernyshevsky, known for his abstract and utopian fictional communes, revealed a more practical side. When informed in prison that his wife was trying out a few lovers in his absence, he defended her strongly on the grounds that if he could and had,

---

10   Clara Zetkin, *Reminiscenses of Lenin*, London, 1929, pp. 64–5.

why shouldn't she? Tolstoy tended to define non-procreative sex as 'lust' and preached the virtues of celibacy, especially in *The Kreutzer Sonata*. Within Russian Social Democracy, Alexandra Kollontai was one of the principal champions of women's social, political and sexual liberation. She became a symbol of 'free love'. For this she was maligned at home and abroad. The vilest slurs were hurled at her and the worst offenders were often Western scholars, otherwise reasonably restrained. Pitirim Sorokin, observing the country post-1917, accused her of 'sexual sadism', writing in his diary that 'her revolutionary enthusiasm is nothing but a gratification of her sexual satyriasis.' For Robert Daniels she was 'the mistress of Shlyapnikov (among others, as she practiced what she preached)'. E. H. Carr found it difficult to mask his hostility, informing readers that she 'preached the uninhibited satisfaction of the sexual impulse, supported by the assumption that it was the business of the state to take care of the consequences'.[11]

Sexuality was not a taboo subject, but Marx, Engels and Bebel had assumed that true liberation on this front would come with the establishment of a Communist society. The victory of a revolution made by Marxists had, according to some, telescoped the process and begun the transition to heterosexual liberation. Kollontai had written essays and fiction in 1922–23 underlining the new moral turn. Sexual intimacy would only be regulated by individual needs. It was not the business of the state or of any authority. She was denounced for preaching a utopian feminism that was impossible to achieve or, for some, simply wrong. Given the chaotic conditions in the country, middle-aged party leaders (among others) would argue that it was the government's duty to discipline or channel youthful energies to prevent the exploitation of young women. Alarmed by the ferocity of the attacks, Kollontai retreated and accepted the post of Soviet ambassador to Norway,

---

11   Carr's hypocrisy is astounding. It's hardly a secret that the old goat found it difficult to control his own 'sexual impulses' and since the British state did not recognise illegitimacy, he would have had a few problems regarding consequences.

becoming the first woman ever to be entrusted with such a senior diplomatic post. Zhenotdel, too, stepped back under attack and agreed to concentrate on more practical and political work, leaving theory aside for the moment. Despite this, they refused to accept Bukharin's views on the transformative capacities of the new state's centralised institutions. For them, self-activity and self-emancipation though democratic debate and collective action was the way forward. In 1927, three years before Stalin disbanded them, a text by Sofia Smidovich (herself a veteran of the revolution) to commemorate the tenth anniversary of the October Revolution spelt out the essentials of Zhenotdel's aims in a single paragraph:

> The satisfaction of all needs; the possibility that every person can develop his or her natural proclivity towards participation in this or that field, his or her corresponding tastes and inclinations; the full freedom from each and every oppression of person by person and the new conquest of all the new possibilities in the struggle with the forces of nature and new victories over it; and the development of the many-sided potentialities of the human personality – these, approximately, are the basic features of that bright, true, still distant future ... Is this possible under conditions of the oppression of women?[12]

It was not to be. The Komsomol and student experiments in 'free love' had, according to some in the Politburo, degenerated into frenzied, free-for-all, male-dominated fornication,[13] though whether this was a balanced view is still the subject of debate. The troika of leaders – Stalin, Zinoviev and Kamenev – had been startled by the number of Communist cells in the universities that

---

12 Quoted in Barbara Evans Clements, 'The Utopianism of the Zhenotdel', *Slavic Review* 51: 3, Autumn 1992, p. 493.

13 And not just young men. The older Anatole Lunacharsky used his position at the Ministry of Culture to prey on as many Bolshoi ballerinas as he could, an old tsarist tradition that continued into the late Brezhnev years and probably still exists.

passed resolutions agreeing with Trotsky's critique in *Pravda* of the growing bureaucratisation of party and state. The Politburo started referring to petty-bourgeois tendencies, to which Trotsky replied that up to the day before they had been referring to the crucial 'barometer of youth' as a necessary guide to judge the progress of the revolution. It is difficult to know the extent to which this affected the line on sexuality as well.

What is undeniable is that more than a few young women did not like the over-casual attitude towards sex imported into the campuses by demobilised soldiers at the end of the civil war. This attitude was also present among more bohemian offenders, members of Proletkult and the Mayakovsky cult who adopted the poet's black leather overcoats, his erect demeanour and the devil-take-you arrogance that made him and his poetry extremely popular with the young. Lenin disliked Mayakovsky's poetry intensely, preferring Pushkin, but the poet was unfazed. He used to ask in public, and rightly, how literary and artistic forms could remain unchanged in the middle of a revolution. Nor was this Lenin's only inconsistency.

All this did not benefit many young women on any level. Contraception was either unavailable or primitive; one woman suggested that the male motto should be 'Liberty, Equality, Maternity'. The 'winged Eros' of Kollontai was conveniently misinterpreted. She had argued for free relationships based on love. But a Komsomol leader portrayed much later in a short story sounded a bit more evocative of the period: 'Down with the capitalist tyranny of parents! Kiss and embrace! ... Free love is for free.' Or did he?

The historian Sheila Fitzpatrick has written convincingly that there was no fixed pattern of sexuality in real, everyday life in the 1920s, though people did feel much freer and less inhibited. Many of the students entering universities, especially from proletarian or Red Army backgrounds, tended to be older and often married. Marital separation was given as the cause for most cases of 'adultery'. Surveys carried out in Moscow, Omsk and Odessa uncovered a great many 'infidelities' and while more men admitted to this than women, the latter were sometimes refreshingly open. A young, 'technically faithful' woman in Odessa confessed that 'besides having a husband, I am attracted to other men who interest me.' Her sexual activities were confined to kissing, since 'the sexual act as such has no particular interest for me. My family relations do not suffer from this.' And her spouse?

> I can't guarantee my husband here, since all are great believers in private property [i.e., wives/partners as property], even the Communists, and they will never draw conclusions. They don't want to understand and agree. Men themselves can sow wild oats but wives, Allah forbid, can't. I am answering in kind; I am behaving as men do.[14]

Same-sex love did not enter the discussion at all. Tsarist laws had been repealed and homosexuals were left alone, though public debate might have benefited many who saw this orientation as an illness, including Gyorgy Chicherin, the commissar for foreign affairs, an authority on classical music, fluent in all the major European languages and one of the most cultivated members of the Bolshevik leadership. This intelligent man, during the prerevolutionary years in exile, spent many hours with German doctors to find a 'cure' for his homosexuality, finally giving up in despair. Kollontai, a close friend, described him sublimating his desires by working long, hard and, no doubt, tormented hours at the foreign ministry and later the Comintern.

Homosexuality was outlawed in Russia by Peter the Great, who mimicked European modernity on every level. He had been told that the discipline of the 'military and naval revolutions' in Great Britain required criminalising sodomy. He followed suit. The Church pressured Nicholas I to extend the law to the male population as a whole and not restrict the ban to the armed services. He did as the Church asked. Naturally none of this had any serious impact on same-sex activities in the navy, the army, the Church or the rest of society. Numerous sites for these pleasures existed in

---

14 Sheila Fitzpatrick, 'Sex and Revolution: Soviet Students in the 1920s', *Journal of Modern History* 50, June 1978, pp. 252–78.

most cities, and coaches were a much-favoured vehicle in this regard for both men and women.

What would the revolution do about it? Apart from decriminalisation (which did not happen in Western Europe and North America till the 1960s), not much. There were debates, and some psychiatrists opined that while it was a 'pathological condition', it need not be stigmatised harshly as had been done before. It was a perversion, but not a perversity. And, in any case, medical advances would solve everything. This was only one view. Decriminalisation was in force from 1918 onwards. Three years after the shuttering of Zhenotdel, homosexuality was, once again, made a criminal offence. The fact that homosexuality existed within the German Nazi Party was utilised in Soviet homophobic rhetoric, which included gems such as implying that gays were more vulnerable to becoming foreign spies, failing to see that criminalisation was more likely to make people susceptible to blackmail. But the upper echelons of the Nazi Party were not staffed by homosexuals, as claimed by some Soviet propagandists. Only in the SA was there a significant number of gay men in leadership positions, due partly to the strong *Männerbund* culture that dated back to the war and partly to Röhm's promotion of like-minded colleagues. In 1934, the celebrated *Brown Book* on the Reichstag trial fostered the 'gay Nazi' myth (Van der Lubbe was falsely characterised as homosexual and 'therefore' linked to the Nazis), and so, ironically, did the explicitly anti-homosexual 'Night of the Long Knives'. Though this served as a justification for Soviet homophobic rhetoric, the Stalin regime's new emphasis on a 'soldierly' male culture (including, for example, its abolition of co-education) was equally responsible for generating it.

Official homophobia reached its polluted peak with the following outburst by Commissar for Justice N. V. Krylenko in March 1936 to the Central Executive Committee:

In our environment, in the environment of the workers taking the point of view of normal relations between the sexes, who are building their society on healthy principles, we don't need little gentlemen [*gospodchiki*] of this type. Who then for the most part are our customers in these affairs? Workers? No! Declassed rabble [*mirth-ful animation in the hall, laughter*]. Declassed rabble, either from the dregs of society or from the remnants of the exploiting classes. [*Applause*] They don't know which way to turn. [*Laughter*] So they turn to . . . pederasty. [*Laughter*][15]

In 1936 the Soviet state banned abortions in order to promote 'family responsibility'. Incentives were provided for childbearing; divorce was made more difficult; enhanced maternity leave was offered for working women; more childcare centres were built and criminal prosecutions were instituted for men who refused to pay alimony. A much-circulated Moscow joke of the period had a judge insisting that more alimony be paid:

'You must pay a second "third",' said the judge.
   'I can't, I'm already paying that too,' the man replied.
   'Well, then you must pay a third "third".'
   'I can't. I'm paying that too.'
   'What do you mean,' asked the judge. 'You're paying all your wages to former wives? Then what are you living on?'
   'I'm living on the alimony my wife is getting from five other men,' the man replied.

---

15   Quoted in Dan Healey, *Homosexual Desire in Revolutionary Russia*, Chicago and London, 2001, p. 196. This is an extremely valuable, well-documented and comprehensive history of the subject, from which I have certainly learnt a great deal. During the Brezhnev period in the late Soviet Union, the homophobic law travelled to Cuba where homosexuality was decriminalised only recently, an outrage when everyone knows that the country's most beloved martyr is José Martí, who was gay. As for Krylenko, he was always slightly deranged, demanding, for instance, a five-year plan to teach Soviet proletarian chess that could never be defeated by the class enemy. Despite his blind loyalty to Stalin, he was arrested in late 1938, confessed to being a foreign agent and was executed. Earlier, his sister had left the country and married Max Eastman, close to Trotsky and his English translator. Might this have been the real reason for charging Krylenko with spying for foreign powers? We'll never know.

It was a Stalinist joke reflecting the undeniable fact that the wheel had turned full circle. The first years of the revolution now appeared utopian to many of its critics, who began to yearn for its uncertainties and debates. The days when cartoonists could depict a heavily pregnant Virgin Mary queuing eagerly for a Soviet abortion were long gone.

A persistent homophobic strand in Russian culture (whether or not a Freudian 'denegation' of widespread homosexual practices among Russian men) remains to this day. The resurgence of Orthodoxy in the post-Soviet era has given this a political voice. The Duma and regional legislatures have passed various anti-gay measures. But calls to ban homosexuality have been rejected by Putin, who has said publicly on several occasions that he has nothing against gay people, and, despite harassment, there is quite a flourishing gay life in major Russian cities.

14

Sunlight and Moonlight

In the course of a mid-nineteenth-century public debate on the need for women's education and reform of the existing system, one of the feminist participants, Nadezhda Stasova, characterised the new generation of Russian women as those who 'desired not the moonlight, but rather the sunlight'. Her niece, Elena Stasova, who joined the Bolshevik Party and served temporarily as its secretary in 1917, felt the same, and even more strongly. Another Nadezhda – Nadya Krupskaya – had, together with Elena, taught workers at a radical Sunday school in St Petersburg before both women joined the Emancipation of Labour Group, the RSDLP and later its Bolshevik faction. Krupskaya agreed to become Lenin's fiancée and accompany him to Siberian exile, but insisted that her mother come too. This was definitely a first in Russian revolutionary history. Exiles were common, and aristocratic wives accompanying their husbands to share a tiny room in a snow desert became the stuff of poetry, fiction and plays, especially in relation to the Decembrists. In a later period, fictitious 'marriages' enabling radical young Populist women to leave home and, often, accompany their 'husbands' to exile were not uncommon. Many of these women remained celibate. They were wedded to the cause, to the revolution and Chernyshevskian ethical principles. But a future mother-in-law accompanying a revolutionary couple? This had not happened before. It puzzled both Lenin and his family. His mother was quite disapproving of the whole business, but accepted that her son needed

Inessa and her children from her marriage to Alexander Armand, Brussels, 1909.

companionship and, since there was no alternative, agreed grumpily to the arrangement.[1]

And young Lenin? He wondered what the future held in store on this front, and booked an extra room for mother and daughter. Obviously he knew Nadya Krupskaya, but as a comrade. He'd been more attracted to three of her friends. Nina Gerd had not shown any interest in him and married Peter Struve instead, Lidya Davidova had preferred Michael Tugan-Barovsky, and Elena Stasova, according to some, did have a brief episode with Lenin which didn't work out, although they remained close comrades until his death. Krupskaya has left no account of this early period of love, courtship or whatever else it might have been. The first time she and Lenin met was at an underground political meeting,

---

1   His mother knew only too well that Lenin was not interested in cooking and that his later verbal references to creating a state that 'even a cook could run' were not references to himself. His insistence on communal kitchens, laundries and so forth was yet another indication of his own shortcomings in the domestic field.

in St Petersburg in 1894, to discuss the role of markets and the economic content of Populism. Not a subject conducive to holding hands under the table. The event was organised as a pancake party. A liberal attendee asked the others to distribute leaflets from the Committee for Ending Illiteracy. Krupskaya herself was very Tolstoyan on such matters and believed in missionary work. She was taken aback by Lenin's sarcastic response to the liberal's request: 'Something evil and arid sounded in his laugh – I never heard him laugh that way again.' Others did. They never forgot it either. Lenin's sarcasm was widely commented on by both comrades and enemies. In her memoirs of Lenin, Krupskaya writes that by 'the winter of 1894–1895, I had already got to know Vladimir Ilyich fairly intimately'. What she meant is that they both taught the same workers at different study circles. The growing intimacy was with his political ideas and methods. There is no indication of anything else. Had there been, one of Lenin's sisters would have informed Krupskaya's mother and a few friends. For unexplained reasons and unlike his younger siblings Maria and Dmitri, Lenin's older sister Anna never became close to Krupskaya. As for passion, there is no hint of it on Lenin's side. On his insistence, Krupskaya burnt all his letters to her that dealt with more personal matters.

The Siberian exile for the young couple was successful. The fictitious was made real on both sexual and legal fronts. The authorities had threatened to end the arrangement unless there was a proper marriage, and a deadline was set. Cheap copper rings made by a local peasant craftsman were found, as was a monk to preside over the ceremony. The couple were undoubtedly attached to each other. One reason for this was her monumental efficiency and organisational skills. The flow of books on which he was dependent for writing *The Development of Capitalism in Russia* rarely stopped.

After he was released, Krupskaya still had time to serve. So they returned to Ufa with her mother. The organisation suggested foreign exile for Lenin, so that political work for the party and his own intellectual work could be continued without hindrances. Production of a Social Democratic newspaper was the main priority. Krupskaya joined him after she was freed, and her mother followed soon after. The exile lasted seventeen years. Munich, Zurich, Brussels, London, Warsaw and Tampere beckoned. As did Paris.

Inessa Armand at the time her relationship with
Lenin began.

It was here in 1909 that he first met Inessa Armand. The moonlight beckoned. She was a Bolshevik feminist who had just lost her equally radical partner (Vladimir Armand). Having gone to visit her in the Artic Circle where she was exiled, he contracted tuberculosis, later dying in the South of France despite his hopes that a sojourn there might help him recover. Inessa Armand decided to stay in Paris for a while and reestablished contact with an old friend, Elena Vlasova, who was living there. Armand had read Lenin's articles and books, and *What Is to Be Done?* in particular had impressed her a great deal. She could almost picture the character of the man who had written those words. She went to hear him speak at the Bolshevik café on Avenue d'Orléans. It was the month of May and Paris was at its most attractive. Before proceeding further, a brief literary digression is necessary.

Some years prior to this fortuitous encounter in Paris, while Krupskaya and Lenin were in Geneva, a handful of young Bolsheviks – Vorovsky, Gusev and Volsky (Valentinov) – were also in the city for political work, which effectively meant listening to Lenin, acting as couriers for illegal documents and papers and so on. Lenin was in a relaxed and open mood in discussions; when the work of Turgenev came up, all agreed that he was a fine writer, despite being a liberal. The following day, Lenin was absent; Krupskaya told the assembled group that she and Lenin had improved their German in Siberia by translating Turgenev into that language. She recounted:

> On Ilyich's insistence we translated with particular care a few pages from *Andrei Kolosov*. He had been particularly drawn to this story as far back as his schooldays and thought very highly of it. He felt that Turgenev showed here, absolutely correctly and in a few lines, how to understand properly what is rather pompously called the 'sanctity' of love. He often told me that his views on this question were exactly the same as those expressed by Turgenev.

This piece of information startled the young men. Volsky recounts that he 'got hold of *Andrei Kolosov* and reread it'. His verdict confirmed the accuracy of his first response. It was 'a weak and insipid story, generally disregarded by everyone'. He was genuinely puzzled as to what Lenin could possibly have found in it to affect him so deeply. The storyline is almost banal. Kolosov is an 'uncommon' man. Why? Because he fell in love with a girl, then fell out of love and left her. What turns out to be 'uncommon' is that he did so boldly and honestly, which impresses Turgenev, one of nature's weaklings. It is the passage below that Lenin obviously liked and described as 'revolutionary', so different from the 'vulgar bourgeois view on relations between men and women':

How many of us have been able to break with the past in good time? Who, tell me, is not afraid of reproaches – I do not mean the reproaches of the woman, but the reproaches of the first fool of an onlooker? Which of us has not yielded to the desire to appear magnanimous, or selfishly to play with the devoted heart of another? Finally, how many of us have the strength not to give way to petty *amour propre* and to such petty feelings as pity and remorse? … A person who breaks with a woman whom he once loved, at that bitter, great moment when he involuntarily recognises that his heart is no longer completely filled by her, that person[,] believe me, understands more deeply the sanctity of love than the faint-hearted who from boredom or weakness continue to play on the half-broken strings of their lukewarm and sentimental hearts … At a certain age, to be natural is to be uncommon.[2]

At the time when Lenin and Krupskaya were translating these lines into German, they had recently become lovers. Was this his way of telling her that when it was over he would be as 'uncommon' as Kolosov? It's difficult to say because she destroyed all the clues, but how did these lines make him feel in Paris when he realised that he'd fallen in love with Armand? Lenin's canonisation has kept most biographers away from such matters. His school

---

2 Nikolay Valentinov (N. V. Volsky), *Encounters with Lenin,* trs Paul Rosta and Brian Pearce, Oxford, 1968. Volsky was a lifelong socialist from an old landed family. He broke with Lenin after a huge row over philosophy and became a stern critic. This is why his memoir of Lenin, despite many disagreements one might have with it, is honest and unaffected compared to the hundreds of hagiographies published after Lenin's death whose only use is as doorstops. For me it's one of the finest books on Lenin. Towards the end, when the subject of his book lay dying, Volsky wrote to him suggesting a short meeting. He got a reply from Lenin's sister, Maria, saying her brother also hoped for a meeting. But it was too late.

adventures have never been written about, though soon after 1917 it would have been relatively easy to interview his friends and acquaintances, both male and female, and get their reminiscences on record. Lenin, who genuinely loathed trivia of every sort, would have raged and roared had he found out, but he had other things on his mind and, in any case, the task of a good biographer is to try and uncover everything. What is actually published is, of course, a matter of judgement. His sister Anna's notes on the family were published in Russian but never translated, and while she provided some interesting material, she kept well away from subjects she knew would annoy him.

The most detailed conversation with him on sexuality, free love, monogamy and linked subjects, including the much-discussed theory of sex being as simple and inconsequential as drinking a glass of water, was published after his death by Clara Zetkin in her seventy-eight-page *Reminiscences of Lenin*, based on two lengthy meetings with him. On the question of sexuality and its transformation in postcapitalist societies, Lenin stood by his traditional Bebel/Engels positions, with a sprinkling of Marx. His prudishness was not uncommon in those times. Despite their relative autonomy from the class struggle, it was still important to view the new struggles for women's rights and sexual liberation within the overall framework of a total social transformation, he argued. Otherwise the debate would become unbalanced. The news that the German comrades in Hamburg were planning a special paper for prostitutes to incorporate them into the revolutionary movement startled him. He wondered aloud whether this should be a priority at the present time. Zetkin agreed that it should not, but insisted that the question of prostitution could not simply be swept under the carpet – there were important issues at stake. Lenin's response was not unthoughtful:

> Rosa acted and felt as a Communist when in an article she championed the cause of the prostitutes who were imprisoned for any transgression of police regulations in carrying on their dreary trade. They are, unfortunately, doubly sacrificed by bourgeois society. First by its accursed property system, and secondly by its accursed

moral hypocrisy. That's obvious. Only he who is brutal and short-sighted can forget it. But still, that is not at all the same thing as considering prostitutes – how shall I put it? – to be a special revolutionary militant section, as organising them and publishing a factory paper for them. Aren't there really any other working women in Germany to organise?[3]

In the same interview Lenin suggested that behaving like either a Don Juan or a monk or the 'middle-road adopted by the German philistines' was unacceptable. One assumes that by the middle-road he meant the hypocrisy and lies on the part of the German SPD leaders. Lenin's own position was one of a mutually agreed-upon monogamy without any legal inhibitions. The glass-of-water debate was raging in the aftermath of the revolution, but no one – not Kollontai, Zetkin or Armand – has ever admitted to having originated the expression. It could have been used verbally in the heat of debate by anyone. Whatever its origin, Lenin used it regularly in his own arguments with the proponents of free love. With Zetkin he suggested that a discussion on the 'real innovation of marriage and

---

3　Clara Zetkin, *Reminiscenses of Lenin*, London, 1929, pp. 50–4. There is a related question. Prostitutes don't constitute a vital segment of either the means or the forces of production, but as working women they are perfectly capable of becoming, and do become, politicised. During the huge uprising in Pakistan in 1968–69, many prostitutes came out to the main streets and joined the demonstrators who brought down the dictatorship.

Some even boasted of going on strike against the pro-dictatorship politicians. During the Vietnam War, many call girls and their colleagues on lower levels worked actively for the political goals of the National Liberation Front, and sent important information on US movements to help the NLF prepare for the next offensive. Similar examples during the Chinese civil war that preceded the revolution have been documented. A series of interviews with prostitutes filmed in Tehran a few decades ago revealed real anger at the hypocrisy of mullahs who come and 'jump on us with their two-ton beards just after returning from Muharram and other religious festivals'. It's the political temperature of a society that determines the consciousness of many different social layers.

sexual relations' after a revolution is badly needed, but should be delayed a bit since 'other problems are more urgent than the marriage forms of Maoris or incest in olden times. The question of Soviets is still on the agenda of the German proletariat', and the effect of the Versailles Treaty imposed on a defeated Germany had been disastrous for working women.

As their conversation shifted to the conditions prevailing in the postrevolutionary Soviet Union, Lenin turned a bit despondent. Of course he agreed on the repulsive hypocrisies of bourgeois marriage, he told Zetkin, but some of 'our most promising young people' are rethinking the 'relations between man and man, between man and woman'. 'Feelings and thoughts are becoming revolutionised,' but 'the matter is still in a state of chaotic ferment.' He knew all this, he told her, but was still disturbed by the fact that sexual obsession had so many young people in its thrall. Partially this was a generational response, but there were some reasons for concern (as discussed above).

Lenin then raised, once again, the never disappearing subject of which Zetkin must have been aware:

The famous theory that in Communist society the satisfaction of sexual desires, of love, will be as simple and unimportant as drinking a glass of water. This glass-of-water theory has made our young people mad, quite mad. It has proved fatal to many young boys and girls. Its adherents maintain it is Marxist.

The latter contention provoked a few characteristic sarcasms such as this: 'But thanks for such Marxism which directly and immediately attributes all phenomena and changes in the ideological superstructure of society to its economic basis.' After this comes the pronouncement: 'I think the glass-of-water theory is completely un-Marxist, and moreover anti-social.' Drinking water is an individual choice, 'but in love two lives are concerned, and a third, a new life arises. It is that which gives it its social interest, which gives rise to a duty towards the community.'

Lenin's partial solution – 'healthy sport, swimming, racing, walking, bodily exercises of every kind and many-sided intellectual interests' – was Victorian in character, and still in force in most English private schools. Its effect, as many have described, was repressive; it drove sex underground, treated it as sordid or linked to procreation and restricted sex before marriage to 'out-of-bounds' brothels. This was obviously not Lenin's design, but, consistent with this attitude, he lambasted a young comrade whose name Zetkin discreetly withheld. The boy was, according to Lenin, 'a splendid boy, and highly talented', but seemed to be in a self-destructive state in which 'he reels and staggers from one love affair to the next.' That 'will not do for the political struggle, for the revolution'.[4] Then, for gender evenhandedness, he 'wouldn't bet on the reliability, the endurance in the struggle of those women who confuse their personal romance with politics'. At this point, Zetkin informs us that he 'sprang up, banged his hand on the table, and paced the room for a while'.

Who was he thinking of? Just the young? Even during this inter-view, as they were discussing the function of women inside the party, he confessed to Zetkin how he wished that Comrade Inessa were present but that unfortunately she was resting in the Crimea. He did not add, '. . . on my instructions'.

So what happened at the Bolshevik Café des Manilleurs, at 11 Avenue d'Orléans in Paris, on that summer's day in 1909 when Armand first heard Lenin speak and was introduced to him after-wards? Nothing, according to her two biographers, and that is undoubtedly the case. One of them, however, insists that nothing ever happened between Armand and Lenin, which raises the ques-tion of why he wrote her biography in the first place. The other pieces together all the circumstantial evidence and states the oppo-site. He has the advantage of having met Armand's direct descend-ants and discovered that within the family, her affair with Lenin was not a secret. Nor was it for a close circle of Lenin's comrades in exile. In fact, the only reason for the mystery is Lenin's

---

4   In Zetkin's place one could have asked: 'What if a young person temporarily gives up on sport and exercises for a while and gets on with sex instead? That would leave him more time for the revolution, wouldn't it?'

secretiveness on *all* matters personal and the hagiographers who transformed him, after death, into a Byzantine saint, holy, infallible, pure and only designed to be worshipped. This is the tragedy of the global Lenin cult.

Armand's story is remarkable. She was born in Paris in an apartment on the Rue de la Chapelle in May 1874. There were railway yards in its vicinity and she grew to like the noise of the trains and the chatter of workmen. Her parents were opera singers, though not stars by any stretch of the imagination. Sometimes her father did a turn at the circus as well. Her parents rehearsed a great deal and music was almost always playing in the background in the tiny apartment. When both parents died, an aunt who worked as a governess and housekeeper for a Franco-Russian family in Pushkino, not far from Moscow, arranged for the nine-year-old Inessa to come and live with her. The Armands were democratic-minded, wealthy industrialists and insisted that the young girl become part of the family. She was an instinctive linguist, picked up Russian rapidly and received the best possible education. She fell for the older of her two Armand brothers, Alexander. They married and had two children, Inessa ('Inna') and Varvara. They and their mother read Chernyshevsky's novel and began to see Armand as Vera Pavlovna. A young medical student hired to tutor the children, as was common in those times, turned out to be a radical. He excited the young couple with tales of courage and the insufferable conditions to which the workers were subjected. The Armand elders treated their workers well, and said as much to their children, but the seeds had been planted. Soon the tutor brought in a small printing press for publishing Social Democratic propaganda. He also brought banned books as gifts. The police raided the premises. The tutor took full responsibility. The Armands paid his bail and he fled abroad. Decades later Armand would second his membership application to join the Bolshevik Party.

By now she was desperate to play a part in radical politics. Doing good deeds locally on behalf of the family had become dull and irritating. She loathed the more reactionary sections in *War and Peace*, especially Tolstoy's descriptions of Natasha becoming a complete woman only after she was married.

Meanwhile Alexander Armand was beginning to fulfil his role as a young capitalist. He was a member of the Duma and various commercial organisations, as well as the English Club in Moscow. The youngest brother, Vladimir ('Volodya') Armand, had become a Bolshevik. Virtually the entire Armand family, apart from the parents, regarded themselves as Marxists of one sort or another. Two were members of the SRs. The others were Social Democrats. Inessa found herself more and more in Volodya's company. She developed a passion for him, very different from the warm affection she retained for her husband. They began an affair. The family found out. At first they were distraught, but Alexander accepted the new situation and insisted that there was absolutely no question of Volodya and Inessa moving out. And so they all lived together like characters from a bourgeois utopian novel, and this excludes the ubiquitous Chernyshevsky. Armand now had three children with Alexander, and became pregnant again with Volodya's child. They all went abroad for a holiday. A new baby was born and the household rejoiced.

Like most people, Armand had her likes, dislikes and weaknesses, but strengths too – strengths she never knew she possessed till history quickened its pace. Strengths she now took for granted, but that made those who loved her nervous. Lenin would warn her to be wary of overestimating them.

There is little doubt that Armand and Lenin fell in love in Paris. There was a Bolshevik education school outside the city for party members and sympathisers, in Longjumeau. They would sometimes disappear for a day, cycling through the countryside and appreciating each other more and more. Lenin once told Maxim Gorky in Capri that to become a revolutionary he had to give up three vices: chess, Latin and music. His famous remark, which had to do with not being able to listen to Beethoven's *Pathétique* because it made him 'soft', is usually distorted through decontextualisation and was sometimes taken literally by many a bourgeois philistine. In fact Lenin never stopped listening to music, as was known to all his circle. Armand herself was a gifted pianist and often played for him. Lenin could sing well and surprised Volsky in Geneva when, climbing a mountain, they came across a vista so stunning that they stopped to observe it in silence. Suddenly Lenin burst into song, a poem by Nekrasov extolling nature, which surprised the party even more. They proceeded in silence for some time as the sight and the sound continued to reverberate in their minds.

The idyllic time Lenin and Armand spent together did not go unnoticed. His mother-in-law glared at him with hawk eyes, making clear her disapproval. He told his wife. She had already guessed, and suggested that they separate so that he and Armand could live together. Was he tempted? We don't know. Did he think about Turgenev and *Andrei Kolosov*? It would have been difficult not to, given the circumstances. Could this dilemma ever be resolved? He was thirty-nine and she thirty-five when they first met. What was to be done? I think the solution he opted for was conservative, but motivated by politics. Any change in the background scenery of the Bolshevik faction would be exploited by factional opponents. His own comrades and the underground networks in Russia would be discomfited. It was Krupskaya who corresponded with them, who looked after their needs when they came to attend clandestine conferences abroad. This could be put at risk, at an extremely difficult time for him and the Bolshevik faction. These must have been the considerations.

Once, in order to test Krupskaya, he had asked: 'Who is more dear to you. Me or the party?' After a long pause, she opted for 'Both of you are dear to me', and failed the test. Had Armand asked him the same question, he would not have hesitated for a second. The party meant more to him than anything else, because it was the instrument necessary to make the revolution. Yes, the revolution. This had become the most important thing in his life soon after his brother had been hanged on the tsar's orders. The trauma hardened him. His adolescence ended the day he heard the news. School flirtations, chasing girls, all this came to an end as he later confessed to Gusev, a fellow exiled Bolshevik stuck in Switzerland. He could not let a romance, however passionate, however deep, come in the way now and disrupt all of them. It is what he undoubtedly explained to Armand as they went for a long break-up walk in Cracow in 1911. That she and Krupskaya spoke about the matter is obvious. Philistine biographers who write that there could have been no affair, because she and Krupskaya remained friends, do so in order to transfer their own values onto the Bolsheviks. Krupskaya, Kollontai, Zetkin, Balabanova and probably Luxemburg knew of Lenin's 'infatuation'. Armand and Krupskaya must have had a fairly free discussion. The only section of Lenin's archive that remains closed is a letter from him to Armand, which, if made public, would likely make it impossible to deny that they were passionate lovers. He asked for a special face-to-face meeting so that she could return his letters, as he did not trust the post, not even the registered post in this instance. It is likely that Lenin burnt these letters. The fragments that survive leave no room for doubt as to the depth of their love for each other. On 12 January 1917 she received a note that included the following paragraph:

Your last letters were so full of sadness, and these aroused such sorrowful thoughts and stirred up such pangs of conscience in me that I simply cannot compose myself. I would like to say at least something friendly and urgently beg you not to sit in virtual solitude in a little town where there is no social life, but to go somewhere where you can find old and new friends and shake yourself out of it.

Given that a letter from her had managed to shake his indomitable will, how easy could it have been for Armand to 'shake herself out of it'? She must have been angry, for she refused to reply even to his 'business' letters that were concerned solely with her activities as a militant – though even in one of these, dated 19 January 1917, he includes a few sentences on personal matters:

I urge you, when choosing your place of residence, <u>not</u> to take into account whether I will come there. It would be quite absurd, reckless and ridiculous if I were to restrict you in your choice of city by the notion that it 'may' turn out in the <u>future</u> that I, too, will <u>come there!!!</u>

Understandably, she did not reply. He asked too many questions without appreciating their impact on her. On 22 January 1917, he wrote again:

Apparently your failure to reply to several of my last letters reveals on your part – in connection with some other matters – a somewhat changed mood, decision or state of affairs. Your last letter contained a word repeated twice at the end – I understood and dealt with it. Never mind. I don't know what to think, whether you took offence at something or were too preoccupied with the move or something else . . . I'm afraid to ask, because I suppose such queries are unpleasant for you, and therefore I'll agree to interpret your silence on this point in precisely this sense, that queries are unpleasant for you, period. Therefore, I beg your pardon for all [the queries] and, of course, will not repeat [them].

We know that they remained close friends till her death. Whether or not they were intimate after the break-up is a matter for speculation. My own hunch is yes, and Kollontai's novella *A Great Love* based on the affair (and she knew everything) tends to confirm my instinct. This scene is after they had officially parted:

'Natalja Alexandrowna! Natalja Alexandrowna!'
Natascha turned quickly.
'Here I am, after all.'
Ssemjon Ssemjonowitsch stood before her, panting heavily, with a whimsical gleam of triumph in his eyes.
'I tore myself away, after all . . . I was actually cruel . . . I'm sorry for Anjuta, but . . .' He took her arm familiarly while Natascha looked in wonderment at the strange expression of crafty exultation that persisted on his face. The railway compartment was already overcrowded, and they were forced to sit very close to each other. Ssemjon Ssemjonowitsch continued to gaze at Natascha with eyes that for the first time betrayed the man behind the gold-rimmed glasses.
Natascha was disconcerted, and it added to her confusion to notice that his hand trembled when he touched her. His

agitation had already infected her calmness with its intensity. Eyes, seeking and precipitously avoiding each other, spoke their own language as the sweet, delirious current, tormenting and enticing alike, bound her more and more closely to the man who sat beside her.

At one of the longer stops they left the car for a breath of air. They breathed its keen, wintry freshness with a sigh of relief because they had escaped from this beautiful but disturbing dream. The smoke-darkened city was far away.

They spoke of indifferent, trivial matters, and the oppressive tension gradually vanished. Neither felt the desire to return to the crowded train.

But, back in the compartment once more, the mischievous boy with his arrow again began to exercise his magic. The sultry atmosphere and the enforced nearness of their bodies evoked an irresistible charm. Ssemjon Ssemjonowitsch sought Natascha's hand and she did not withdraw it.

Even in the published letters the tenderness never quite disappears, as when he's trying to persuade her to moderate a pamphlet on free love. One can see from his letters that he's annoying her, but her responses have not been published. After the attempt on Lenin's life by SR terrorist Fanny Kaplan in 1918 (reminiscent of the Girondin Charlotte Corday and the radical Marat), when a bullet lodged near his collarbone and another in his shoulder, an immediate operation was considered too dangerous and Lenin was forced to rest. He explained to Krupskaya that he needed Armand close to him. Not in the Kremlin, but not far away either. A suitable apartment was found and they saw each other regularly. A direct phone line was installed that connected Lenin's office to Armand's apartment.

She had been appointed the head of Zhenotdel and worked all hours as ferociously as Lenin himself. He was so shocked by how tired she looked that he insisted she leave Moscow and go to the Caucasus for a rest. Despite her own instincts to the contrary, she capitulated. They kept in touch. The last letter he sent her, in March 1920, speaks for itself:

Dear Friend,

So, the doctor says pneumonia. You have to be *extra*-careful. You must make your daughter phone me every day (12–4). Write, *frankly, what do you need?* Do you have wood? Who makes the fire? *Do you have food? Who prepares it?* Who makes you compresses? You are evading the questions – that's not good. Answer straightaway on the same sheet, answer ALL MY POINTS. Get well!

Your Lenin.

Is the telephone repaired?

She wrote a reply, sent it via her daughter and asked it to be delivered to Lenin's sister, who would make sure it reached him. Hearing their leader's panic, the doctors shifted her to another hospital. There she caught typhus and died. They brought her coffin back to Moscow. The Bolshevik feminists provided an honour guard. Lenin, grieving and broken, walked behind it on his own. The description left by Angelica Balabanoff is haunting:

I saw Lenin at the funeral of someone particularly dear to him. I never saw such torment; I never saw any human being so completely absorbed by sorrow, by the effort to keep it to himself, to guard it against the attention of others, as if their awareness could have diminished the intensity of his feeling ... I found myself in the immediate vicinity of Lenin. Not only his face but his whole body expressed so much sorrow that I dared not greet him, not even with the slightest gesture. It was clear he wanted to be alone with his grief. He seemed to have shrunk; his cap almost covered his face, his eyes drowned in tears held back with effort.

Armand had kept a diary in her last few weeks of life, a reflection of how exhausted she was and on every level. The letter she wrote him could have been along similar lines:

The only warm feelings I have left are for the children and V. I. In all other respects it's my heart that has died; as if, having given up all my strength, all my passion to V. I. and the work, I have exhausted

Inessa Armand's funeral in Moscow.

all sources of love towards people to whom previously I was so richly open. I have no one apart from V. I. and my children ... For romantic people love takes first place in the life of a person. Love is higher than anything else. And until recently I was nearer to this idea than I am now ... Together with love there was always the cause and in the past there were many times when I sacrificed my happiness and love for it ... It is true that in my life even now love has a big place ... But not for a moment do I cease to recognise that, however painful for me, love and personal relationships are nothing compared to the needs of the struggle.[5]

5   Michael Pearson, *Inessa*, London, 2001, p. 218. Another biography of Armand is by the Canadian historian R.C. Ellwood: *Inessa Armand: Revolutionary and Feminist*, Cambridge, 1992.

SECTION FIVE

The Last Fight Let Us Face

15

Till the Bitter End

A rmand's death had a similar effect on Lenin as that of Sasha all those years ago. In both cases he masked his grief and threw himself into work. In the first instance he had chosen to read on a vast scale, starting with Chernyshevsky (whose novel had been Sasha's favourite) and moving on to anything and everything by Marx that was available in Russian. After this he had established contact with clandestine People's Will circles in Kazan.

Now a return to work was compulsory. However much he mourned the loss of Armand in private (and this should never be underestimated), he was aware that she was but one casualty out of 3 million. He and Krupskaya adopted the Armand children, which brought him some solace. He set young André chess tests and made sure Varvara was doing well at university, creating a pandemonium by turning up unannounced to her classroom at the university one day and chatting to the students about literature. When he asked the students to name their favourite poet, they replied in unison: '**MAYAKOVSKY**'. As a classicist with conservative literary and artistic tastes, he was shocked. He could never appreciate Mayakovsky. They laughed when he said that Pushkin was the best and always would be. They calmly informed him that Mayakovsky was the poet of Bolshevism. Lenin snorted contemptuously. He had argued in the same fashion against Lunacharsky at the Commissariat of Enlightenment, and had been similarly overruled.

There was only one occasion when he found himself in complete agreement with the poet:

Yesterday I happened to read in *Izvestia* a political poem by Mayakovsky ['Incessant Meeting Sitters']. I am not an admirer of his poetical talent, although I admit that I am not a competent judge. But I have not for a long time read anything on politics and administration with so much pleasure as I read this. In this poem he derides the meeting habit, and taunts the communists with incessant meetings. I am not sure about the poetry; but as for the politics, I vouch for their absolute correctness. We are indeed ... in a very absurd position of sitting endlessly at meetings, setting up commissions and drawing up plans without end.

The poem reads as follows:

> No sooner the night turns into dawn
> when everyone whose job it is:
> goes to the 'firm'
> to the 'Co'
> to the 'trust'
> to the 'Corp'
> they all disappear into offices.
> Paper business pours
> like a torrent,
> no sooner than you get into the offices.
> Pick out from a hundred –
> the most important! –
> employees disappear into conferences.
>
> Then I appear and ask:
> 'To whom can I refer?
> Been here since once upon a time.'
> 'Comrade Ivan Ivanich has gone to
> confer with the People's Commisar of Teetotal Wine.'
>
> Crippled by countless stairs.
> Light barely blinks.
> Again:
> 'Asks you to come back in an hour or so.

In conference: –
Re the purchase of inks
For the All-in Co-op, Corp and Co.'

In an hour –
not a clerk
not an office boy
appears . . .
bare!
Everyone up to twenty-two years is at the
Komsomol conference upstairs.

Night is falling.
I still climb on
to the highest floor of my temporary
home.
'Has Comrade Ivan Ivanich come in?'
'Still in conference
with the A-B-C-D-E-F-G-Com.'

Into that conference,
I burst like a lava
with savage oaths the path is strewn.
And see:
people are sitting there in halves.
Heavens above!
Where've their other halves gone?
'Slaughtered!
Murdered!'
Running about like mad I shout.
At such a picture I go out of my mind.
Then I hear the calmest of clerks
point out:
'They're in two conferences at the very
same time.'
Twenty conferences
we have to attend

every day –
and more to spare.
So we're forced to split ourselves in
Two!
Here to the waist,
and the rest –
over there.

Can't sleep for suspense.
I meet the dawn with frenzied senses.
'Oh for just
one
more conference
regarding the eradication of all
conferences!'

This reminds Lenin of the eternal eponymous anti-hero portrayed in Goncharov's masterpiece, who 'typified Russian life – Oblomov'. Lenin's image of him is that of a man 'always lolling on his bed and mentally drawing up schemes'. But then he moves in for the kill. Despite the three revolutions, 'the Oblomovs have survived.' They might have been portrayed in the novel as lazy landowners, but Oblomovs also 'existed among the peasants . . . the intellectuals . . . also among the workers and communists'. He's been watching them 'at our meetings, at our work on commissions, to be able to say that <u>old Oblomov still lives; and it will be necessary to give him a good washing and cleaning, a good rubbing and scouring to make a man out of him.</u>' Lenin concludes, as was his wont, with an appeal to the authority of Marx, who once wrote 'that many foolish things are done during a revolution, perhaps more than at any other time. We revolutionaries must learn to regard these foolish acts dispassionately and fearlessly.'[1]

On personal matters there was nothing to hide now. Young Inessa was in and out of their tiny Kremlin apartment. She had

---

1 V. I. Lenin, *Collected Works*, vol. 33, trs David Skvirsky and George Hanna, Moscow, 1966, pp. 223–4. Emphasis in original.

been the favourite child, sharing her mother's indomitable spirit and politics, and had adopted Krupskaya as a substitute mother. Lenin never really recovered from Armand's death. His last letters to her were unusually signed 'Your Lenin', and that is what he had felt. Deeply felt. How often must he have thought that if he hadn't insisted so strongly that she have a rest cure in the Caucasus, she would probably still be alive. Apart from their love for each other, she was also a very close and trustworthy comrade and friend with whom he could discuss everything. Her opposition to him on Brest-Litovsk and the decree ending workers' control had not damaged anything. Her positions on these subjects were not too different from those of Kollontai, but Armand would not join any factional opposition. Lenin had an uncanny knack for being proved correct by events, and that had certainly been the case with Brest-Litovsk. Many observed that immediately after her funeral, where his emotions had been uncontrollable, he had walked straight back to his office and resumed his duties. It was totally in character. There was much to do.

The European crisis had not yet abated. Lenin remained obsessed with the situation in Germany. How could the Comintern help generalise the 1918 mutiny of the 20,000 German soldiers occupying Kharkov, who had turned their backs on their officers and marched through the town carrying red flags and declaring solidarity with the Russian revolution? An uprising in Germany was not pure fantasy, even after the failed attempt in Berlin. At home the civil war was almost over. A few stragglers here and there, especially in the Caucasus and a final reckoning with Wrangel in the Crimea, but Denikin and Kolchak defeated them together with the help of the Entente powers. What if they had taken Petrograd in 1919? He had been wrong to suggest an evacuation of the city. Trotsky had convinced him that it would be a huge blow if the cradle of the revolution fell to the counterrevolution. The resistance of the citizens and the newly created Red Army had saved the day. Now he could even smile at the thought of Trotsky on horseback addressing the Red troops without pause, making sure the defensive front did not collapse and turning back the Whites. A fortnight after Armand's death, Lenin wrote an appeal to the Ukrainian peasants. These civil war appeals were designed not just for the addressees but for the Bolshevik agitators of the Red Army, to provide them with a political line and a few pithy sentences.

TO THE POOR PEASANTS OF THE UKRAINE

Comrades, the tsarist general Wrangel is building up his offensive against the Ukraine and Russia. With backing from the French capitalists, he is pushing forward, threatening the Donets Basin and Ekaterinoslav. The danger is grave. Once again the landowners are trying to re-establish their power, get their estates back, and re-enslave the peasants.

Comrades, the Ukrainian countryside has endured unparalleled sufferings under the yoke of the landowners. The latter have more than once been able to overthrow the Soviets, the workers' and peasants' power; more than once they have been helped by the kulaks, the rich peasants, who either went over openly to their side or hampered the poor and working peasants' efforts to introduce the new order, the new way of life, the new organisation in the villages. Each such attempt to restore the rule of the landowners has ended in a new victory for the workers and peasants. Today, all over the Ukraine, the poor villagers have begun to set up their committees so as to smash the resistance of the handful of the rich, and finally to establish the rule of the working people. Wrangel, general of the landowners, is increasing his pressure with the intention of routing these organisations of the working people.

Comrades, rise up to a man to hurl Wrangel back. Let all committees of poor peasants bend every effort to help the Red Army crush Wrangel. Not a single working peasant should stand aside in the struggle for the cause of the workers and peasants, or remain inactive or indifferent. Comrades, remember that this is a matter of saving the lives

of your families, of defending the peasants' land and their
rule.

Rally for aid to the Red Army! Death to the oppressor
landowners!

2.10.1920

Lenin[2]

The new state was almost secure. Lenin understood very well
that it had been the refusal of the poor peasants to back the Whites
that had turned the tide. Not that they had been happy with the
permanent requisitions carried out by the Red Army, but in the last
analysis they knew that a return of the Whites would bring with it
a new wave of savagery, exploitation and landlords. The image of
a strikingly attired landed family, replete in cream silk and straw
hats, walking to the meadow on their estate, casually taking their
seats on both sides of a long table dressed with pristine tablecloths
and napkins and being served by a horde of servants was not
something the former serfs and poor peasants of Russia wanted to
see again. Wrangel was defeated in the autumn of 1920.

In 1921 the Bolsheviks won the civil war. Three million people
had died, amongst them the cream of the Russian working class;
its most politically conscious members were annihilated. Trotsky's
military triumph was an amazing feat of arms, carried out by a
newly formed army. The political price was high. Lenin wrote
that while they had defeated the capitalists in Russia, the latter's
friends abroad had punished them without mercy via the economy and the civil war. The fact that they had retained state power
'was due to the split of world imperialism into two predatory
groups' who had fought each other almost to the end. As a result,
'neither group could muster large forces against us, which they
would have done had they been in a position to do so.' The civil
war had shown that both Entente weaknesses and the growth of

---

2   V. I. Lenin, 'To the Poor Peasants of the Ukraine', *Kommunist*
(Kiev) 199, October 13, 1920, in *Collected Works*, 4th ed., vol. 31, tr.
Julius Katzer, Moscow, 1965, pp. 314–15.

a solidarity movement with Russia in Britain, France and Germany had made the imperialists' work much harder. In Washington, Woodrow Wilson faced strong opposition to any new war in Europe from both the soldiers' families and dissident congressmen. The small expeditionary force dispatched to Archangel had been welcomed by the wealthy and a section of the intelligentsia, but these groups were disappointed that a proper army had not been sent to defeat their Bolshevik enemy, while the US consul Felix Cole reported to the State Department that 'the working class was patently absent' from the welcome party. The Entente dispatched more soldiers to boost the counter-revolution. The Soviet leaders had attempted to divide European imperialism from its American ally and future rival, but with new landings, Lenin lost his patience and on 20 August 1918 drafted his 'Letter to American Workers' in which he denounced Wilson as the 'head of the American multi-millionaires and servant of the capitalist sharks'. In October that same year, as more US troops arrived, Lenin suggested a few lines for foreign minister Chicherin to send to Wilson, thanking him for helping to revive the 'Russian counterrevolution that had already become a corpse', since this had 'opened the eyes of the workers and peasants of Russia as to the aims of the Russian counterrevolution and of its foreign assistants'. As a result they were fighting back with an even greater determination.

The American public was getting nervous. On 12 December 1918, Republican senator Hiram Johnson of California proposed a resolution in the Senate asking the State Department for an explanation as to why US soldiers were fighting in Russia, despite its own press release that rejected armed intervention. Johnson's speech in the Senate was scathing, openly mocking Wilson for his hypocrisy and the dissonance between his words and deeds. The US ambassador in Russia demanded 50,000 US troops and as many Allied auxiliaries to 'restore order in the interests of humanity and to suppress bolshevism'. But the tide was turning and the US ambassador in Paris refused to see Kerensky, who was also there to request more troops. He was denied a US visa. Wilson was worried by growing anti-interventionist fervour at home and told his man in Moscow that, while he shared his opinions, it would simply be 'very unpopular in America'.[3] Large-scale US military intervention did not take place, but a transmission belt was established for dispatching US and Entente weapons and food supplies to the White Armies for most of the civil war, while maintaining an effective blockade against the Bolsheviks.

The three key features of the Russian civil war – forced requisitions from the countryside, iron discipline and leadership to transcend the chaos that all civil wars produce and, most importantly, a politicised proletariat prepared to sacrifice its life for the revolution – are depicted with stunning clarity in the short stories of Isaac Babel, who was embedded with the Red Army. The system that prevailed during this period – 'war communism' – was harsh but maintained a rough equality. It also helped mask the realities of the economic crisis. Factories were closing down while the workers either fought in the civil war or returned to their villages to be able to eat at least one meal a day. Even before the civil war started in earnest, Lenin was aware that 'an extraordinarily difficult, complex and dangerous situation' existed internationally and at home. After the civil war he understood very clearly that the commune-state they had all wanted from the minute they had gained power was now impossible. Those workers who had not perished were interspersed in the party and state bureaucracies. Industrialisation had to start as soon as possible, not just for the needs of the country but also to create a new proletariat, without whom they were doomed. The New Economic Policy (NEP) was designed to relax state controls and permit a degree of capitalism to kick-start the economy. There was no other credible alternative. But in order to make sure that the state was not infected, it was not the time to implement the commune-state ideas embodied in *State and Revolution*. To preside over this new transition, the revolutionary dictatorship had to be tough-minded and make sure that the revolution did not collapse. Workers' control in the

---

3   David S. Foglesong, *America's Secret War Against Bolshevism*, North Carolina and London, 1995, pp. 224–30.

factories had to be abandoned. Experts must be brought in regardless of their class or political background, so the economy could grow and the 'task of peaceful reconstruction begin.' This is how Lenin reasoned.

It was a huge risk and the problems were discussed openly at the Ninth Party Congress in 1920, with the Lenin–Trotsky leadership uniting against strong rank-and-file criticism. Some of it was expressed mildly, but all speakers were clear in their opposition to the new turn and the regime being suggested for the factories. A delegate asked Lenin where one-man leadership would end. Would it not travel fast from the factories to the party? 'Who will elect the Central Committee?' The same delegate prophesied that the result of all this would be 'the dictatorship of the party bureaucracy'. Lenin had to fight hard to convince them that it was a temporary phase, that this was the wrong time to indulge in theory. There were important '*practical* tasks' ahead, and the same energy that had defeated the Whites was needed to rebuild the country.

NEP worked, but even a little bit of capitalism brings with it an increasing quota of inequality. And added to that, as a special bonus, were hidden 'gifts' or bribes to party officials. The corruption particularly angered party members and helped to fuel the Workers' Opposition, that of smaller groups inside the party and the Kronstadt uprising outside of it. Civil war veterans, too, despised this aspect of the NEP.

Two episodes symbolised the period. A shipment marked 'military supplies' and addressed to Abel Enukzide, a member of the Central Committee, was opened and inspected at the Kazan railway station. The military supplies consisted of wines, cognacs, flour, sugar, tobacco and other items unavailable to ordinary citizens. One party leader (a loyal apparatchik till the end of her life) was livid and registered a strong protest. It was, argued Rozalia Zemlyachka, in addition to all other issues, discrediting the party in the eyes of non-party workers. The Central Committee's Orgbureau saved Enukzide's skin by informing her that the alcohol was destined for use by the Health Commissariat in hospitals. Another scandal revealed that a mansion attached to a large estate and redesigned as a centre for children had been sequestered by a general as his country retreat. He needed a rest after the civil war. The Bolshevik daily, *Pravda*, published a number of sharp exposés of corruption, and a Commission of Enquiry prepared an equally scathing report for the next party congress. The congress organisers could find no time to discuss the report, distracted as they were by more important issues. One of these was a tightening of the screws: a formal ban on all party factions, and an intemperate proposal from Lenin to expel the leaders of the Workers' Opposition.

This last proposal the conference refused to accept. A party without Kollontai and Shlyapnikov (two of the very few Bolshevik leaders who had supported the *April Theses* in 1917) was unthinkable. The ban on factions was accepted. It was the ultimate logic of the course on which the Bolsheviks had embarked soon after the revolution. Once they established a rigid monopoly of political representation in the soviets, so much so that not even loyalist pro-revolution (but not pro-Bolshevik) groups such as the left Mensheviks led by Julius Martov were barred, it was only a matter of time before opposition within the Bolshevik party itself would be disallowed. It was certainly logical, but a tragedy nonetheless and some of the most politically conscious party members dropped out. Lenin would realise this error in a very short space of time, but it would be too late. He was dying. So was the party.

On 26 May 1922, at the age of fifty-two, Lenin suffered his first stroke. He recovered fairly soon, but was prescribed complete rest. His brain was functioning as usual, but it was now overpowered by a sense of urgency. There was too much to do and too little time. He knew he did not have long to live. His father had died from a brain haemorrhage at roughly the same age and had a similar build. To the stresses and strains of the revolution and the civil war had been added the untimely and unnecessary death of Armand. When he had turned fifty, his comrades in the Moscow party had insisted on a celebration. Lenin resisted this and stayed out of the room while Lunacharsky, Gorky and Stalin, amongst others, made speeches. Only after they had finished did Lenin enter

Lenin in 1922 after his first stroke.

the room.[4] He did not speak for long on that occasion. He quoted from a prescient text by Kautsky published in *Iskra* in which the German socialist had written that the Slavs might well be the carriers of the socialist revolution in Europe:

---

4 There is an excellent account of the birthday party in Valentino Gerratana's exemplary text on how 'Leninism' was manufactured and became a football in the inner-party debates after Lenin's death: 'Stalin, Lenin and "Leninism" ', *New Left Review* I: 103, May–June 1977, pp. 59–71.

At the present time [in contrast with 1848] it would seem that not only have the Slavs entered the ranks of the revolutionary nations, but that the centre of revolutionary thought and revolutionary action is shifting more and more to the Slavs. The revolutionary centre is shifting from the West to the East. In the first half of the nineteenth century it was located in France, at times in England. In 1848 Germany too joined the ranks of the revolutionary nations ... The new century has begun with events which suggest the idea that we are approaching a further shift of the revolutionary centre, namely, to Russia ... Russia, which has borrowed so much revolutionary initiative from the West, is now perhaps herself ready to serve the West as a source of revolutionary energy. The Russian revolutionary movement that is now flaring up will perhaps prove to be the most potent means of exorcising the spirit of flabby philistinism and coldly calculating politics that is beginning to spread in our midst, and it may cause the fighting spirit and the passionate devotion to our great ideals to flare up again. To Western Europe, Russia has long ceased to be a bulwark of reaction and absolutism. I think the reverse is true today. Western Europe is becoming Russia's bulwark of reaction and absolutism ... The Russian revolutionaries might perhaps have coped with the tsar long ago had they not been compelled at the same time to fight his ally – European capital. Let us hope that this time they will succeed in coping with both enemies, and that the new 'Holy Alliance' will collapse more rapidly than its predecessors did. However the present struggle in Russia may end, the blood and suffering of the martyrs whom, unfortunately, it will produce in too great numbers, will not have been in vain. They will nourish the shoots of social revolution throughout the civilised world and make them grow more luxuriantly and rapidly. In 1848 the Slavs were a killing frost which blighted the flowers of the people's spring. Perhaps they are now destined to be the storm that will break the ice of reaction and irresistibly bring with it a new and happy spring for the nations.[5]

---

5   Karl Kautsky, 'The Slavs and Revolution', *Iskra* 18, March 10, 1902.

Lenin had dug out the quotation for a pamphlet he was writing
– '*Left-Wing' Communism: An Infantile Disorder* – but, probably
irritated by the self-congratulatory atmosphere amongst the party
leaders at his fiftieth, he read it in its entirety. No doubt they smiled
and nodded as he did so. Then came the stiletto:

> These words lead me to think that our Party may now find itself in
> a very dangerous position – the position of a man with a swollen
> head. It is a very stupid, shameful and ridiculous position. We know
> that the failure and decline of political parties have very often been
> preceded by a state of affairs in which a swollen head is possible.
> And, indeed, what was expected of the Russian Revolution by the
> man I have quoted, and who is now our bitterest enemy, was
> immense beyond measure.

Of course there had been brilliant successes, but these had been
against the traditional enemies of Russian socialism.

> The tasks that are the substance of the socialist revolution had to
> be postponed in order to grapple with the task of organising the
> struggle against the common, everyday manifestations of petty-
> bourgeois instincts, division and disunity, that is, against every-
> thing that would drag us back to capitalism. These tasks were post-
> poned both in the economic and political spheres; we were unable
> to tackle them properly ... Let me conclude with the hope that
> under no circumstances will we allow our Party to contract a swol-
> len head.[6]

As he recovered slowly from his stroke, he had time to reflect
on the revolution that he, above all others, had made possible. He
had been so sure that knowledge of Marxism would be sufficient
to solve everything and anything, but the problems that arose
proved the opposite. Marxism was only an approximation. How
could it be otherwise? On three important subjects he took issue
with the general secretary he had approved: Stalin. Enraged when

---

6   Lenin, *Collected Works,* vol. 30, p. 528.

he heard that Stalin, Dzerzhinski (the head of the Cheka) and Ordzhonikidze (a Central Committee member) had visited Georgia and physically attacked the local Bolshevik leaders, he demanded an immediate repudiation of this type of behaviour, denounced Russian chauvinism and recalled how Tatars and Georgians had been treated and referred to during the tsarist period. He suggested a common bloc to Trotsky, sending him an ultra-friendly note that he insisted be read out to Trotsky on the phone:

> I earnestly ask you to undertake the defence of the Georgian affair at the Central Committee of the Party. That affair is now under 'prosecution'; at the hands of Stalin and Dzerzhinski and I cannot rely on their impartiality. Indeed, quite the contrary! If you would agree to undertake its defence, I would be at rest. If for some reason you do not agree, send me back all the papers. I will consider that a sign of your disagreement. With the very best comradely greetings, LENIN.[7]

Kamenev was despatched to Georgia to apologise, with a personal letter from Lenin inviting the Georgians to complain to the party and informing them that he was preparing notes for them and a speech. He knew that his life was ebbing away, but still he fought this last battle against Stalin and his cohort. In his notes on the national question, he apologised to the workers for 'not having intervened energetically and decisively enough on the notorious question of autonomisation'. He blamed this deficiency on his ill health and recounted that the report from Dzerzhinski had woken him up with a jolt. He demanded that Ordzhonikidze be suspended from the party for having struck another comrade. He declared his hatred for 'that really Russian man, the Great Russian chauvinist, in substance a rascal and a tyrant, such as the typical Russian bureaucrat is': this disease had infected the upper

---

7 Moshe Lewin, *Lenin's Last Struggle*, London, 1969. This work by a Polish historian remains the most perceptive study of Lenin's last two years.

echelons of the Bolshevik Party and the top leaders had behaved in a thoroughly 'imperialist fashion'. He accused Stalin and Ordzhonikidze, regardless of their own Caucasian origins, of having acted like typical Great Russian bullies. The Soviet Union should be maintained, he wrote, but its unionism should only operate in the fields of foreign policy and defence. Otherwise non-Russians must be given autonomy to run their own countries. At the next conference, Lenin demanded that Stalin be removed from his post as general secretary and that the party replace him with someone more capable. He had 'concentrated too much authority in his hands'.

In February 1923, Lenin had written his message to the forthcoming party conference and what would be his last text for *Pravda*. The Politburo delayed its publication and an up-and-coming apparatchik, Kubishyev, suggested publishing a fake issue of the paper to deceive Lenin. The Politburo rejected this solution and the article was finally published with Lenin's title intact: 'Better Fewer, but Better'. Why were they so worried? The 5,000 words were impersonal but damning. Lenin and others had assumed that Marxism offered a sufficient basis to solve all the problems that lay ahead, but this had turned out not to be the case.

Marx and Engels's ideas, brilliant though many of them were, offered only an approximation in relation to what needed to be done. Marx did not conceptualise the structures of a socialist state. The theory of proletarian revolution is what differentiated them from all precursors or contemporaries. Machiavelli's political theory was based on the manipulation of elite politics; Rousseau's theory of the general will, while decrying inequality, denied all political representation; Bakunin did not believe in the state at all. Marxist politics could not spring fully formed from the heads of Marx and Engels. It required long and patient stretches of involvement in the workers' movement. It required experimenting with a wide variety of tactics before a successful revolution erupted. Once this happened, it would be rapidly confronted with a powerful enemy in the shape of the world capitalist system. Experience alone would determine how proletarian democracy could be established. There was no conceptualisation of politics as they had conceptualised philosophy, economics or history, but the clarity and vigour of their political interventions can be read in numerous essays, published in three volumes.[8]

It was Lenin who developed Marx's ideas and politicised them further, stressing the autonomy of the political and how in times of political crisis, 'politics is concentrated economics'. This applied to bourgeois revolutions even if their leaders were not conscious of it, and was definitely the case for proletarian revolutions. Describing them as such is in itself an assertion of the fact that they were conscious revolutions. October 1917 was the first such upheaval, followed by October 1949 in Beijing.

'Better Fewer, but Better' is a balance sheet of the Russian experience after six years of revolution and civil war. It's a bleak document whose importance lies in the fact that as he lay convalescing, Lenin fully understood the scale of the problem. The rot lay within. The causes were both objective and subjective, each playing on the other and making matters worse. The first key point has often been underestimated or even ignored. It is concerned with a word he used more and more after the civil war: *culture*. He complained that despite the revolution, the revolutionaries were not 'abreast of the times', that their culture was 'much inferior' to the best Western European standards and till they had overtaken the West, a serious transformation on every level would be difficult. The use of the word *culture* was a variant of what the Italian thinker, Antonio Gramsci, would later refer to as *hegemony*. Lenin wrote that the Communists had won political power, but that this was not sufficient either at home or abroad:

> For a socialist republic this condition is, of course, too modest. But our experience of the first five years has fairly crammed our heads

---

8   Karl Marx, *The Revolutions of 1848*, *Surveys from Exile* and *The First International and After*, ed. David Fernbach, London and New York, 2010.

with mistrust and scepticism. These qualities assert themselves involuntarily when, for example, we hear people dilating at too great length and too flippantly on 'proletarian' culture. For a start, we should be satisfied with real bourgeois culture; for a start we should be glad to dispense with the crude types of pre-bourgeois culture, i.e., bureaucratic culture or serf culture, etc. In matters of culture, haste and sweeping measures are most harmful. Many of our young writers and Communists should get this well into their heads.

From this starting point he moves to the heart of the matter with a startling sentence both in terms of its content and its length:

Our state apparatus is so deplorable, not to say wretched, that we must first think very carefully how to combat its defects, bearing in mind that these defects are rooted in the past, which, although it has been overthrown, has not yet been overcome, has not yet reached the stage of a culture, that has receded into the distant past.

He then explains why this is the case and why he uses the word *culture* deliberately and consciously:

Because in these matters we can only regard as achieved what has become part and parcel of our culture, of our social life, our habits. We might say that the good in our social system has not been properly studied, understood, and taken to heart; it has been hastily grasped at; it has not been verified or tested, corroborated by experience, and not made durable, etc. Of course, it could not be otherwise in a revolutionary epoch, when development proceeded at such breakneck speed that in a matter of five years we passed from tsarism to the Soviet system.

Something needed to be done about this. Scepticism and doubt needed, in Lenin's view, to replace the boasting that was only too common. What the Party claimed to have achieved was, on closer inspection, 'flimsy, superficial and misunderstood'; therefore, 'we must come to our senses in time.' Lenin had a few sharp sentences in particular for the swollen-headed party bureaucrats constantly trying to please:

The worst thing of all would be haste. The worst thing of all would be to rely on the assumption that we know anything, or that we are well provided with the elements necessary for the building of a really new state apparatus, one really worthy to be called socialist, soviet, etc.

That this was a turnaround from his own earlier position is beyond dispute. He was not merely criticising others, but rapping himself on the knuckles as well. Had he not said in 1918 that the entire countryside was on the socialist path? Had he not led the charge to a commune-state? What had happened? Had the wings burnt out in the flight to paradise? The defeats in Germany, Hungary and Poland had necessitated applying the brakes before the locomotive went off the tracks altogether. And too many committed supporters of the revolution had perished in the civil war. The European revolution would revive and, if it didn't, the revolution might move eastwards as a result of imperialism's impact on India and China. Those would be a good substitute for Europe, but the martyred Soviet comrades were a huge loss. Substituting them with new recruits from the countryside was not going to be sufficient. These recruits would lack the experiences of 1905 and 1917, experiences that could not be replicated. Patience, diligence, vigilance, learning – these were the virtues Lenin was preaching in his last sermon to the Bolshevik Party as he argued that the existing apparatus was 'ridiculously deficient'. It had to be completely rebuilt. Here, too, there were problems and he was not shy in enumerating them:

What elements have we for building this apparatus? Only two. First, the workers who are absorbed in the struggle of socialism. These elements are not sufficiently educated. They would like to build a better apparatus for us, but they do not know how. They cannot build one. They have not yet developed the culture required for this; and it is culture that is required. Nothing will be achieved in this by doing things in a rush, by assault, by vim or vigour, or in general, by any of the best human qualities. Secondly, we have elements of knowledge, education and training, but they are ridiculously inadequate compared with all other countries . . .

In order to renovate our state apparatus we must at all costs set out, first, to learn, secondly, to learn, and thirdly, to learn, and then see to it that learning shall not remain a dead letter, or a fashionable catch-phrase (and we should admit in all frankness that this happens very often with us), that learning shall really become part of our very being, that it shall actually and fully become a constituent element of our social life . . . In order that it may attain the desired high level, we must follow the rule: 'Measure your cloth seven times before you cut.'

All the attempts, 'the bustling' to improve the state apparatus, had proved useless in these five years, 'or even futile, or even harmful. This bustle created the impression that we were doing something, but in effect it was only clogging up our institutions and our brains.'

Rarely has a confession of failure by a revolutionary political leader been so complete. Rarely can a leader have regretted so deeply that his time was up, that he could no longer walk up to the podium, say all this to the assembled delegates and win their support. They would be shocked, of course, but they needed to be. Since this was no longer possible, he was writing to them just as he had written his *Letters from Afar* from exile, prior to the revolution. This time he was writing from the Kremlin, but he felt alone. He knew that Trotsky, Bukharin and a few others would not disagree with what he had written, but Stalin and the apparatus he commanded were a different matter altogether. He doubted that they would be able to grasp the importance of all this and the necessity to push new measures through for the health of the revolution. He had managed to conquer most of the dilemmas that confronted him during his adult life. The party and state bureaucracy that he now wanted to curb, to reduce in size, to punish for breaching norms, to place under the permanent watch of a Workers' and Peasants' Inspectorate consisting only of tried and trusted veterans known for their fearlessness and integrity – this bureaucracy would fight back, would wriggle out of what was being suggested. He wrote as much in this, his last appeal to fellow Bolsheviks:

> We must follow the rule: better fewer, but better. We must follow the rule: better get good human material in two or even three years than work in haste without hope of getting any at all. I know that it will be hard to keep to this rule and apply it under our conditions. I know that the opposite rule will force its way through a thousand loopholes. I know that enormous resistance will have to be put up, that devilish persistence will be required, that in the first few years at least work in this field will be hellishly hard. Nevertheless, I am convinced that only by such effort shall we be able to achieve our aim; and that only by achieving this aim shall we create a republic that is really worthy of the name of Soviet, socialist, and so on, and so forth.

No such effort was ever made and those who might have fought for all this were gradually neutered, weeded out from the party or simply killed. There was also a weakness in Lenin's appeal. The scale of the problem he had outlined was huge, but this was not something that could be solved by even the purest of comrades serving in the Workers' and Peasants' Inspectorate. Who would implement their critical reports? The Politburo? Who would elect it? Delegates chosen by then local party bureaucracies who had the power of life and death – or, to put it less dramatically, the officials with the most influence – were those who authorised jobs, food, factory positions and so on. Lenin had demanded the total reconstruction of the state, without specifying the proper instrument to start the process. In his 1919 lectures 'On the State' at Sverdlov University, he had stressed time and time again that the central question for politics in revolutionary, prerevolutionary or peaceful times was the state. Its nature and 'the attitude of our Party' were of crucial importance, because if one did not study this question 'several times, return to it again and again and consider it from various angles in order to attain a clear understanding of it', one could never understand the question of political power. He had been looking at every angle, which is why the solution suggested is so weak and slightly pathetic. Perhaps he thought that this would do as a start and the rest would follow, or perhaps he understood only too well that the party and its structures also posed a huge problem. He had hinted as much in a number of texts. The dream of a commune-state had been replaced by the reality of a party-state, and both suffered from bureaucratic deformations because the old tsarist state machine had not been destroyed. Its foundations were still there. All they had done was to rebuild the odd room and change the furniture everywhere else.

The solution was to make the party accountable to the soviets, but these were dead institutions. To bring them back to life required free elections and, yes, the right of other soviet parties to exist. This had been the crux of the debate between Lenin and the left Menshevik leader Julius Martov. Lenin was not convinced that this was a solution because of the level of culture of the Bolsheviks and society as a whole. As a result, nothing changed.

This was a tragedy, for enhancing the culture of the population raises many issues.[9] The open debates between Bolshevik leaders and the number of letters from ordinary readers to the press from all over the country were a strong indication of this fact. Many prefer to and actually do learn more from the expression of contrarian opinions than from even the most intelligent or sophisticated repetitions of the dominant ideology, whatever that might be. A

---

9 In 1938 the head of the Propaganda Section in Gorky reported to Stalin a huge problem that they faced: 'Often a semi-literate propagandist with a secondary education or none at all consults an engineer with higher education, who is well-read and has a better understanding of Marxist-Leninist theory; the latter asks questions the educator can't answer.' The low cultural level of the 'cadres' in the propaganda departments, the publishing houses and the provincial newspapers registered a sharp decline from the 1920s. One reason given by Stalin himself was the 'loss of cadres', i.e. the people who he had imprisoned or killed.

spirited, impolite conversation that hovers on the edge of heated polemic is much more educative than a polite agreement to disagree. Genuine debate fortifies the mind. Agreement often conceals the inability to challenge views that one knows to be wrong. That is why, even on a personal level, it is the duty of close friends to speak the truth to each other, whatever the cost, because silences can erode a friendship from within. The story of Lenin and Martov is instructive in this regard.

16

Friends and Enemies

One of Rumi's verses nicely encapsulates a mystical view of friendship: 'Out beyond ideas of doing wrong and doing right there is a field,' he writes. 'I'll meet you there. When the soul lies down in that grass the world is too full to talk about.' What if the soul is very political? Mysticism finds such a question inexplicable; but close friendships between people of strongly opposed political views are not that common, and sometimes what two friends regard as opposing views are not that different after all. This is especially the case in present times when liberals, conservatives and social democrats pretend to be enemies, but, without proper theatrical training, end up exposing themselves as bad actors. Serious political rifts, despite shared literary or cinematic tastes, can wreck even long-lasting friendships.

For Lenin's generation, discordant attitudes towards the First World War broke numerous close relationships, personal and political, across the continent. Many who were theologically on the left turned out to be temperamentally on the right. And virtually all the socialists who backed their 'own' imperialisms during that war moved on afterwards to help sustain capitalism, defend imperial wars large and small and, in some cases, become public ideologues for their erstwhile enemies. It is a process that continues to this day.

All this is understandable, but there is another category applicable only to politicals. This is factional battles inside the same party. Here, too, old friendships can be wrecked by a moment's rashness or uncertainty. The RSDLP was not immune to the process and, because it was a party either in exile or underground in Russia, divisions sometimes assumed an importance that was out of proportion. The arguments within Russian Marxism were the subject of much mockery and negative comments in the corridors outside the meeting halls of the Second International, but those who expressed the greatest irritation – the German SPD – themselves ended up in a gruesome civil war with the party paper *Vorwarts,* when it celebrated the murders of Rosa Luxemburg and Karl Liebknecht that some of its leaders had made possible.

Lenin and Martov were two of the founding members of the Emancipation of Labour Group, launched in St Petersburg in 1899, that played a decisive role in laying the foundations for the RSDLP. They were almost the same age, though Lenin was three years older (a difference that seems much greater in one's twenties). They were to be close comrades and friends for the next five years. Martov was the only male friend to be addressed with the familiar *ty* by Lenin, and vice versa. Temperamentally they could not have been more dissimilar. Lenin has been discussed at some length. His defeated opponent has been treated with what the English historian Edward Thompson in another case once referred to as the 'enormous condescension of posterity'.

Lenin and Martov: Friendly times as founders
of the RSDLP.

Lenin and Martov came from different backgrounds. Julius Martov Tsederbaum was born into an enlightened Jewish family based in Odessa. Four generations of Tsederbaums had been products of the Haskalah, an assimilationist current within Judaism that stressed the vital role of education in lifting Jews out of the ghetto, despite all restrictions. Martov, like all Jews in the tsarist empire, had no illusions regarding his status and was accustomed to the casual anti-Semitism that dominated everyday life in Russia. Interestingly enough, there were never any pogroms in Georgia, where Babylonian Jews had been settled for over two millennia. It was the cruder, Russian varieties of prejudice that young Jewish men, regardless of class, faced at school and university. Martov was shocked by his headmaster's racism at what was regarded as the best *gymnasium* (high school) in Odessa.[1]

The relentless oppression of the Jews in tsarist times pushed many intellectuals and workers towards Social Democracy. Martov himself wrote that he wondered what his biography might have been had he not been a Jew. He recalled how his mother used to put large cauldrons of water to boil when news of a pogrom spread. She would send the servants home and prepare to pour the water from the windows on the anti-Semitic gangs gathering below. The harrowingly powerful descriptions of these pogroms by both Martov and Trotsky stand in a league of their own. Martov, on his way back to Russia in October 1905, saw Jewish refugees from the recent pogroms in Russian cities crowding the platforms on the station at Vilno. It brought back memories of the Odessa pogrom of 1881, of the old Jew he had encountered on the train from that blood-drenched city to St Petersburg, 'the same dim eyes, the same submission to fate and the same story . . . of a human

---

1   The only existing biography of Martov is Israel Getzler, *Martov: A Political Biography of a Russian Social Democrat*, Cambridge, UK, 1967. Getzler is by no means uncritical of his subject, but concludes that it was Martov's belief in Marxism and the proletariat that kept him in Lenin's broad sphere of influence, if not his bed. The book contains a great deal of valuable information besides a portrait of the man Trotsky referred to as the 'Hamlet of democratic socialism'.

whirlwind which burst over peacefully sleeping people and cast them into an abyss of filth and blood.'[2] These images never left him; many years later, during the civil war, he shouted angrily at Gregory Aaronson, a leader of the Jewish Bund, when he suggested that perhaps the Bundists should remain neutral given that the White Armies, though led by tsarist generals, had the support of large sections of the peasantry resisting Bolshevik oppression. Martov reminded him of the pogroms that the Whites left behind them everywhere and exclaimed:

> Don't you remember, in the past, when we had to make up our minds whether a political movement was progressive or reactionary, we found that 'Jew-baiting' was a pretty good acid test? Should I have to remind you, who are a Bundist, of this litmus test?[3]

The early collaboration between young Lenin and young Martov was exemplary. They worked well together on *Iskra* and both Lenin and numerous others admired the fierce moral tone in Martov's articles denouncing various aspects of the autocracy. He was often referred to as 'our Dobryulov'. Differences between the two men grew, though it must be said that it was not Lenin who initially took the offensive. And for some time Martov would convince himself that it was Lenin's personality, his bossy style, his refusal to compromise, his supreme belief that he was right, rather than any major political issue, that was responsible for the rift. Lenin was sure of the opposite. It was Martov's increasingly divergent approach to politics that had driven them apart, though neither ever regarded the other as a complete enemy. Gusev and Volsky, two younger Bolsheviks in exile with Lenin in Geneva, found him quite relaxed and expansive on non-political matters. Volkov (in his memoir of Lenin written under the pseudonym Valentinov) recounted how when Lenin was describing his life in London, he said:

---

2   Getzler, *Martov*, p. 110.
3   Ibid, p. 191.

It is impossible to live in a house where the windows and doors are never closed, where they are completely open to the street and where every passer-by considers it necessary to look in and see what you are doing. I should go mad if I had to live in a commune similar to the one which Martov, Zasulich, and Alekseyev organised in London in 1902. This was more than a house with open windows – it was a public thoroughfare. Martov could be with people all day. I simply can't. Altogether Martov is a phenomenon. He can simultaneously write, smoke, eat, and converse continuously with up to a dozen people. Chernyshevsky was quite right when he said that everyone has a corner in his life which should never be penetrated by anyone, and everyone should have a special room completely to himself.[4]

The split between the Bolsheviks and the Mensheviks was in a class of its own. Not because their growing political differences were unique – reformist and semi-revolutionary currents existed in virtually every Social Democratic party bar the British – but because in Russia, the Menshevik majority could not easily espouse liberalism. *Reforming* the autocracy was viewed as a collaborationist exercise within the tsarist camp or on its fringes. As a result, the debate between the two currents in Russian Social Democracy was centred on what type of revolution was needed – bourgeois-democratic or socialist – and what would be its likely instrument – peasants, workers or a combination of both. Positions on this were more or less fluid till April 1917, but the direction in which these two currents were moving had become obvious much earlier after the famous split in 1903 on an organisational question related to the tasks of a party member. Lenin later wrote that a compromise on this question was perfectly possible, but the Mensheviks and their allies were determined to remove him from the editorial board of *Iskra* because he had ruffled too many feathers. This had been necessary, he argued, because the three-person editorial board that he proposed was the only efficient way to produce the paper. His worry was that Martov would not be able to manage this on

4   Nikolay Valentinov, *Encounters with Lenin*, Oxford, 1968, p. 43.

his own and the paper would collapse, which is, in fact, what happened soon afterwards. Whatever the real motive, the more interesting question is, if there were no substantive political differences, why did the split develop into a permanent breach?

And here there can only be one answer. Deep down in the Mensheviks, there was an unexpressed divide that first came to the surface after the 1905 revolution, when armed pro-Bolshevik workers set up barricades and fought against tsarist troops. Lenin insisted on an immediate conference to discuss the 1905 events and make plans for what was bound to follow. Martov, too, was in favour of unification and prepared to accept the organisational clause that had supposedly been the main point of contention in 1903. But he was not in favour of the conclusions reached by Lenin after the 'dress rehearsal'. A joint conference took place in London in April 1907. The debate was productive on many levels. The Mensheviks stressed the need to work in the existing Duma (the tsarist pseudo-parliament), and, since they believed the revolution had to be bourgeois-democratic, argued consistently that an alliance with the liberal-conservative Kadets was necessary. Not simply Lenin, but Trotsky and Rosa Luxemburg as well had opposed any such notion, declaring that the Russian bourgeoisie was counterrevolutionary and had moved on since the English and French revolutions. The Bolsheviks insisted that the question of an armed insurrection should be put on the agenda. Martov fought hard to get this proposal defeated, using the kind of Martovian contortion that often enraged both his comrades and his opponents: 'A social democratic party may take part in an armed uprising, may call upon the masses to rise ... but cannot *prepare* an uprising if it is to remain faithful to its programme of not becoming a party of "putschists."' On every issue apart from the 'armed insurrection', the Bolsheviks' arguments triumphed. Six weeks after the conference, Prince Stolypin dealt a fatal blow to the Mensheviks by banning trade unions, all Social Democratic factions inside and outside the Duma and the legal Social Democratic press, and embarking yet again on repression and pogroms as Lenin and others had predicted. Martov raged, but the facts had to be faced. His statement on May Day 1908 acknowledged the reality:

From the rear the socialist proletariat is threatened by bands of Black Hundreds and pogromists unleashed by the government; from above – from the milieu of the Russian intelligentsia which once 'adulated' it – comes the cynical laughter of petty-bourgeois self-intoxication; and in the far background of the scene darken the silhouettes of Nicholas II's five thousand gallows.

At the outbreak of the war, a majority of the Menshevik leadership and the SRs maintained that tsarist Russia had to be defended. They were for the war effort. This led to a division within their ranks: the left Mensheviks led by Martov now realised that they held positions closer to those of the Bolsheviks than their own comrades, though they blanched when they first read Lenin's call for transforming the imperialist war into a civil war – a continental revolution against capital and empire, in other words. Martov believed that they should not sabotage the war but just vote against war credits. The symbolism, he felt, would be sufficient to alert the masses that Social Democracy was opposed to the war. Again, Lenin was vindicated by the outbreak of a new revolution in Russia.

Lenin got back from exile in April, Martov in June. Both men were confronted with political parties very much under the influence of presentism, a failure to look ahead. In this case it was partially justified, as the internal parties were in the throes of a revolution and resented newly arrived exiles who thought they knew everything. Lenin won his party back and prepared them for the October Revolution. Martov's left Mensheviks failed to win the party till December 1917. Martov was criticised by his own party allies, who wanted him to be tougher with the right-wing Mensheviks and, if necessary, break with them. Sukhanov, a member of Martov's own faction, was livid at the indecisiveness shown when, instead of remaining in the Congress of Soviets, the left Mensheviks had followed the right-wing, counterrevolutionary parties out of Smolny. The historian wrote:

By quitting the Congress . . . we gave the Bolsheviks with our own hands a monopoly of the Soviet, of the masses, and of the revolution . . . We ensured the victory of Lenin's whole line . . . I consider my greatest and most indelible crime the fact that I failed to break with the Martov group immediately after our faction voted to leave the Congress. To this day I have not ceased regretting this October 25th crime of mine.

Histrionics aside, this criticism of Martov is fully justified. At a pivotal moment he failed to support the revolution, which harmed his own stature and, more importantly, ended all serious possibility of a united government with the Bolsheviks. The left SRs had supported the revolution; if Martov had followed suit, he would have enjoyed a much greater influence.

Isolated, ill and worn out, the Menshevik leader reflected on how his faction had been outwitted and outvoted by Lenin. He knew they had lost the argument back when the Bolsheviks had won a majority in the Petrograd and Moscow soviets in 1917, reducing the Mensheviks to a rump. He knew after the elections to the Constituent Assembly that his faction was nowhere. The SRs dominated the countryside and had won a majority; the revolution had the cities and the working class. Ten million had voted for the Bolshevik Party. The Bolsheviks disbanded the Assembly and opted for a revolutionary dictatorship, stating that this was the case and not pretending otherwise. This is how they finally outwitted the German high command and won the Entente-supported civil war. Contrary to the central Bolshevik demand that the Treaty of Brest-Litovsk bring the war to an end, Martov backed the anti-treaty Bolsheviks and demanded militias to fight the Germans everywhere on Russian soil. Lenin appealed to the German soldiers, sailors and workers to topple the kaiser (which they did), to set up soviets (which they did) and to make a revolution, at which they baulked.

In March 1919, Trotsky who, during his Menshevik years, had worked closely with Martov, wrote a profile of his one-time comrade which, while not inaccurate, lacked generosity:

Without doubt Martov represents one of the most tragic figures in the revolutionary movement. A talented writer, a resourceful politician, a penetrating mind and a graduate of the school of Marxism, Martov will nevertheless enter the history of the workers' revolution as an enormous minus. His thought lacked courage, his incisiveness lacked will. Tenacity was no substitute. It destroyed him. Marxism is a method of objective analysis and at the same time a prerequisite for revolutionary *action*. It presupposes a balance of thought and will which can communicate physical force to thought itself and can discipline the will with the dialectical coordination of the subjective and the objective. Deprived of the will's mainspring, Martov's thought consistently directs all the force of its analysis towards theoretically justifying the line of least resistance. There scarcely is or could be at any time another socialist politician who could exploit Marxism with such talent to justify deviations from and direct betrayals of it. In this respect Martov could be called without any irony a virtuoso. Hilferding, Bauer, Renner and Kautsky himself though more educated in their own fields were in comparison with Martov but clumsy apprentices when it was a question of the *political* falsification of Marxism, i.e. the theoretical presentation of passivity, adaptation and capitulation as the supreme forms of the irreconcilable class struggle.

A revolutionary instinct doubtless lay in Martov. His first reaction to great events always revealed a revolutionary aspiration. But after every such effort, his thought, not being sustained by the mainspring of will power, disintegrated and sank back. This could be observed at the first glimpses of the waves of revolution (*Iskra*), and then in 1905, then again at the start of the imperialist war and in part yet again at the beginning of the 1917 revolution. But it was in vain. The resourcefulness and flexibility of his thought was expended entirely on evading the fundamental questions and seeking out yet more pretexts in favour of what was indefensible. Dialectics became in his hands the most refined casuistry. An unusual, quite cat-like tenacity, the wilfulness of indecision and the stubbornness of hesitation allowed him for months and years on end to adhere to the most contradictory and insoluble positions. Though revealing in the face of the decisive historical tremors a desire to take up a revolutionary position and arousing hopes, each time he was disappointed: his sins were not forgiven. And as a result he slid still further downhill. Finally Martov became the most cultivated, the most refined, the most elusive and the most incisive politician of the stupid, banal and cowardly petty-bourgeois intelligentsia. And the fact that he himself did not see nor understand this indicates how mercilessly his Mosaic incisiveness was laughing at him. Nowadays in a period of the greatest tasks and possibilities that history has at any time opened up and posed, Martov is stretched between Longuet and Chernov. It is sufficient to mention these names in order to gauge the depth of the ideological and political fall of this man who was more greatly gifted than many others.[5]

Martov's illness worried Lenin and he made sure the Bolshevik leadership sent the best available doctors to help treat him. He recovered enough to travel and accepted an invitation to speak at the Halle Congress of the USPD, which was debating whether or not to join the Communist International. Martov was opposed. There was dissension within the Bolshevik leadership, but Lenin insisted that he be given a Soviet passport and allowed to attend. Martov's illness returned and he was never to come back. Lenin insisted that he be sent money for food and medicine, to which David Ryazanov replied, 'He won't accept it if he thinks it's from you.'

It was dispatched nonetheless. Martov was slowly dying when Lenin had his first stroke. He muttered sadly to Krupskaya: 'They say Martov's dying too.' Martov was already dead when Lenin had a second stroke, but the news was kept from him out of concern for his condition. When Krupskaya told him, Lenin broke doctors' rules and demanded to be wheeled into the Kremlin office, where he read the mostly favourable obituaries of Martov in the Soviet press. A very old family friend of the Ulyanov family and commissar for agriculture, A. I. Svidersky, who visited Lenin during his last months, reported that Lenin was obsessed

---

5 Leon Trotsky, *World Revolution*, vol. 1, 18 March 1919/24 April 1922.

with going to see Martov. Incapable of speech and paralysed, Lenin would point at Martov's books and gesture that a driver take him to see their author immediately. Krupskaya would gently tell him once again that Martov was dead. Was he thinking of Martov's desperate plea to the Bolsheviks to let the left Mensheviks serve as a 'loyal opposition' in the soviets? Martov had insisted that this would be beneficial for the revolution and the Bolsheviks, only to be shouted down.

Given Lenin's political thrust in his last essays – 'We don't know anything' – it's very likely he was thinking of what Martov had said on some of these questions.

Lenin died on 21 January 1924, eight months after Martov. The Menshevik paper in exile, *Socialist Courier,* published an obituary referring to him as the 'outstanding figure in the working-class movement' and 'Martov's comrade-in-arms' … Other opponents, including the two major anti-Communist Western biographers, Richard Pipes and Robert Service, would write similarly long treatises after his death. While they could never support any element of Lenin's 'monstrous' politics, it had to be admitted, according to Service, that Lenin

> would have been as ashamed as was Krupskaya at the ludicrous uses made of his name, ideas and activities … The irony was that the man who, more than any other, presided over the prettification and exaggeration of his own role in the socialist movements world-wide was none other than he whom Lenin had sought to discharge from the seat of power in the Bolshevik party. Thus Lenin underwent posthumous humiliation at the hands of his latter-day enemy.

Service concludes:

> On his death-bed Lenin did not envisage a strategy of liquidating millions of innocent and hard-working peasants. Nor did he aim to exterminate his enemies, real and imagined, in the party … His vision of a future for mankind when all exploitation and opposition would disappear was sincere. This surely is the central point about his life.[6]

---

6   Robert Service, *The Iron Ring,* vol. 3 of *Lenin: A Political Life,* London, 1995, pp. 322–3.

Stalin at the height of his power: feared and loathed by most
of his closest colleaques, he is a Putin favourite today.

Richard Pipes attaches more importance to Lenin's missives revealed
after the fall of Communism than he should. Most of the texts to
which he refers as evidence of Lenin's inherent cruelty were written
during the civil war, when the infant Soviet Republic was fighting for
its life. Civil wars, as American academics should know, are never
pretty affairs, regardless of which side one supports. To take a high
moral tone in relation to Lenin but not to Lincoln smacks of hypocrisy. It was not always thus for Pipes. In an earlier book he was far
more balanced, writing that had Lenin not died prematurely, 'the final
structure of the Soviet Union would have been quite different from
that which Stalin ultimately gave it.'[7] That much is obvious.

---

7   Richard Pipes, *Formation of the Soviet Union*, Cambridge, MA,
1964, p. 276. The horror movie version is *The Unknown Lenin*, New
Haven, 1998.

Everything Lenin had feared came to pass, starting with what was done to his dead body by Stalin and the Politburo. The entire Ulyanov family and especially his widow remained strongly opposed to embalming Lenin. The official funeral oration was delivered by a former seminarian, Joseph Stalin, in tones harshly reminiscent of the Orthodox Church. The revolutionary was being transformed into a Byzantine saint. A more powerful speech was made that same day and in her own quiet way by Nadya Krupskaya, standing by her husband's bier at the memorial:

> Comrades, working men and women, peasant men and women! I have a great request to make of you: do not raise statues of him, name palaces for him, or stage pompous solemn festivals to his memory – all these were to him in life of little significance, even a burden. Remember how many are impoverished and in disarray in our country. You wish to honour the name of Vladimir Ilyich – then establish infants' homes, kindergartens, houses, schools, libraries, ambulances, hospitals, homes for invalids; and above all create a living testament to his ideals.

This would be ignored as well. Having mummified Lenin, within a few years the committee men and their leader would mummify his ideas as well. In that odd way of his, Lenin had foreseen this possibility too. And all one can hope is that, by the time his body is finally buried, some of his ideas, especially those related to the primacy of politics, imperialism, self-determination and the commune-state, are revived. Whether this happens or not, the following warning should serve as his real epitaph:

> After their death, attempts are made to convert revolutionaries into harmless icons, to canonise them, so to say, and to hallow their names to a certain extent for the 'consolation' of the oppressed classes and with the object of duping the latter, while at the same time robbing the revolutionary theory of its substance, blunting its revolutionary edge and vulgarising it.

EPILOGUE

On Climbing a High Mountain
By V. I. Lenin

Lenin scouring the press: he intensely disliked his personality cult.

Let us picture to ourselves a man ascending a very high, steep
and hitherto unexplored mountain.[1] Let us assume that he has
overcome unprecedented difficulties and dangers and has succeeded
in reaching a much higher point than any of his predecessors, but
still has not reached the summit. He finds himself in a position
where it is not only difficult and dangerous to proceed in the

---

1   This is the first section, titled 'By Way of Example', of Lenin's *Notes
of a Publicist*, written at the end of February 1922 and first published in

direction and along the path he has chosen, but positively impossible. He is forced to turn back, descend, seek another path, longer, perhaps, but one that will enable him to reach the summit. The descent from the height that no one before him has reached proves, perhaps, to be more dangerous and difficult for our imaginary traveller than the ascent – it is easier to slip; it is not so easy to choose a foothold; there is not that exhilaration that one feels in going upwards, straight to the goal, etc. One has to tie a rope round oneself, spend hours with an alpenstock to cut footholds or a projection to which the rope could be tied firmly; one has to move at a snail's pace, and move downwards, descend, away from the goal; and one does not know where this extremely dangerous and painful descent will end, or whether there is a fairly safe detour by which one can ascend more boldly, more quickly and more directly to the summit.

It would hardly be natural to suppose that a man who had climbed to such an unprecedented height but found himself in such a position did not have his moments of despondency. In all probability these moments would be more numerous, more frequent and harder to bear if he heard the voices of those below, who, through a telescope and from a safe distance, are watching his dangerous descent, which cannot even be described as what the *Smena Vekh* people call 'ascending with the brakes on'; brakes presuppose a well-designed and tested vehicle, a well-prepared road and previously tested appliances. In this case, however, there is no vehicle, no road, absolutely nothing that had been tested beforehand.

The voices from below ring with malicious joy. They do not conceal it; they chuckle gleefully and shout: 'He'll fall in a minute! Serve him right, the lunatic!' Others try to conceal their malicious glee and behave mostly like Judas Golovlyov.

They moan and raise their eyes to heaven in sorrow, as if to say: 'It grieves us sorely to see our fears justified! But did not we, who

---

Pravda on 16 April 1924. This version of the text is taken from V. I. Lenin, *Collected Works*, vol. 33, trs David Skvirsky and George Hanna, Moscow, 1965, pp. 204–11, available on the V. I. Lenin Internet Archive at marx. org. This was Brecht's favourite Lenin text and for good reason.

have spent all our lives working out a judicious plan for scaling this mountain, demand that the ascent be postponed until our plan was complete? And if we so vehemently protested against taking this path, which this lunatic is now abandoning (look, look, he has turned back! He is descending! A single step is taking him hours of preparation! And yet we were roundly abused when time and again we demanded moderation and caution!), if we so fervently censured this lunatic and warned everybody against imitating and helping him, we did so entirely because of our devotion to the great plan to scale this mountain, and in order to prevent this great plan from being generally discredited!' Happily, in the circumstances we have described, our imaginary traveller cannot hear the voices of these people who are 'true friends' of the idea of ascent; if he did, they would probably nauseate him. And nausea, it is said, does not help one to keep a clear head and a firm step, particularly at high altitudes.

GLOSSARY OF
PERSONAL NAMES

Tsar Alexander II (1818–1881): Emancipated the serfs in 1861. Twenty years later he was assassinated by the anarcho-terrorist organisation the People's Will.

Tsar Alexander III (1845–1894): Counter-reformist and 'semi-literate bore', he opted for repression and avoided the fate of his father.

Inessa Armand (1874–1920): Longtime Bolshevik feminist. Armand met Lenin in 1910 in Paris. They soon became lovers and remained close friends and comrades till her death in 1920.

Mikhail Bakunin (1814–1876): Anarchist theoretician and Marx's chief political rival in the First International.

August Bebel (1840–1913): Founding member of the German Social Democratic Party and Marxist theorist. For many years the most-read book in the socialist canon was not Marx and Engels's *Communist Manifesto* but Bebel's *Women and Socialism*.

Otto Bauer (1881–1938): Austro-Marxist political leader and theoretician. He and his colleagues helped to diffuse serious unrest in Austria following the Bolshevik revolution. The Austrian socialists, like their German counterparts, failed to confront and defeat fascism.

Napoleon Bonaparte (1769–1821): The personification of a stable and sated bourgeois class after the turbulence of the Jacobin period in France. He restored the Church and the aristocracy and crowned himself emperor. His dream of a French-dominated Europe died on the battlefields of tsarist Russia.

Amadeo Bordiga (1889–1970): Highly gifted leader of the ultra-left faction of the Italian Communist Party.

Nikolai Bukharin (1888–1938): Referred to by Lenin as the 'favourite of the party', he was an intelligent economist and politician (and a very fine painter), but was easily manipulated by Stalin and finally executed on his orders after a rigged trial.

Nikolay Chernyshevsky (1828–1889): Author of *What Is to Be Done?*, a novel of remarkable influence in the late nineteenth and early twentieth centuries among the Russian revolutionary milieu. It was this book that radicalised Lenin and sent him off in search of Marx.

Gyorgy Chicherin (1872–1936): Commissar for foreign affairs, an authority on classical music, fluent in all the major European languages and one of the most cultivated members of the Bolshevik leadership. He was tormented by his homosexuality.

Carl von Clausewitz (1780–1831): Prussian general and military theorist whose work had a tremendous impact on the thinking of Lenin, Trotsky and Mao, as well as Carl Schmitt.

Gustave Courbet (1819–1877): Painter and radical. Elected as a delegate to the Paris Commune, he spearheaded a series of art initiatives in the city. These included the democratisation of museum administration, reserving space in galleries for minority artistic tendencies, and iconoclastic destruction of public memorials to imperial conquest.

Eugene V. Debs (1885–1926): Founding member of the International Workers of the World and five-time Socialist Party candidate for the US presidency, winning 6 percent of the votes in 1912. His influence was so pronounced that one of the nineteenth century's most raucous industrial actions – the Pullman Strikes – are now better known as 'Debs's Rebellion'.

Friedrich Ebert (1871–1925): Leader of the German Social Democrats, he approved the assassination of revolutionaries Karl Liebknecht and Rosa Luxemburg in 1919.

Friedrich Engels (1820–1895): Son of a wealthy industrialist, he wrote *The Condition of the English Working Class* which caught the eye of Karl Marx. The two developed a lifelong intellectual partnership.

Vera Figner (1852–1942): Leader in the clandestine organisation the People's Will. She was one of the chief architects of the successful assassination of Tsar Alexander II.

Mikhail Frunze (1885–1925): Leading figure in the 1905 revolution and an esteemed military commander and strategist in the civil war following the Russian Revolution. While Trotsky argued forcefully that the frontiers of historical materialism stopped short of military strategy, Frunze emphasised the decisive importance of the army's 'class character', advocating for democratisation of the armed forces. He was supposedly poisoned on Stalin's orders.

Olympe de Gouges (1748–1793): Playwright, poet and polemicist. She authored *Declaration of the Rights of Woman and the Female Citizen*, which forcefully posed the questions of universal emancipation and women's liberation. She was executed for her political writings as a Girondist, one of the three women put to death during the reign of terror. Over a century later, her legacy inspired the women involved in Zhenotdel, the Soviet Union's women's bureau.

Antonio Gramsci (1891–1937): Revolutionary Marxist and leader of the Italian Communist Party. Jailed by Mussolini, he wrote some of his finest texts in prison, in an elliptical style designed to deceive the censor.

Ho Chi Minh (1890–1969): Communist revolutionary and political leader of Vietnam, who led his country to independence. Rebuffed by President Wilson at Versailles, he helped found the French Communist Party before leading the Vietnamese revolutionary forces to a cascade of victories against the Japanese, French and American empires.

John A. Hobson (1858–1940): Liberal theorist of imperialism. He exercised tremendous influence over the classical Marxist accounts by Luxemburg, Lenin, Bukharin and Hilferding.

Abe Iso (1865–1949): Socialist. He returned to Japan after training in a New England seminar school with two key imports from the Western world: Fabian socialism and baseball, neither of which shook the foundations of capitalism.

Ernest Jones (1819–1869): A prominent figure in the Chartist movement, to which he devoted his life. From an aristocratic background, he poured his considerable wealth into sustaining the Chartist newspaper.

Lev Kamenev (1883–1936): 'Old Bolshevik' and longtime collaborator with Lenin. Opposed to the 1917 insurrection and briefly to Stalin in the mid-1920s, he was executed on Stalin's orders after a show trial.

Alexander Kerensky (1881–1970): Leader of the Socialist Revolutionaries. He was named prime minister of the Duma in July 1917 and deposed in October of that same year. His father had taught Lenin and his son worked for the *Financial Times*.

Alexandra Kollontai (1872–1952): Early member of the Bolshevik Central Committee, and the only member to support Lenin's theses on insurrectionary strategy following the mass uprising of July 1917. She was a leading theorist on women, sexuality, the family and socialism and a pioneering organiser of the Zhenotdel.

Lavr Kornilov (1870–1918): General in the tsar's and later the White Russian armies, who briefly served as commander-in-chief in July 1917 before the 'Kornilov Affair' in August, when he was arrested for attempting a coup. Killed by a shell in battle during the civil war.

Peter Kropotkin (1842–1921): Anarchist theorist of aristocratic descent and author of an influential history of the French Revolution, who returned to Russia following the revolution there. His state funeral was attended by thousands of people, including an official representative of the Bolsheviks.

Nadya Krupskaya (1869–1939): Bolshevik activist and longtime militant, who married Lenin in 1898. She served as the Soviet government's deputy minister of education from 1929 until her death. Her Tolstoyan educational recipes often irritated her spouse.

Eugen Levine (1883–1919): German Communist leader who was reluctantly, though courageously, involved in the Bavarian Soviet Republic. At his trial he declared, 'We communists are dead men on leave', and was executed soon afterwards.

Karl Liebknecht (1871–1919): Lifelong militant who helped launch both the Socialist Youth International and the Spartacusbund. His father was a founding member of the German Social Democratic Party. Initially sceptical of the general strike and armed insurrection launched by workers in July 1917, Liebknecht and Rosa Luxemburg belatedly joined the uprising. With no strategy in place, the insurrection was crushed within a week and its leaders assassinated.

Prosper-Olivier Lissagaray (1838–1901): Renowned historian and rank-and-file participant in the Paris Commune. He remained a passionate defender of that revolutionary experiment, challenging journalists in the bourgeois press to duel whenever they slandered its name and memory. Marx foolishly forbade his daughter Eleanor from marrying the Frenchman.

Rosa Luxemburg (1871–1919): Polish revolutionary and theorist, who was one of the most creative Marxists of her time. She was murdered by the Freikorps with the support of Ebert and Noske.

Julius Martov (1873–1923): Popular leader of the Menshevik faction of the Russian Social Democratic Labour Party and close friends with Lenin. While in opposition to the party's governing right wing after the February Revolution, he also refused an alliance with the Bolsheviks. Such vacillations cemented Martov's reputation as 'the Hamlet of democratic socialism'.

Sergei Nechaev (1847–1882): Terrorist. A theology teacher in a parish school by day, he devoured the texts of the French Revolution by night. He became a close collaborator of Bakunin's and together they wrote *The Revolutionary Catechism*, an instruction manual for radical anarchists.

Tsar Nicholas II (1868–1918): Last tsar of Russia. He abdicated in March 1917 and was put under house arrest with his family. He was executed by the Bolsheviks in July 1918 at the height of the civil war.

George Odger (1813–1877): Shoemaker and founder of the London Trades Council. He was elected the first president of the General Council of the International Working Men's Association.

Emmeline Pankhurst (1858–1928) and Sylvia Pankhurst (1882–1960): Suffragettes. When the First World War broke out, Emmeline demobilised the mass suffrage movement and instructed women to knit socks for soldiers. Her daughter, Sylvia, continued to oppose the war, eventually becoming a Communist.

Sofiya Perovskaya (1853–1881): Russian revolutionary and member of the People's Will. She orchestrated the successful assassination of Alexander II and was the first woman activist to be hanged.

Georgy Plekhanov (1856–1918): Founder of the Emancipation of Labour group in 1883 and the preeminent Russian Marxist theorist from the 1880s to the 1900s. He initially sided with Lenin in the split with the Mensheviks in 1903 but soon moved to the right, becoming an outspoken supporter of Russia's participation in the First World War.

Karl Radek (1885–1939): Bolshevik journalist, who was close to both Lenin and Trotsky and known for his wit and sarcasm. Unsurprisingly, he died in a Stalinist prison.

Fyodor Raskolnikov (1892–1939): 'Old Bolshevik' drawn from the ranks of sailors radicalised during the First World War. He commanded the Red Navy on the Caspian and Baltic Seas during the civil war.

Elena Stasova (1873–1966): Secretary of the Bolshevik Party in 1917 and member of the Central Committee. She was a close friend of Lenin's.

Two unnamed women typists at the Turkestan section of the Ministry of Agriculture in St Petersburg: When Menshevik organiser N. N. Sukhanov overheard two women discussing the imminent revolution, he laughed it off. It turns out that they were entirely clairvoyant, with a demonstrably better analysis of the political situation than their esteemed eavesdropper.

Mikhail Tukhachevsky (1893–1937): Captured as a prisoner of war, he shared a cell with Charles de Gaulle, who could not tolerate his nihilism. After being released from prison, he returned home, joined the Bolshevik Party and became the most gifted military commander of the Red Army during the civil war. He was executed on Stalin's orders.

Woodrow Wilson (1856–1924): American president of the so-called 'progressive' era, he resegregated the federal civil service and lionised the Ku Klux Klan. This was wholly consistent with his international politics, which included sending US soldiers to

Mexico, Cuba, Haiti and Nicaragua. Freud drew a scathing portrait of him.

Varvara Yakovleva (1884–1941): Prominent Bolshevik Party member and the third woman to join its governing Central Committee, she served as minister of education and of finance for the USSR. She supported Trotsky after Lenin's death and was executed in prison after being found guilty of 'terrorist conspiracy'.

Vera Zasulich (1849–1919): First woman to fire a revolver in Russia, she was later a member of the *Iskra* editorial board and later still a leading Menshevik.

Clara Zetkin (1857–1933): Leading light in European Marxism, she was a deft organiser with the German Social Democrats before founding the country's Communist Party in 1918. As with many of her peers, her political leadership was coupled with theoretical acumen; she was an indispensable thinker on 'the question of women'.

Arthur Zimmermann (1864–1940): Senior state official in the German Foreign Office. He is best known for two acts of subterfuge during the 'Great War': the telegram that urged the Mexican government to invade the United States and the smuggling of Lenin and other exiles into revolutionary Russia.

Grigory Zinoviev (1883–1936): Founding member of the Bolshevik Party and leading figure in the Communist International. His show trial in 1936 – nine years after he was expelled from political leadership – was a harbinger of the terror that was to follow. He was executed on Stalin's orders.

FURTHER READING

Anderson, B. (2007). *Under Three Flags: Anarchism and the Anti-Colonial Imagination*. London: Verso Books.

Anderson, P. (1976). *Considerations on Western Marxism*. London: Verso Books.

Anderson, P. (2014). *American Foreign Policy and Its Thinkers*. London: Verso Books.

Bolsinger, E. (2001). *The Autonomy of the Political: Carl Schmitt's and Lenin's Political Realism*. California: Praeger Publishers.

Broido, V. (1987). *Lenin and the Mensheviks: The Persecution of Socialists Under Bolshevism*. Colorado: Westview Press.

Clements, B. E. (1997). *Bolshevik Women*. Cambridge, UK: Cambridge University Press.

Deuschter, I. (1970). *Lenin's Childhood*. Oxford: Oxford University Press.

Deuschter, I. (2003). *The Prophet Armed*. London: Verso Books.

Dostoevsky, F. (1959). *The Possessed*. New York: Heritage Press.

Dostoevsky, F. (2015). *Notes From Underground and Other Stories*. London: Wordsworth Classics.

Erickson, J. (2006). *The Soviet Command: A Military-Political History, 1918–1941*. London: Routledge.

Fitzpatrick, S. (2002). *The Commissariat of Enlightenment: The Soviet Organization of Education and the Arts under Lunacharsky, October 1917–1921*. Cambridge: Cambridge University Press.

Fitzpatrick, S. (2008). *The Russian Revolution*. Oxford: Oxford University Press.

Fitzpatrick, S., and K. Slezkine, eds (2000). *In the Shadow of Revolution: Life Stories of Russian Women from 1917 to the Second World War*. Princeton: Princeton University Press.

Ferguson, N. (2000). *The Pity of War: Explaining World War One*. New York: Basic Books.

Geras, N. (1986). *Literature of Revolution: Essays on Marxism*. London: Verso Books.

Getzler, I. (1967). *Martov: A Political Biography of a Russian Social Democrat*. Cambridge: Cambridge University Press, and Port Melbourne: Melbourne University Press.

Ginzberg, M. (1982). *Style and Epoch*. Cambridge, MA: MIT Press.

Goldmann, W. Z. (2008). *Women, the State and Revolution: Soviet Family Policy and Social Life, 1917–36*. Cambridge: Cambridge University Press.

Gregory, P. R., and N. Naimark, eds (2014). *The Lost Politburo Transcripts: From Collective Rule to Stalin's Transcripts*. New Haven: Yale University Press.

Harding, N. (2010). *Lenin's Political Thought: Theory and Practice in the Democratic and Socialist Revolutions*. New York: Haymarket Books.

Hirsch, S., and L. van der Walt, eds (2010). *Anarchism and Syndicalism in the Colonial and Postcolonial World, 1870–1940*. Leiden: Brill.

Kollontai, A. (1978). *Love of Worker Bees*, tr. Cathy Porter. London: Virago Press.

Kollontai, A. (2011). *The Autobiography of a Sexually Emancipated Communist Woman*. London: CreateSpace Independent Publishing Platform.

Krupskaya, N. (2004). *Reminiscences of Lenin*. Honolulu: University Press of the Pacific.

Lansbury, G. (2016). *What I Saw in Russia*. South Yarra, Australia: Leopold Classic Library.

Lieven, D. (2015). *Towards the Flame: Empire, War and the End of Tsarist Russia*. London: Allen Lane.

Lenin, V. I. (1899). 'Development of Capitalism in Russia'. Available at the Marxists Internet Archive, marxists.org/archive/lenin/works.

Lenin, V. I. (1901). 'What Is to Be Done?'. Available at the Marxists Internet Archive, marxists.org/archive/lenin/works.

Lenin, V. I. (1905). 'Two Tactics of Social-Democracy in the Democratic Revolution'. Available at the Marxists Internet Archive, marxists.org/archive/lenin/works.

Lenin, V. I. (1914–1915). *Collected Works*, vol. 21. Available at the Marxists Internet Archive, marxists.org/archive/lenin/works.

Lenin, V. I. (1917). 'The Tasks of the Proletariat in the Present Revolution [A.K.A. The April Theses]'. Available at the Marxists Internet Archive, marxists.org/archive/lenin/works.

Lenin, V. I. (1918). 'The State and Revolution'. Available at the Marxists Internet Archive, marxists.org/archive/lenin/works.

Lenin, V. I. (1923). 'Better Fewer but Better'. Available at the Marxists Internet Archive, marxists.org/archive/lenin/works.

Lewin, M. (1975). *Lenin's Last Struggle*. London: Pluto Press.

Liebman, M. (1975). *Leninism under Lenin*. London: Cape.

Lissagaray, P. (2014). *History of the Paris Commune of 1871*. London: CreateSpace Independent Publishing Platform.

Losurdo, D. (2014). *Liberalism: A Counter-History*. London: Verso.

Mantel, H. (2006). *A Place of Greater Safety*. New York: Picador.

Mayakovsky, V. (2013). *Selected Poems*. Evanston: Northwestern University Press.

McNeal, R. H. (1973). *Bride of the Revolution: Lenin and Krupskaya*. Ann Arbor: University of Michigan Press.

Mirsky, D. S. (1964). *A History of Russian Literature*. New York: Knopf.

Nabokov, V. (1981). *The Gift*. London: Penguin.

Pearson, M. (2002). *Lenin's Mistress: The Life of Inessa Armand*. London: Random House.

Pearson, M. (1974). *The Sealed Train*. London: Putnam.

Pipes, R. (1999). *The Unknown Lenin*. New Haven: Yale University Press.

Porter, C. (1976). *Fathers and Daughters: Russian Women in Revolution*. London: Virago.

Porter, C. (2014). *Alexandra Kollontai: A Biography*. London: Merlin Press.

Pushkin, A. (2014). *Collected Poems, 1813–1820*. Milton Keynes: JiaHu Books.

Rabinowitch, A. (2009). *The Bolsheviks Came to Power*. New York: Haymarket Books.

Robespierre, M. (2007). *Virtue and Terror*. London: Verso.

Rowbotham, S. (2014). *Women, Resistance and Revolution*. London: Verso Books.

Serge, V. (2015). *Year One of the Russian Revolution*. New York: Haymarket Books.

Service, R. (1994). *Lenin: A Political Life*. London: Palgrave Macmillan.

Smith, S. (2008). *Revolution and the People in Russia and China: A Comparative History*. Cambridge: Cambridge University Press.

Solzhenitsyn, A. (1976). *Lenin in Zurich*. New York: Farrar, Straus and Giroux.

Steinberg, J. (2013). *Bismarck: A Life*. Oxford: Oxford University Press.

Stites, R. (1978). *The Women's Liberation Movement in Russia: Feminism,*

Nihilism and Bolshevism, 1860–1930. Princeton: Princeton University Press.

Stites, R. (1989). *Revolutionary Dreams: Utopian Vision and Experimental Life in the Russian Revolution*. Oxford: Oxford University Press.

Trotsky, L. D. (1925). 'Lenin'. Available at the Marxists Internet Archive, marxists.org/archive/trotsky.

Trotsky, L. D. (1930). 'The History of the Russian Revolution'. Available at the Marxists Internet Archive, marxists.org/archive/trotsky.

Trotsky, L. D. (1972). *The Young Lenin*. New York: Doubleday.

Tukhachevsky, M. (1969). 'Revolution from Without'. *New Left Review* 55, May–June 1969.

Venturi, F. (2001). *Roots of Revolution: A History of the Populist and Socialist Movements in 19th Century Russia*. London: Phoenix.

Weiss, P. (2005). *The Aesthetics of Resistance*. Durham: Duke University Press.

Williams, A. R. (1969). *Journey into Revolution: Petrograd, 1917–1918*. Chicago: Chicago Quadrangle Books.

Woodcock, G. (1970). *Anarchism*. London: Penguin.

Zetkin, C. (1924). 'Reminiscences of Lenin'. Available at the Marxists Internet Archive, marxists.org/archive/zetkin.

Žižek, S. (2011). *Revolution at the Gates: Žižek on Lenin and the 1917 Writings*. London: Verso Books.

INDEX